To Hermann!

Andrew
Koh

The Gleam of Distance

An Amulet of planet Ith,
forged by Tion,
goddess of the moon,
granting divine might.
Long sought
by Ka'ii warlords
in the Age of Blood,
where legions fell
until The Broken Few
forged peace.
Now, tribes flourish
in the Days of Calm.
But The Gleam remains distant...

For now...

Andrew Kafoury's
No'madd
City of Empty Towers

WRITER
ANDREW KAFOURY

ART
TODD HERMAN (THE VOYAGE)

SCOTT ROLLER (THE TOWERS)

CHRIS FACCONE (THE TOTEMS)

DESIGN
TODD HERMAN

LETTERS
ANDREW KAFOURY & SCOTT ROLLER
(RINGBEARER MEDIUM FONT BY PETE KLASSEN
ALEX TOTH FONT BY DANIEL WERNECK)

MAP
SCOTT ROLLER

COVER
TODD HERMAN

ISBN: 978-0-615-92455-7
Copyright (c) 2013 Andrew Kafoury
All rights reserved. The stories,
characters, and incidents, featured in
this publication are entirely fictional.
No'madd, and all related characters
featured in this publication, the
distinctive likeness thereof, and all
related incidia are trademarks of
Andrew Kafoury.

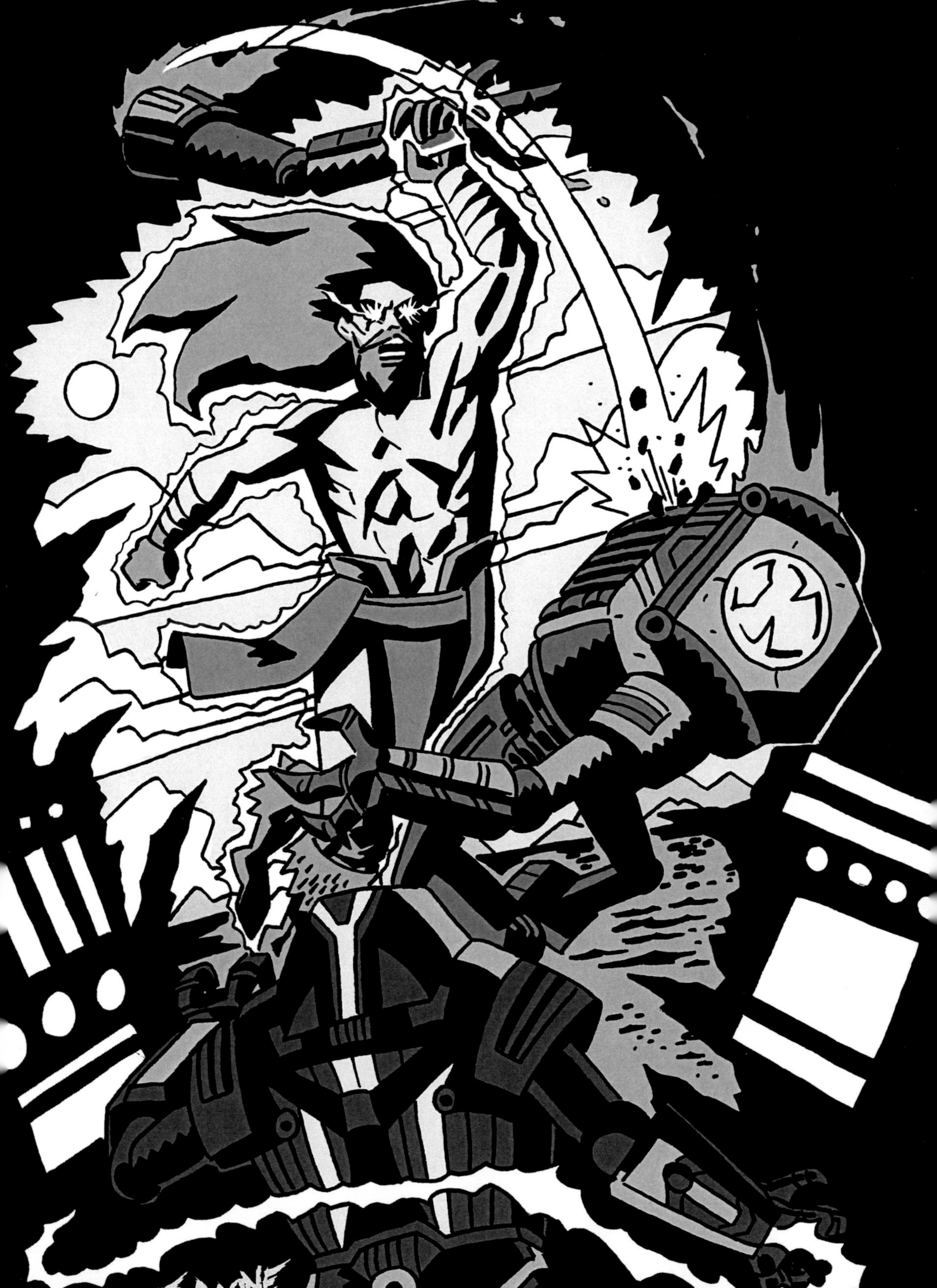
FACCONE

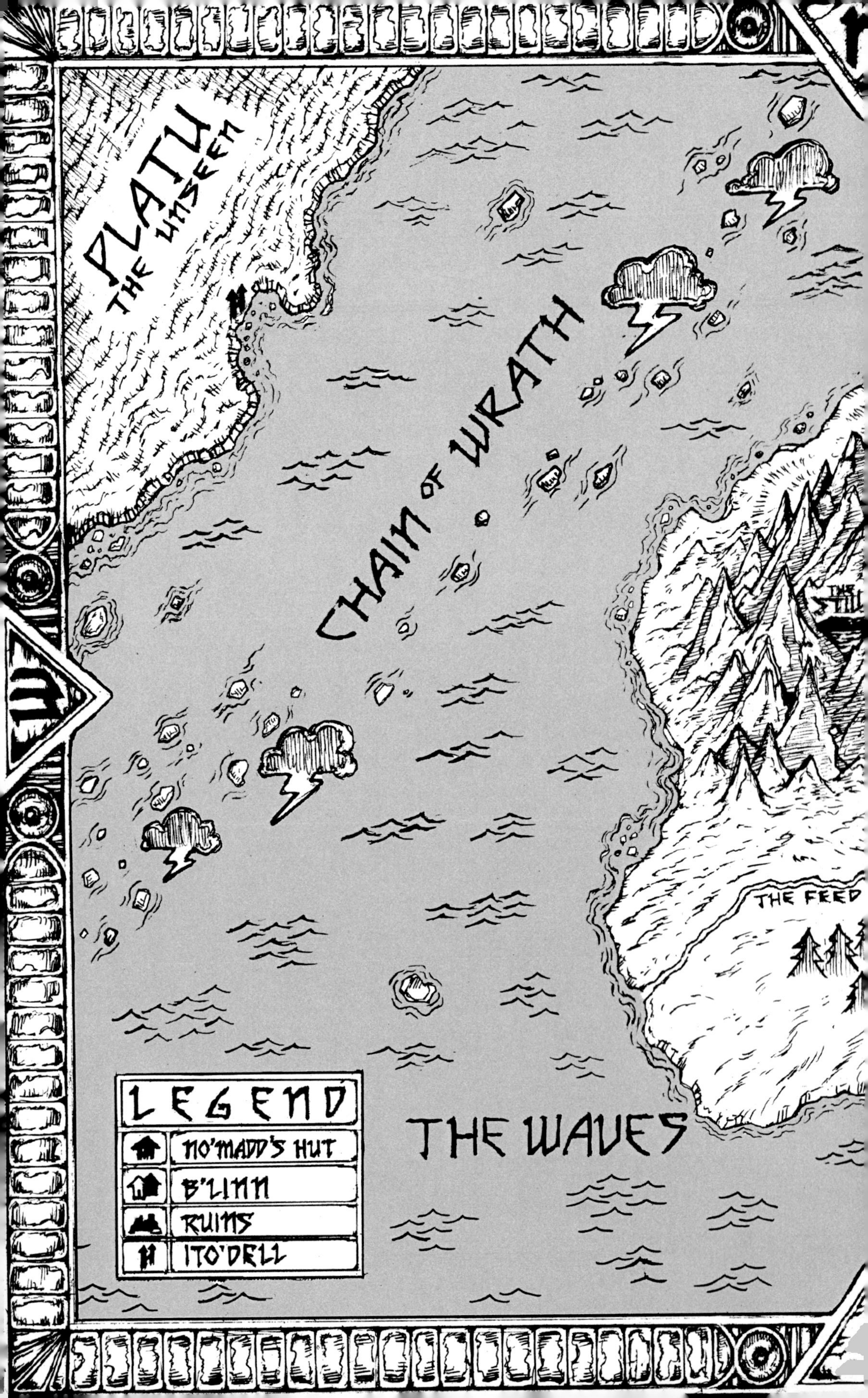
PLATU
THE UNSEEN
CHAIN OF WRATH
THE FEED
THE WAVES
LEGEND
NO'MADD'S HUT
B'LINN
RUINS
ITO'DELL

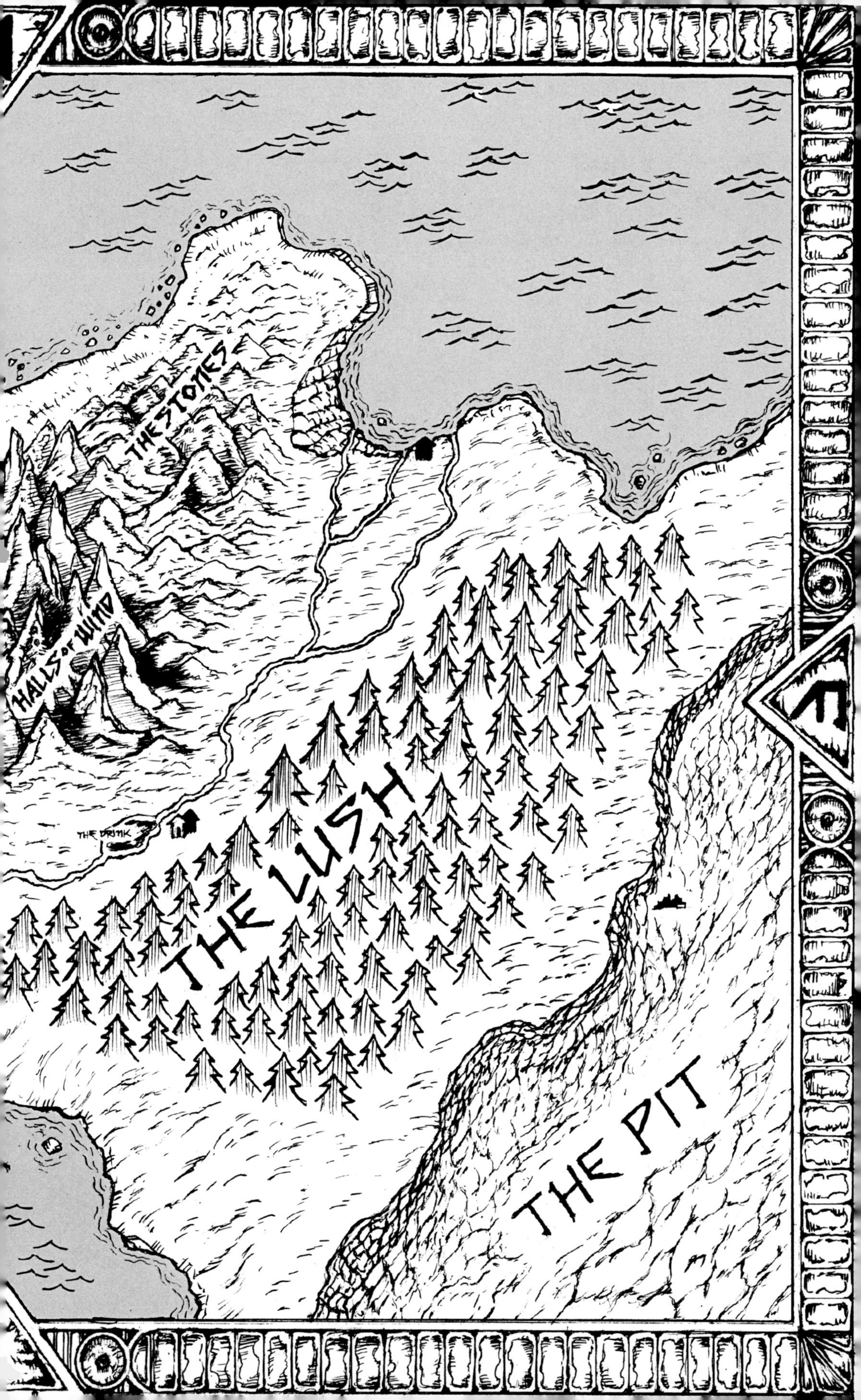
THE STONES
HALLS OF WIND
THE DRINK
THE LUSH
THE PIT

Lands

Barrox

KNOWN AS THE ARM

Platu

KNOWN AS THE UNSEEN

Realms

Chain of Wrath

UNCONQUERABLE BARRIER

Halls of Wind

PERILOUS TRENCH

Roar of Waves

COASTAL PATH

The Still

MOTIONLESS LAGOON

The Steep

WARLORD PALACE

DIETIES

ARIZ

HE IS THE SUN, KNOWN AS THE BRIGHT

TION

SHE IS THE MOON, KNOWN AS THE DISTANT

ITH

SHE IS THE PLANET, KNOWN AS THE SPHERE

TONN

HE IS THE GALAXY, KNOWN AS THE VAST

CLANS

AH'KEE

ANCIENT RULERS

KA'II

TRIBAL SECTS

FOR JOEY, WHO DANCED ACROSS THE CHAIN.
- DREW

CHAPTER ONE

NO'MADD

"HOME.

WHAT A BEAUTIFUL WORD..."

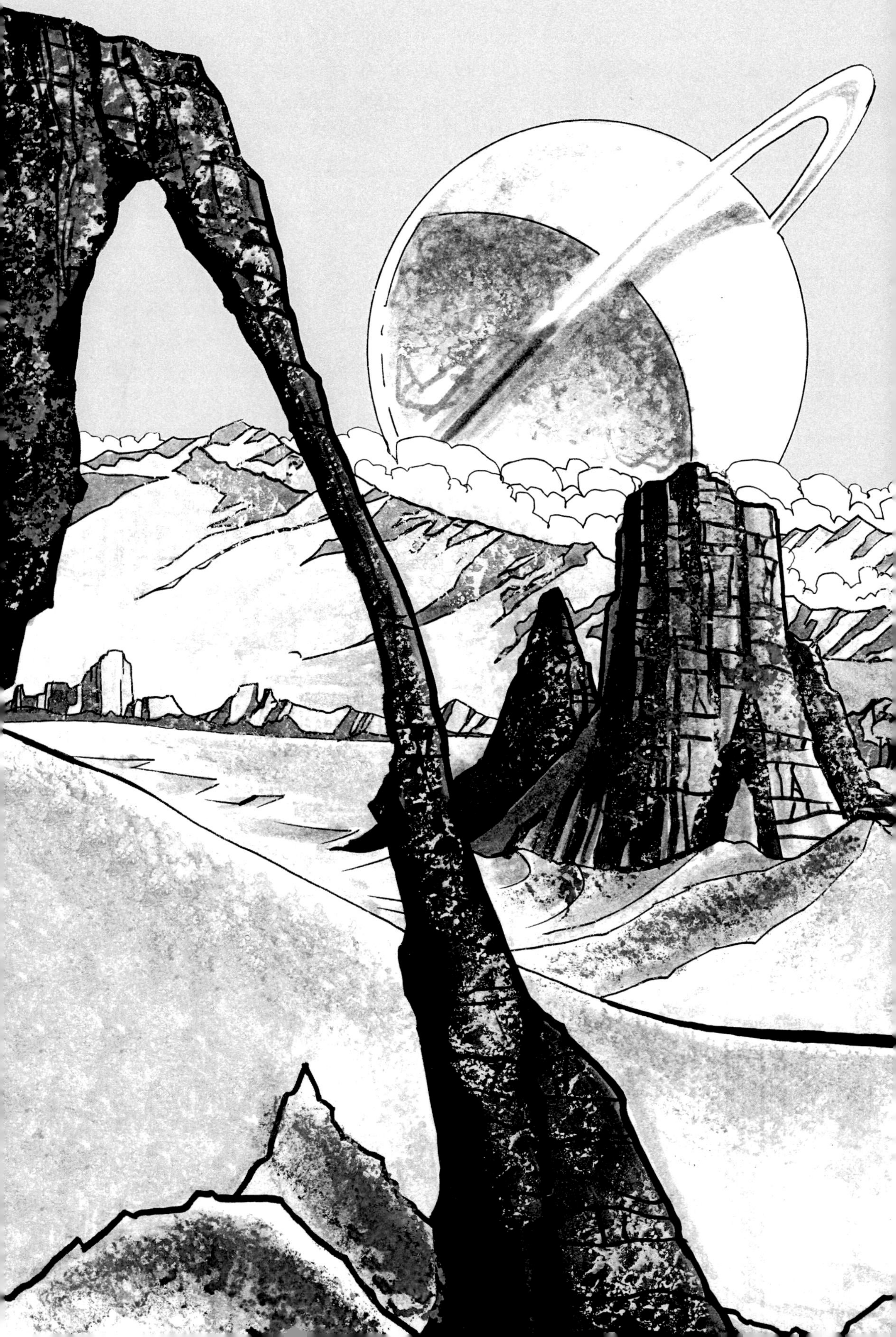

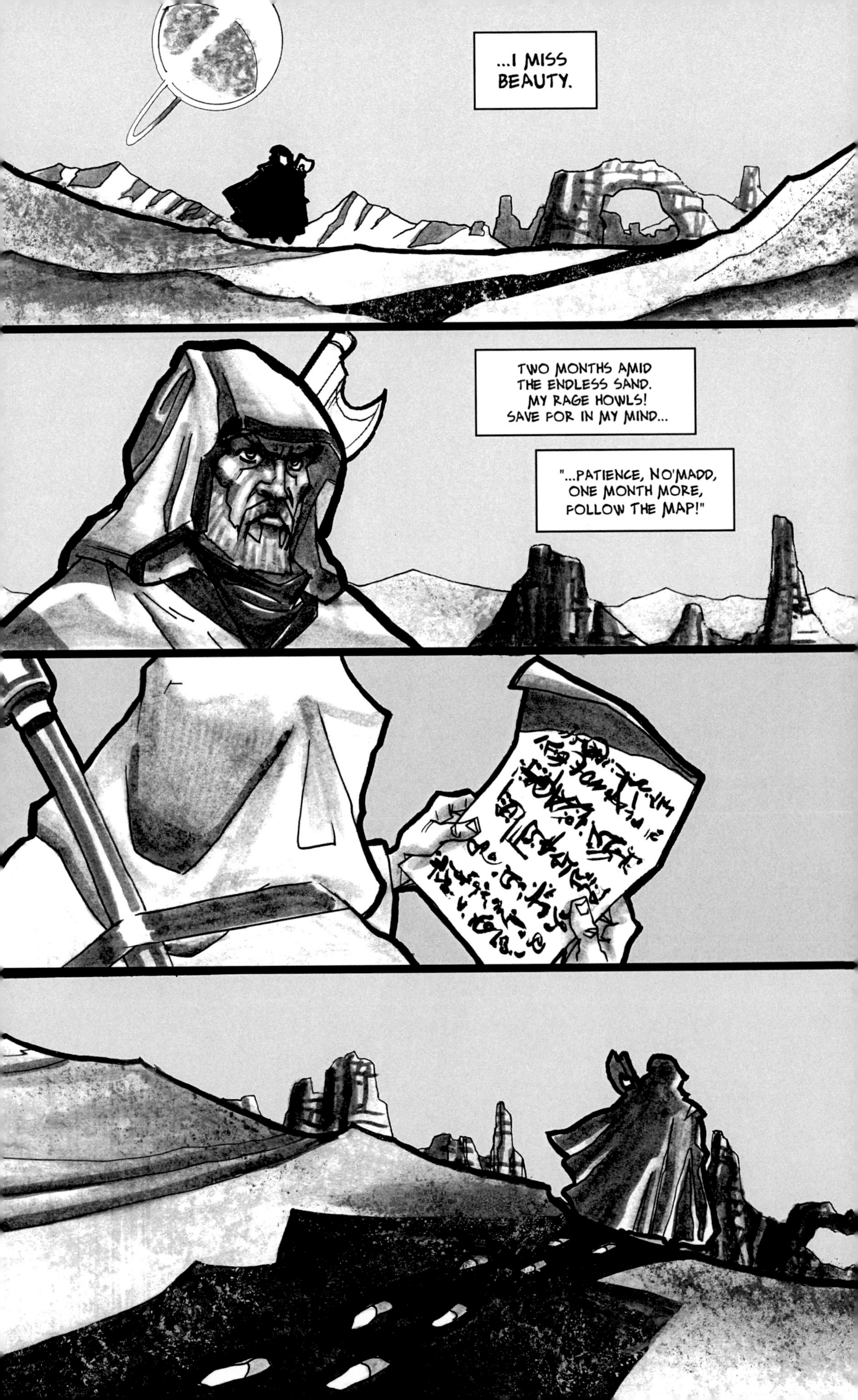
...I MISS BEAUTY.
TWO MONTHS AMID THE ENDLESS SAND. MY RAGE HOWLS! SAVE FOR IN MY MIND...
"...PATIENCE, NO'MADD, ONE MONTH MORE, FOLLOW THE MAP!"

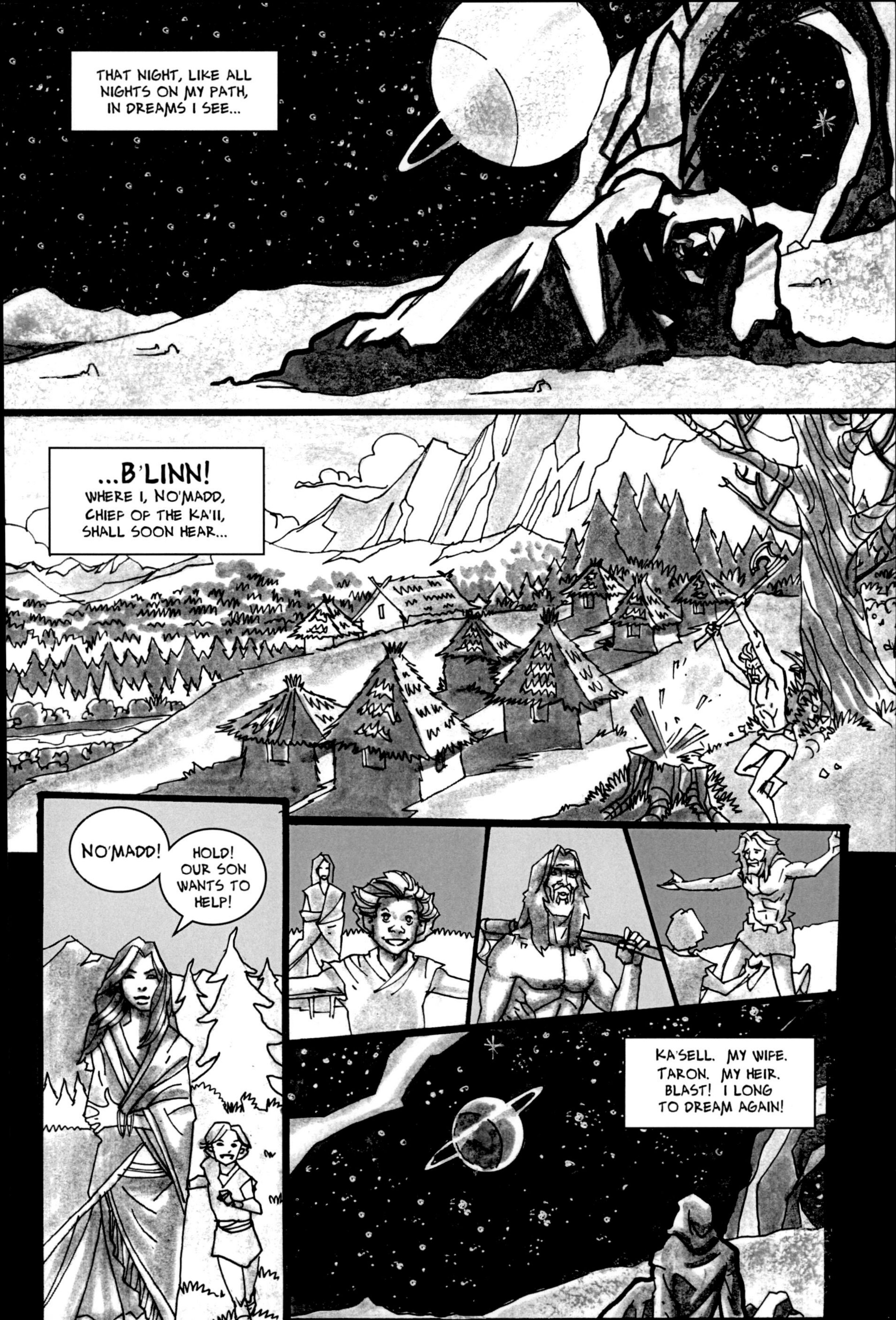
THAT NIGHT, LIKE ALL NIGHTS ON MY PATH, IN DREAMS I SEE...
...B'LINN!
WHERE I, NO'MADD, CHIEF OF THE KA'II, SHALL SOON HEAR...
NO'MADD!
HOLD! OUR SON WANTS TO HELP!
KA'SELL. MY WIFE. TARON. MY HEIR. BLAST! I LONG TO DREAM AGAIN!

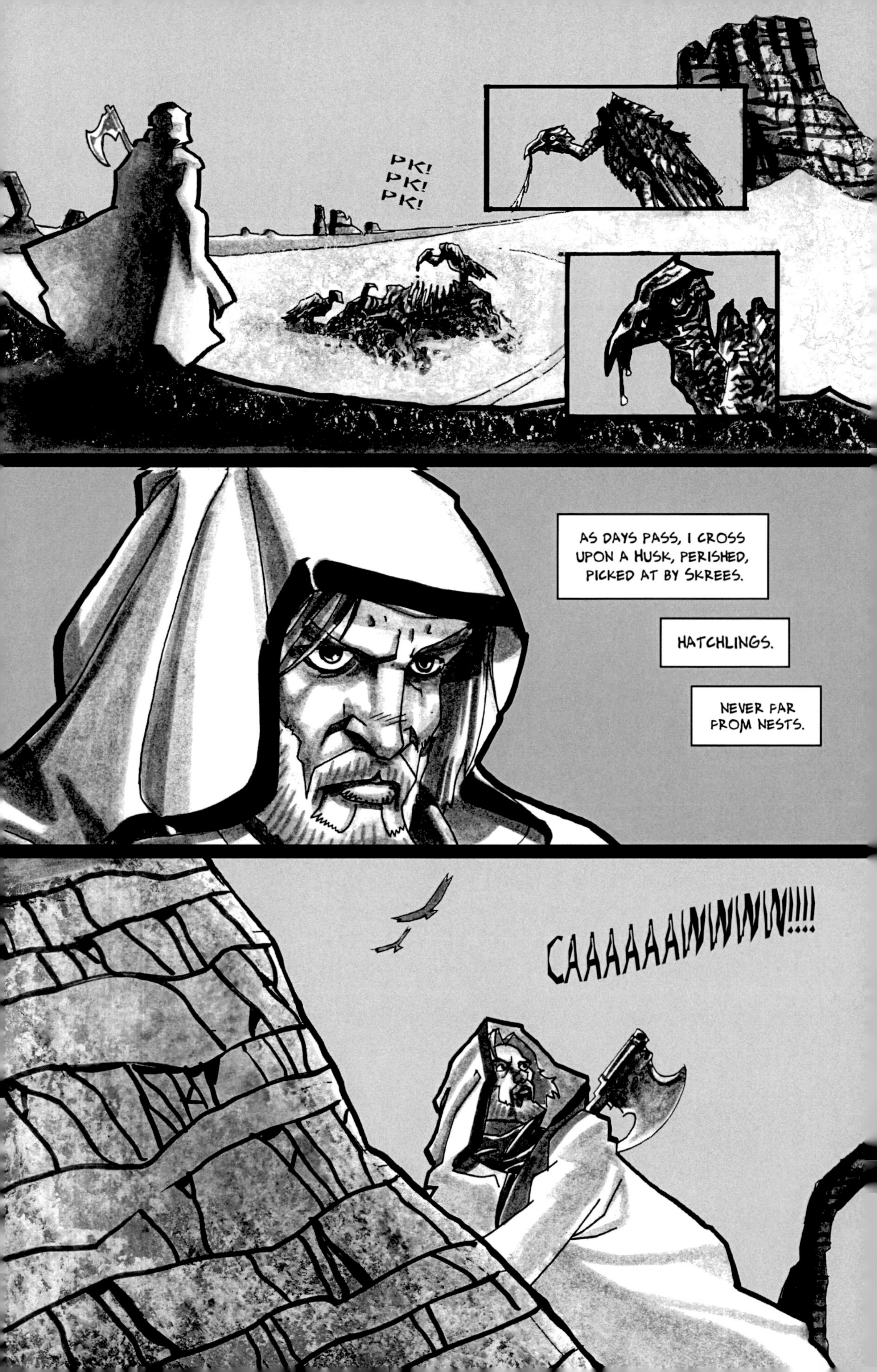
PK! PK! PK!
AS DAYS PASS, I CROSS UPON A HUSK, PERISHED, PICKED AT BY SKREES.
HATCHLINGS.
NEVER FAR FROM NESTS.
CAAAAAAWWWW!!!!

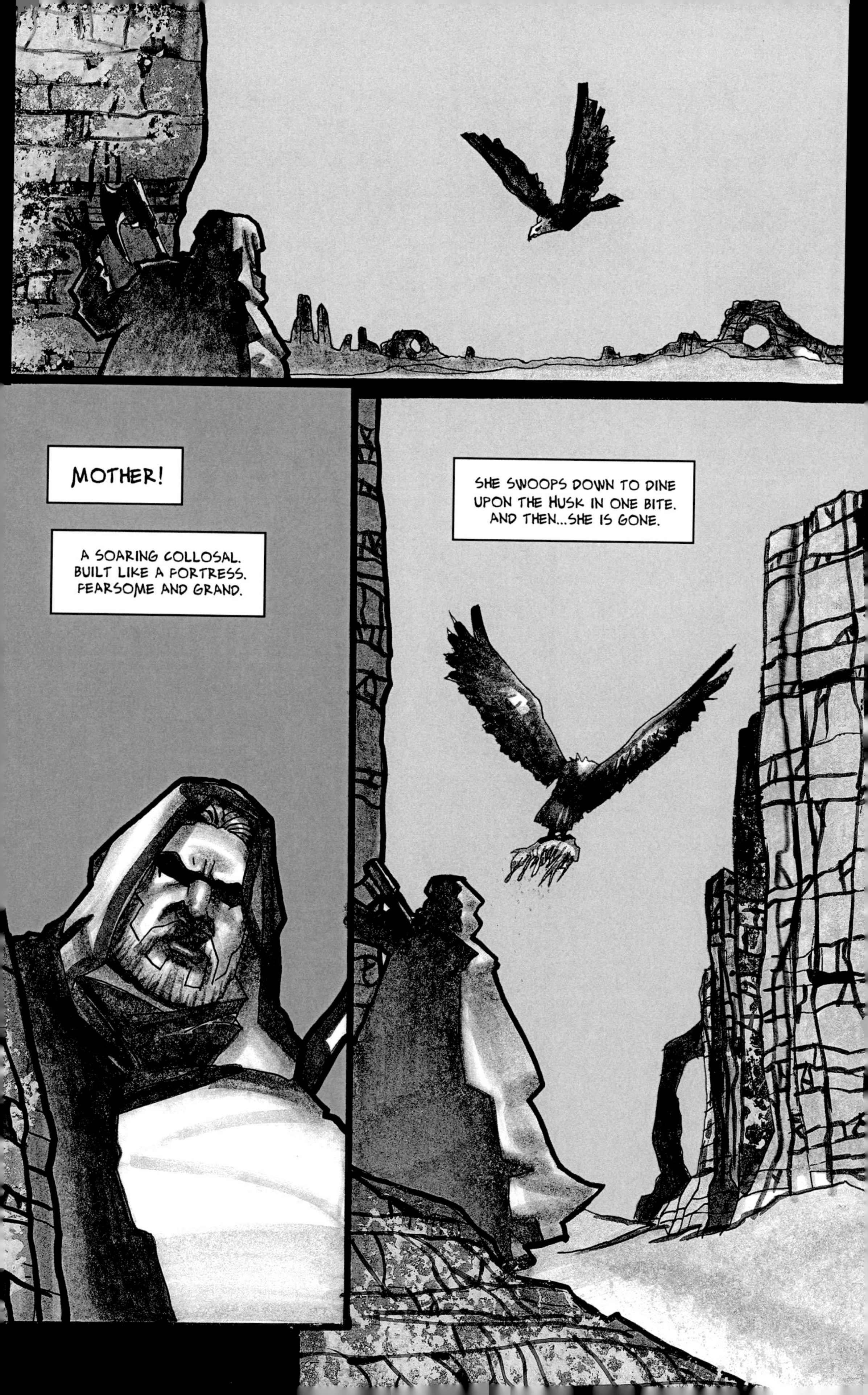
MOTHER!
A SOARING COLLOSAL. BUILT LIKE A FORTRESS. FEARSOME AND GRAND.
SHE SWOOPS DOWN TO DINE UPON THE HUSK IN ONE BITE. AND THEN...SHE IS GONE.

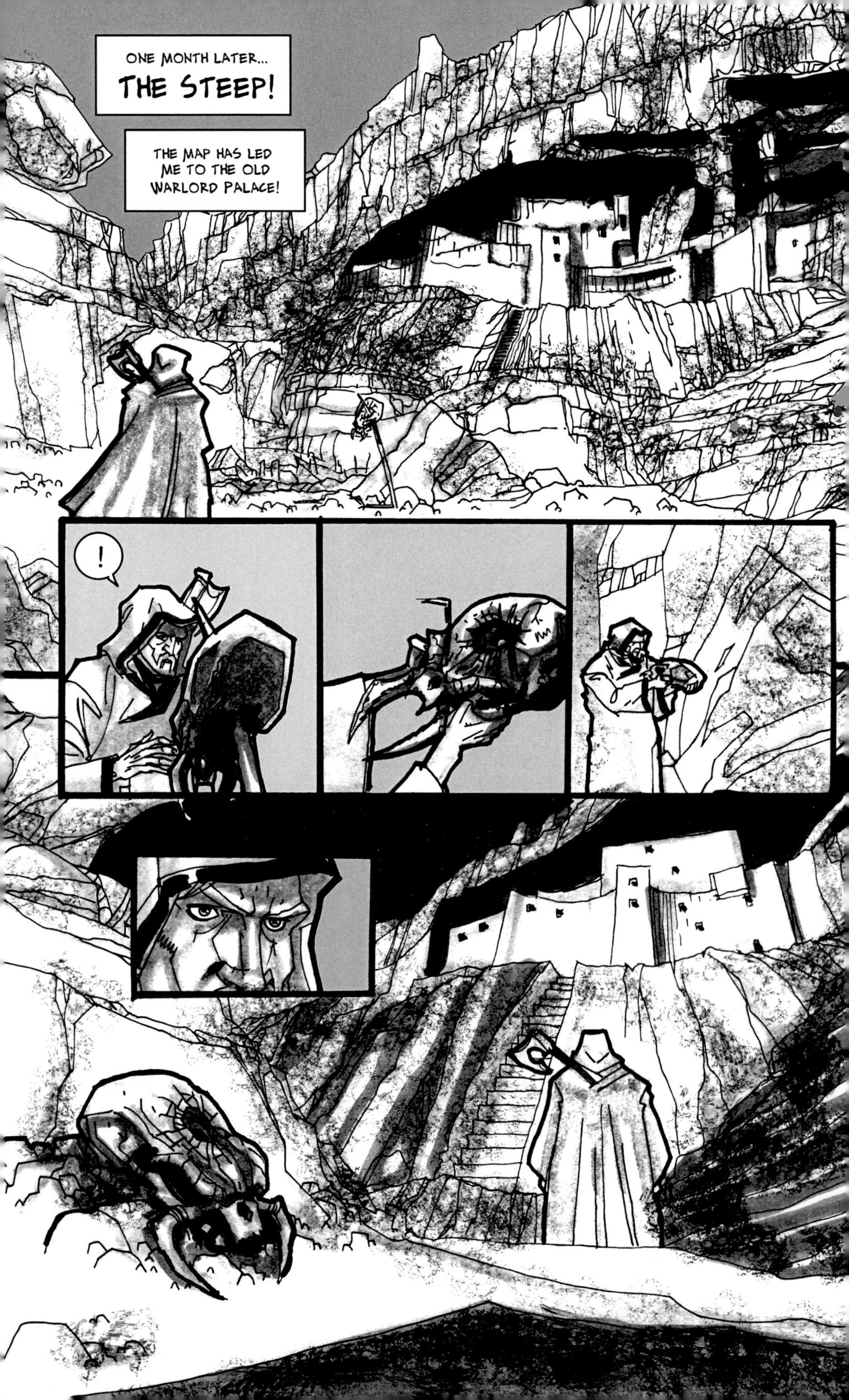
ONE MONTH LATER...
THE STEEP!
THE MAP HAS LED ME TO THE OLD WARLORD PALACE!
!

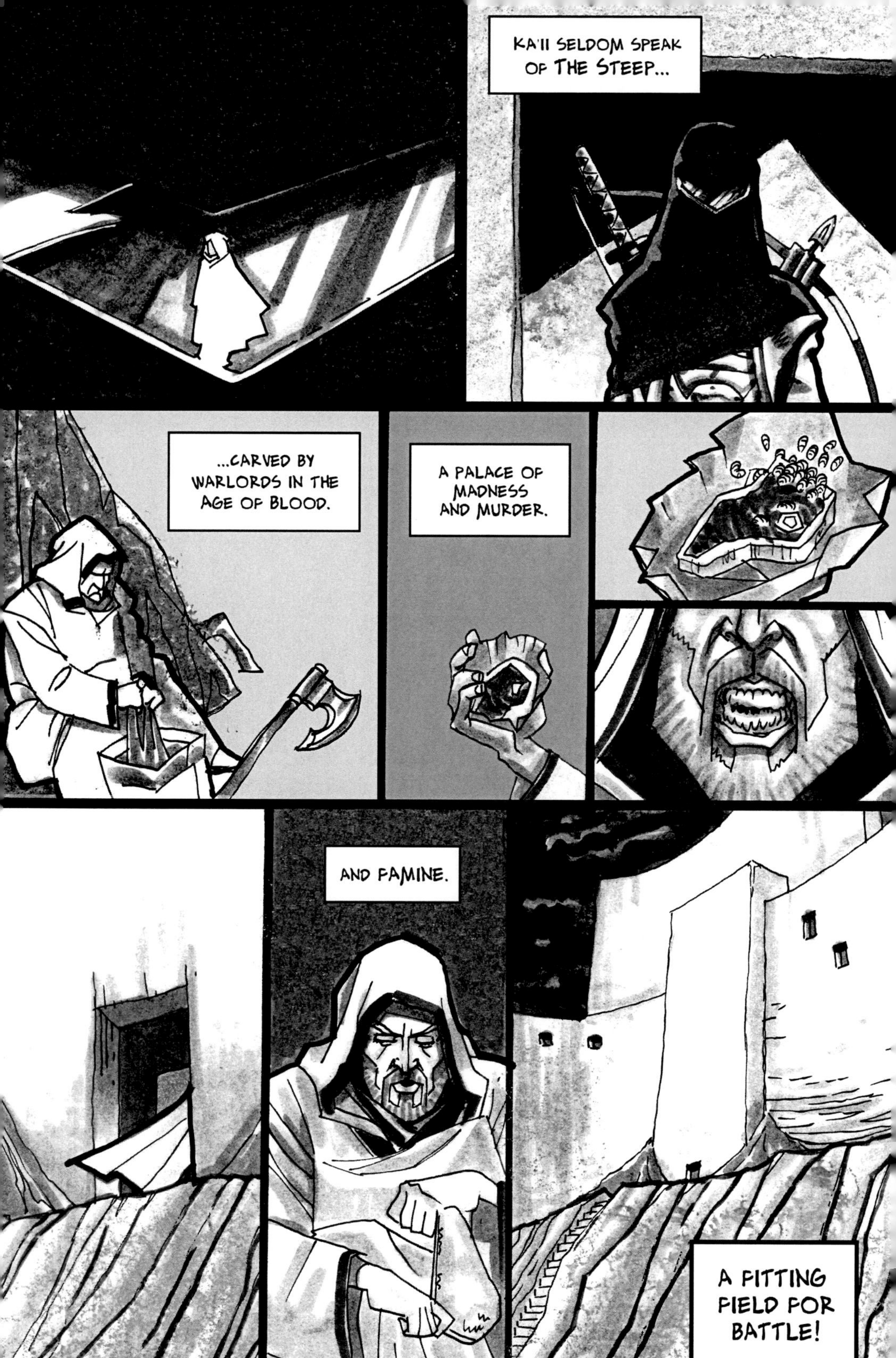
KA'II SELDOM SPEAK OF THE STEEP...
...CARVED BY WARLORDS IN THE AGE OF BLOOD.
A PALACE OF MADNESS AND MURDER.
AND FAMINE.
A FITTING FIELD FOR BATTLE!

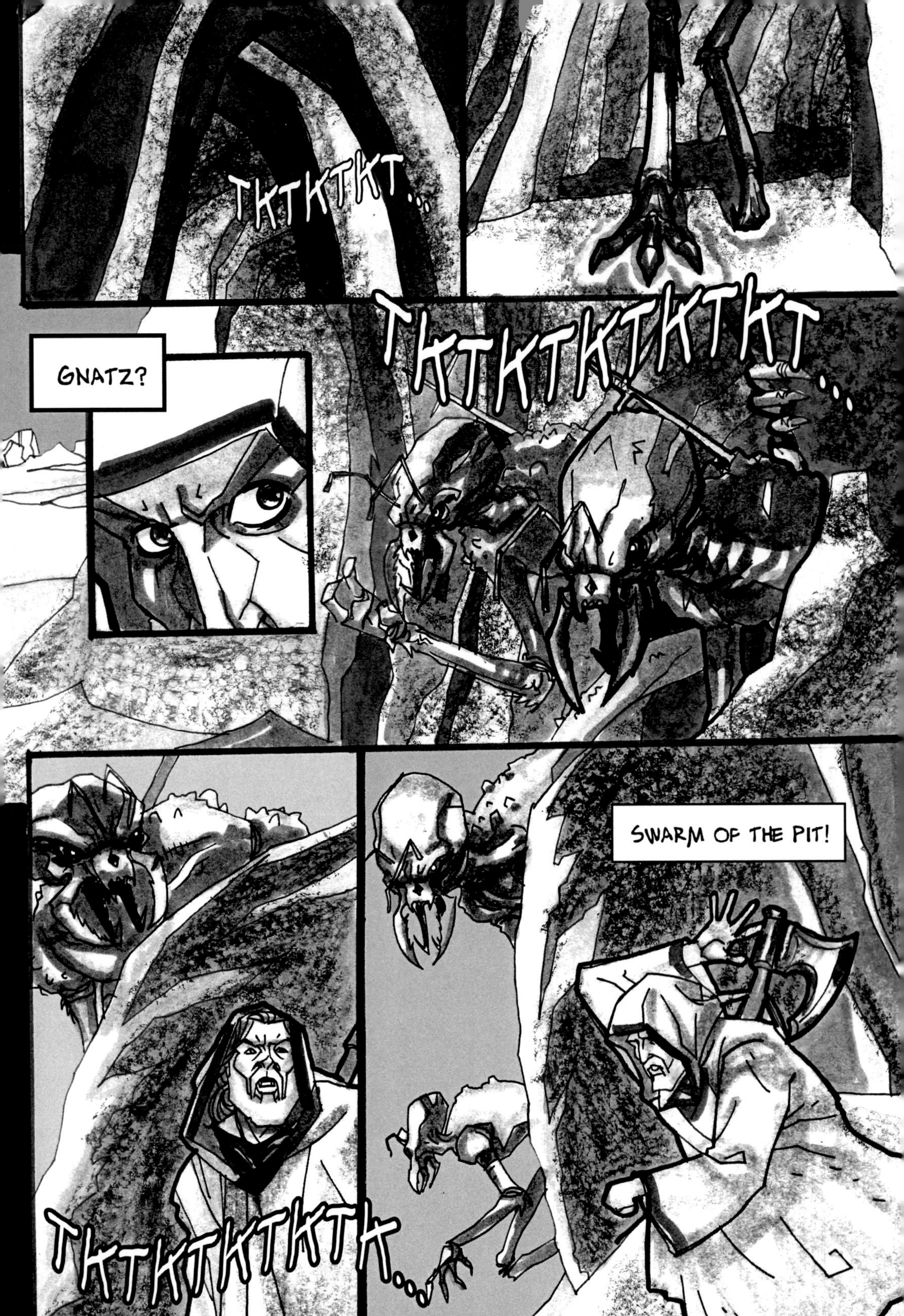
TKTKTKT...
TKTKTKTKTKT...
GNATZ?
SWARM OF THE PIT!
TKTKTKTKTK...

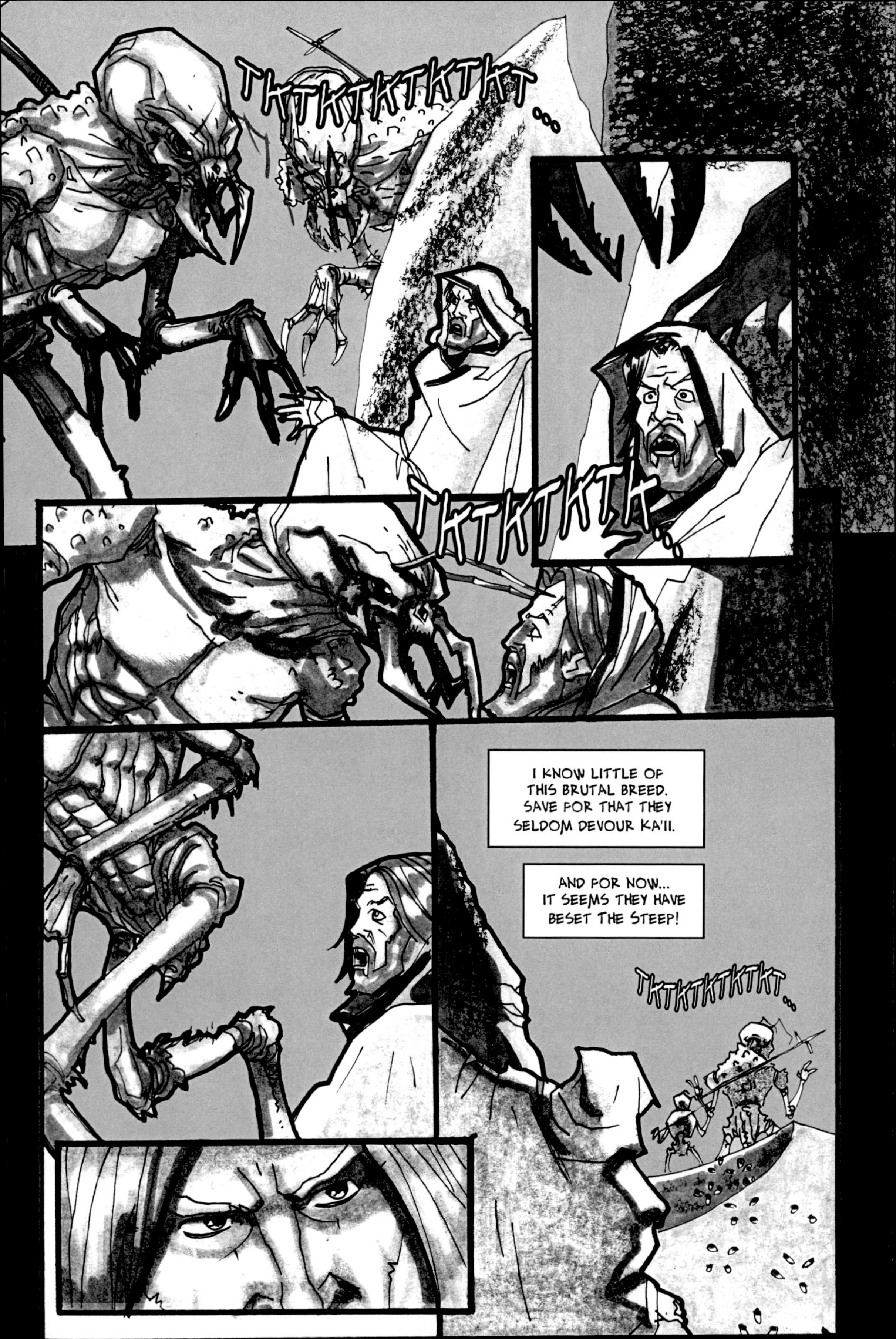
TKTKTKTKTKT...
TKTKTKTK...
I KNOW LITTLE OF THIS BRUTAL BREED. SAVE FOR THAT THEY SELDOM DEVOUR KA'II.
AND FOR NOW... IT SEEMS THEY HAVE BESET THE STEEP!
TKTKTKTKTKT...

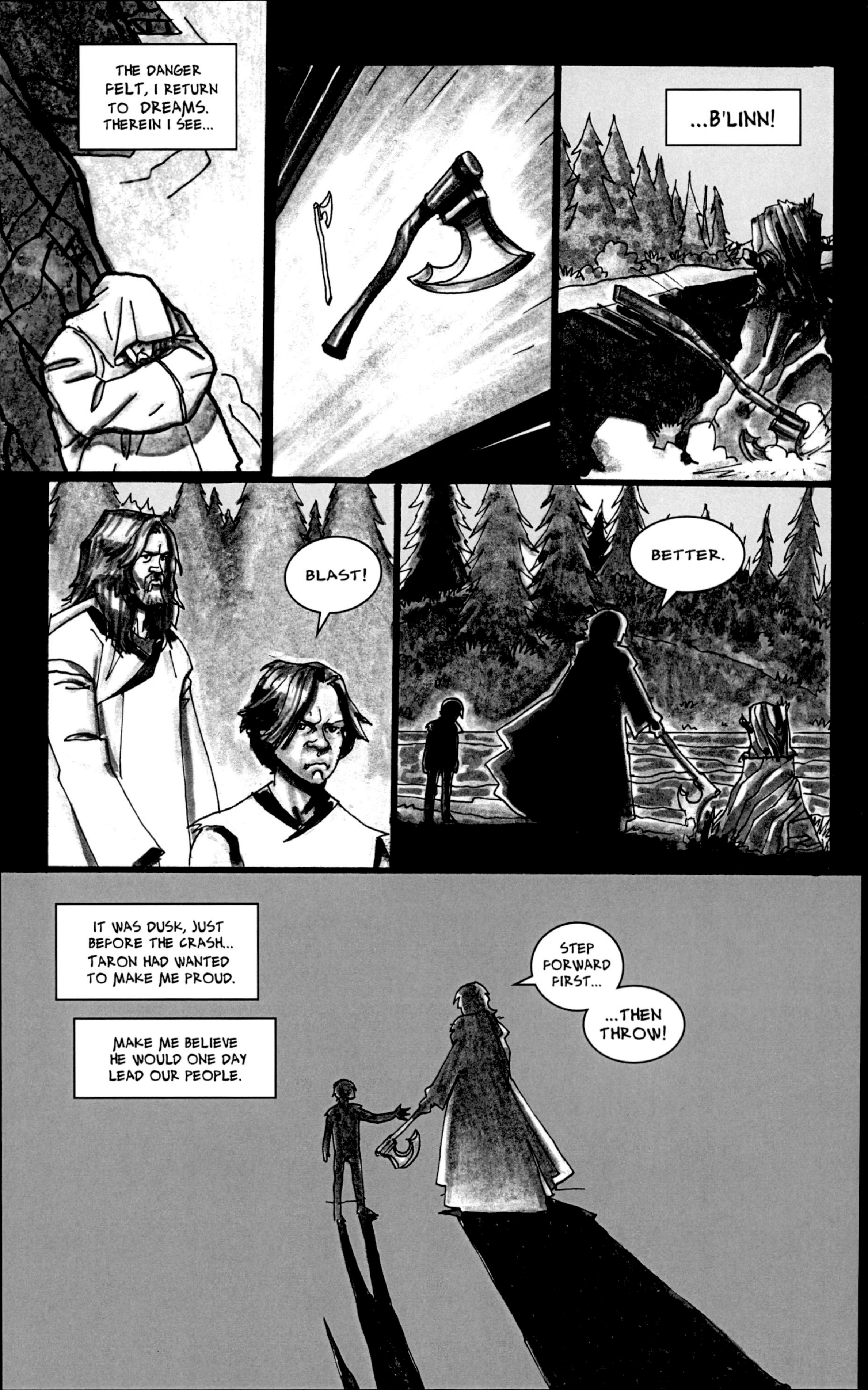
THE DANGER FELT, I RETURN TO DREAMS. THEREIN I SEE...
...B'LINN!
BLAST!
BETTER.
IT WAS DUSK, JUST BEFORE THE CRASH... TARON HAD WANTED TO MAKE ME PROUD.
MAKE ME BELIEVE HE WOULD ONE DAY LEAD OUR PEOPLE.
STEP FORWARD FIRST...
...THEN THROW!

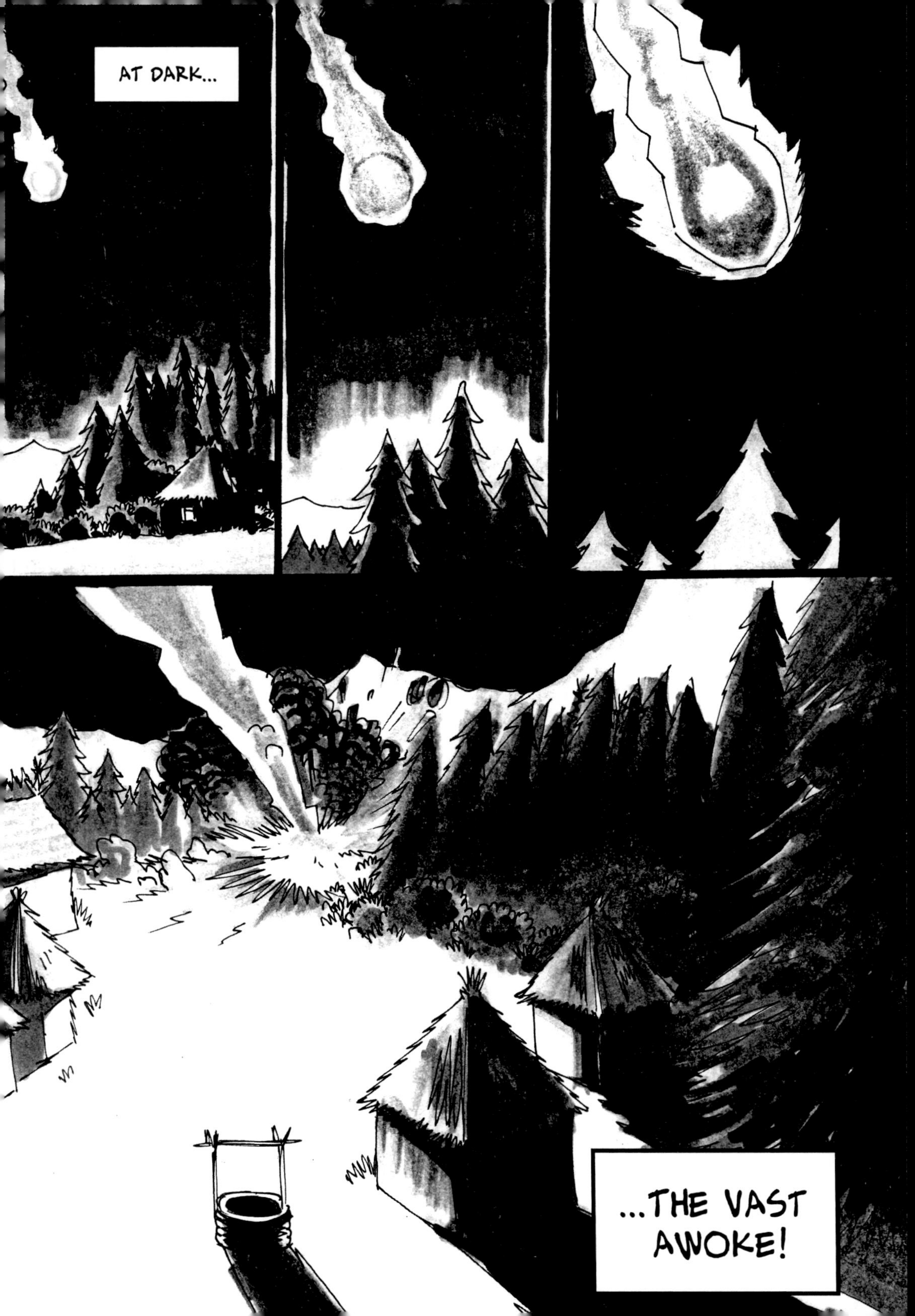
AT DARK...
...THE VAST AWOKE!

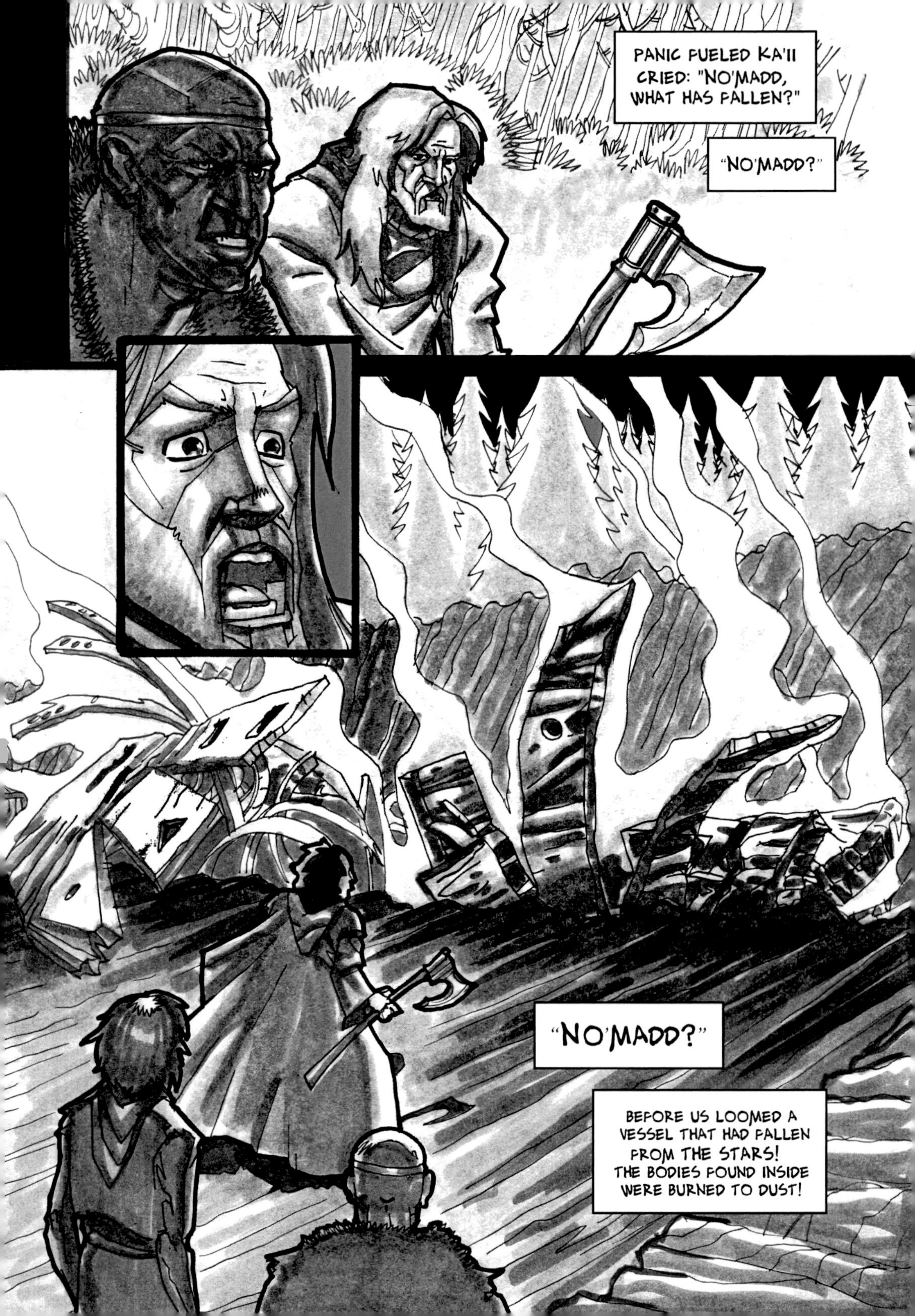
PANIC FUELED KA'II CRIED: "NO'MADD, WHAT HAS FALLEN?"
"NO'MADD?"
"NO'MADD?"
BEFORE US LOOMED A VESSEL THAT HAD FALLEN FROM THE STARS! THE BODIES FOUND INSIDE WERE BURNED TO DUST!

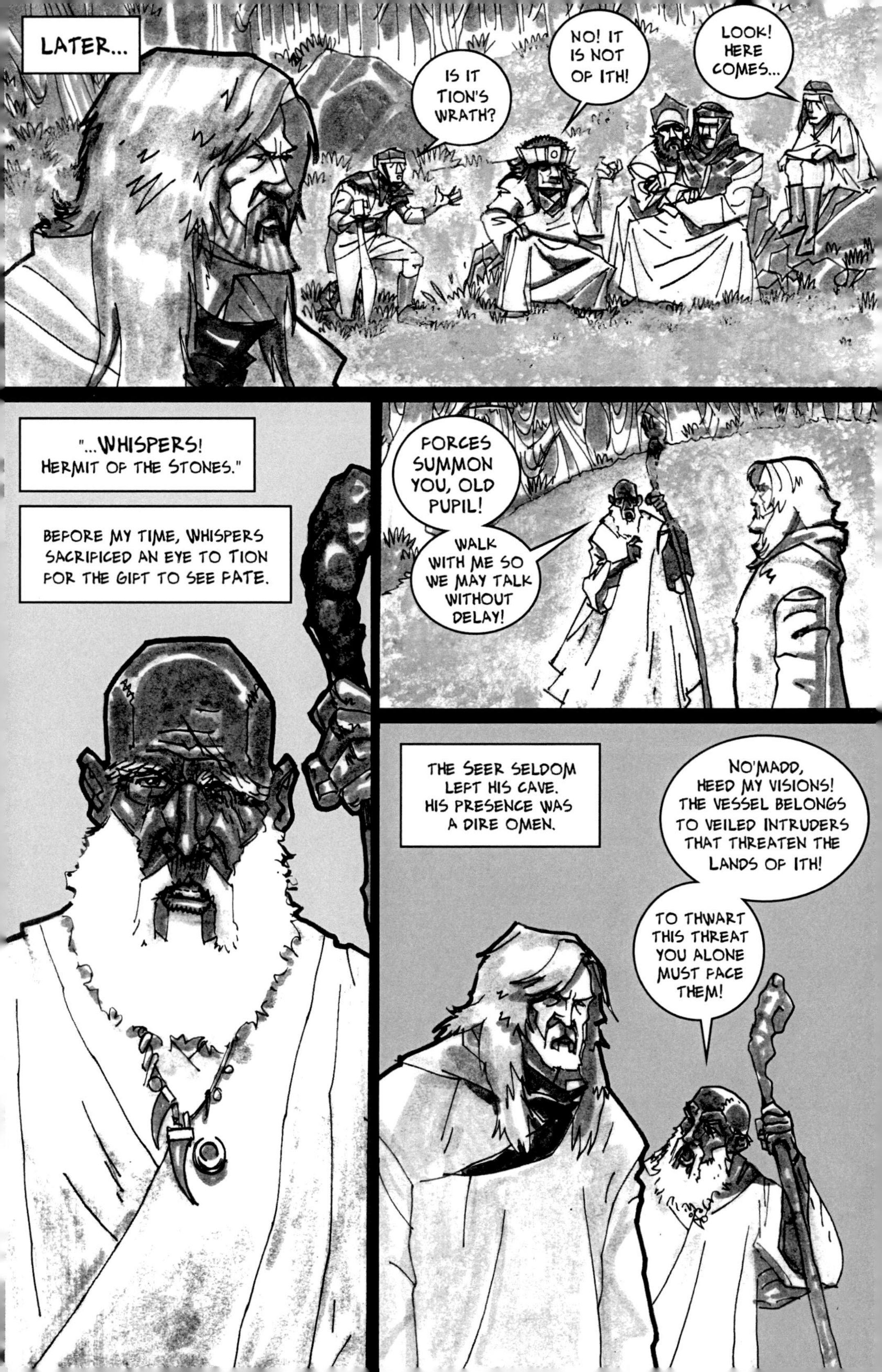
LATER...
IS IT TION'S WRATH?
NO! IT IS NOT OF ITH!
LOOK! HERE COMES...
"...WHISPERS! HERMIT OF THE STONES."
BEFORE MY TIME, WHISPERS SACRIFICED AN EYE TO TION FOR THE GIFT TO SEE FATE.
FORCES SUMMON YOU, OLD PUPIL!
WALK WITH ME SO WE MAY TALK WITHOUT DELAY!
THE SEER SELDOM LEFT HIS CAVE. HIS PRESENCE WAS A DIRE OMEN.
NO'MADD, HEED MY VISIONS! THE VESSEL BELONGS TO VEILED INTRUDERS THAT THREATEN THE LANDS OF ITH!
TO THWART THIS THREAT YOU ALONE MUST FACE THEM!

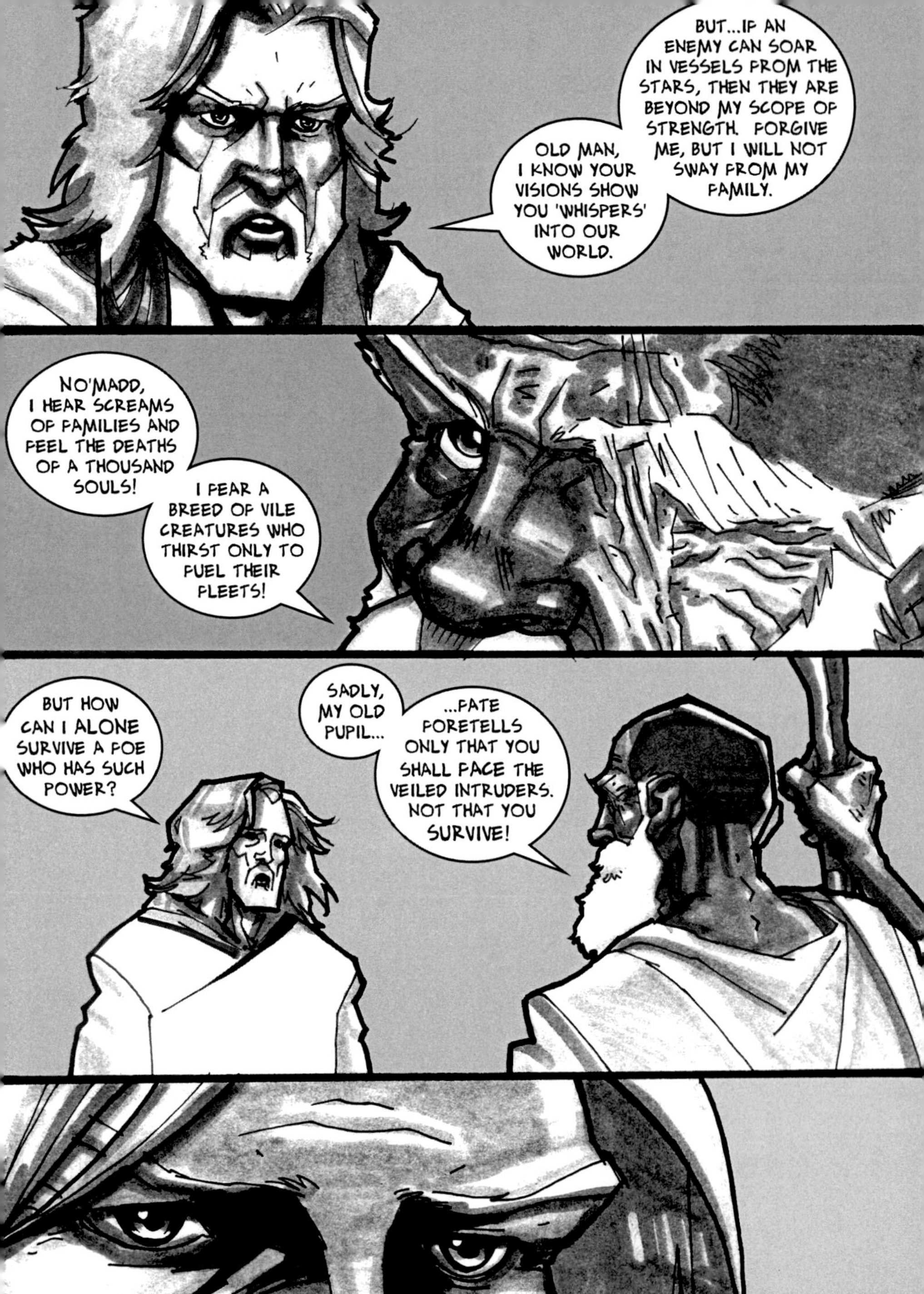

OLD MAN, I KNOW YOUR VISIONS SHOW YOU 'WHISPERS' INTO OUR WORLD.
BUT...IF AN ENEMY CAN SOAR IN VESSELS FROM THE STARS, THEN THEY ARE BEYOND MY SCOPE OF STRENGTH. FORGIVE ME, BUT I WILL NOT SWAY FROM MY FAMILY.
NO'MADD, I HEAR SCREAMS OF FAMILIES AND FEEL THE DEATHS OF A THOUSAND SOULS!
I FEAR A BREED OF VILE CREATURES WHO THIRST ONLY TO FUEL THEIR FLEETS!
BUT HOW CAN I ALONE SURVIVE A FOE WHO HAS SUCH POWER?
SADLY, MY OLD PUPIL...
...FATE FORETELLS ONLY THAT YOU SHALL FACE THE VEILED INTRUDERS. NOT THAT YOU SURVIVE!

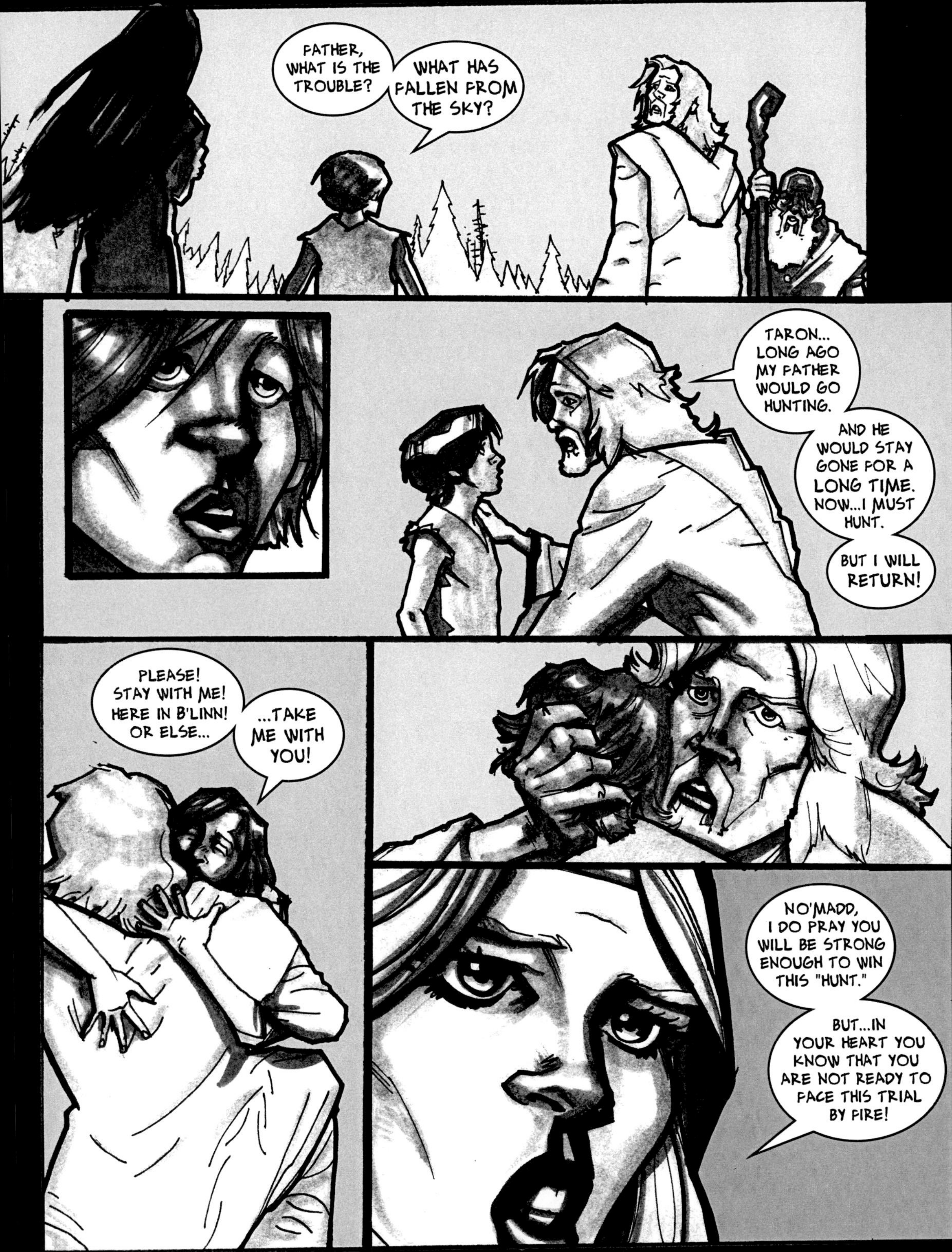
FATHER, WHAT IS THE TROUBLE?
WHAT HAS FALLEN FROM THE SKY?
TARON... LONG AGO MY FATHER WOULD GO HUNTING.
AND HE WOULD STAY GONE FOR A LONG TIME. NOW...I MUST HUNT.
BUT I WILL RETURN!
PLEASE! STAY WITH ME! HERE IN B'LINN! OR ELSE...
...TAKE ME WITH YOU!
NO'MADD, I DO PRAY YOU WILL BE STRONG ENOUGH TO WIN THIS "HUNT."
BUT...IN YOUR HEART YOU KNOW THAT YOU ARE NOT READY TO FACE THIS TRIAL BY FIRE!

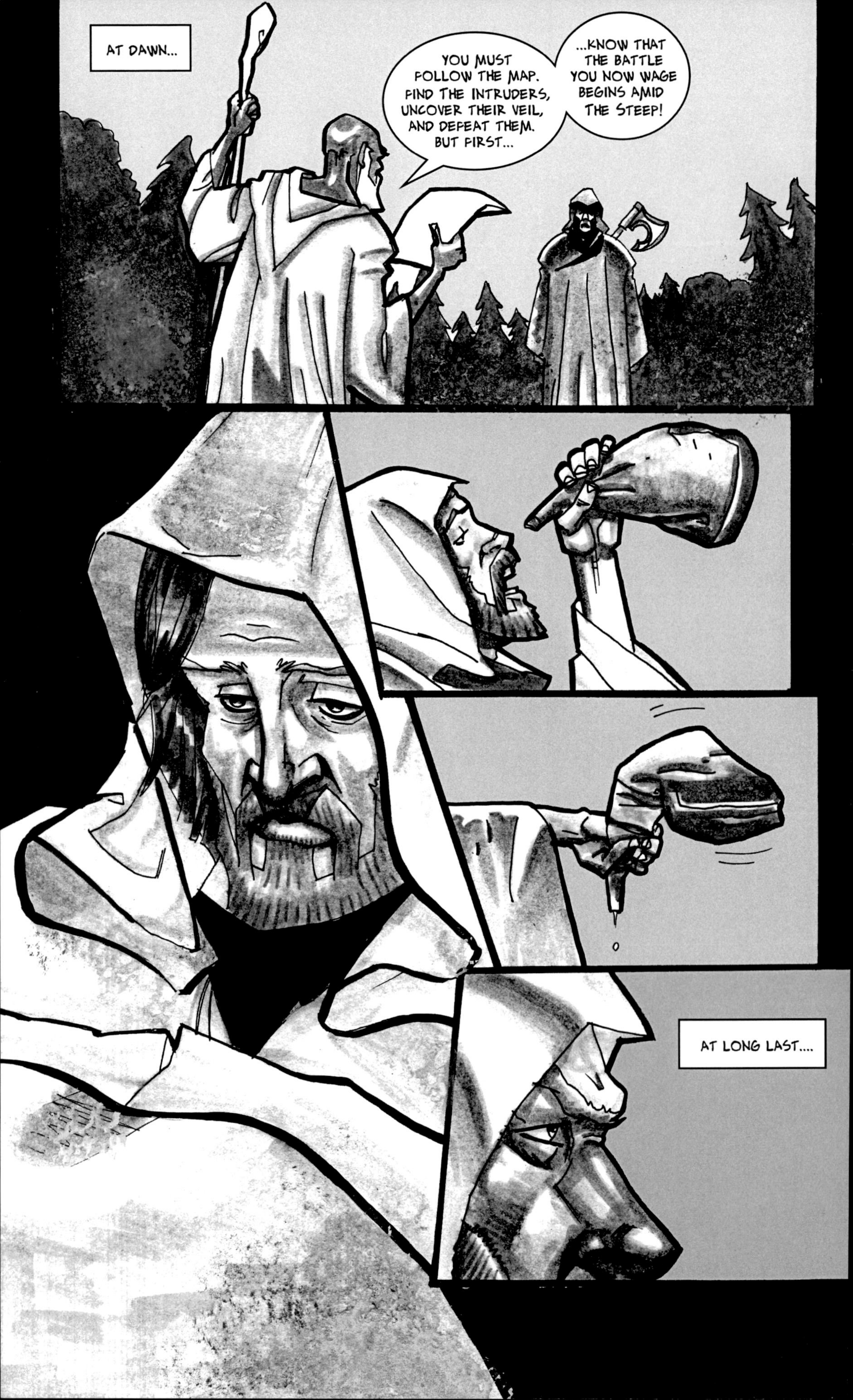
AT DAWN...
YOU MUST FOLLOW THE MAP. FIND THE INTRUDERS, UNCOVER THEIR VEIL, AND DEFEAT THEM. BUT FIRST...
...KNOW THAT THE BATTLE YOU NOW WAGE BEGINS AMID THE STEEP!
AT LONG LAST....

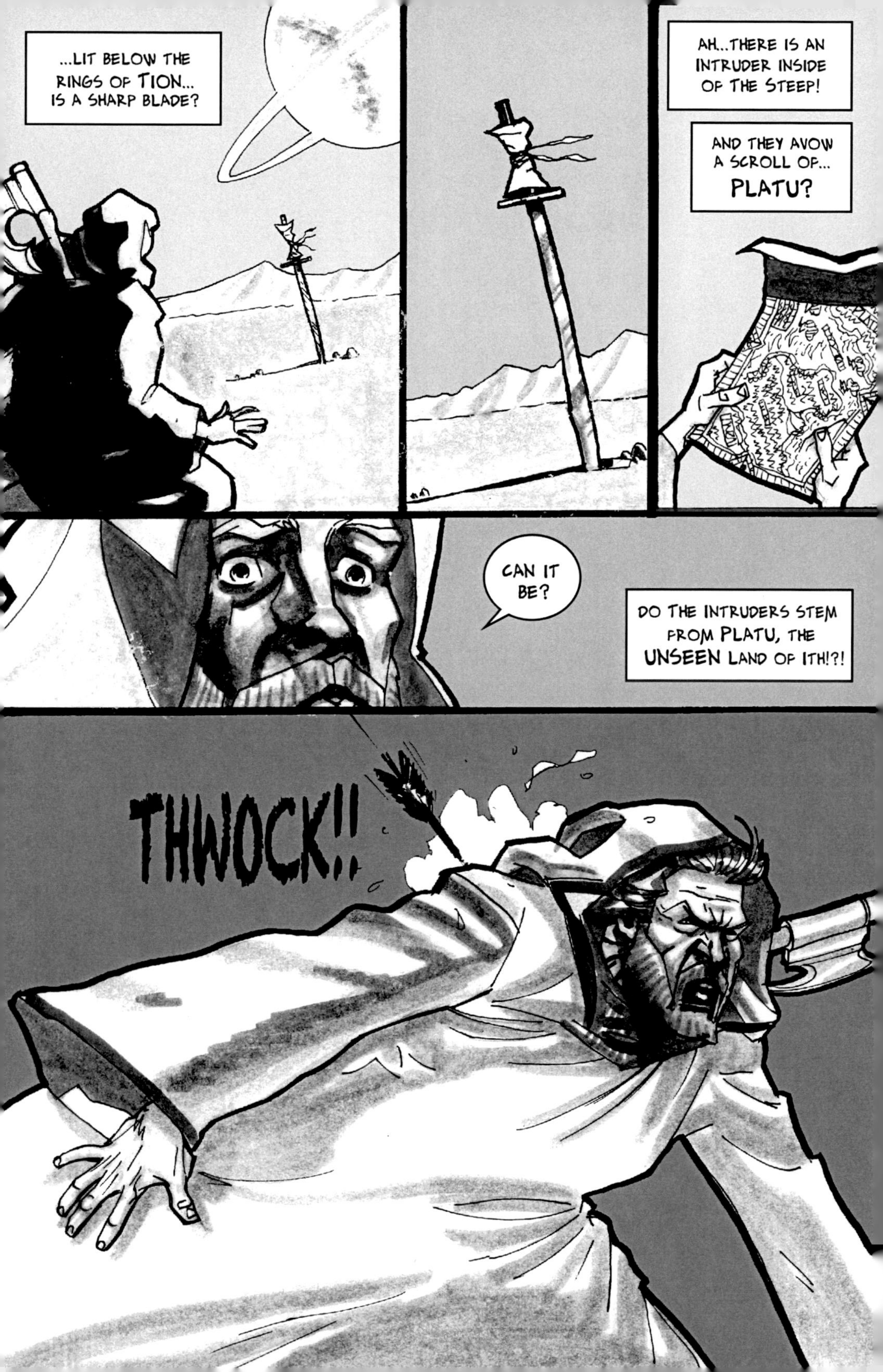
...LIT BELOW THE RINGS OF TION... IS A SHARP BLADE?
AH...THERE IS AN INTRUDER INSIDE OF THE STEEP!
AND THEY AVOW A SCROLL OF... PLATU?
CAN IT BE?
DO THE INTRUDERS STEM FROM PLATU, THE UNSEEN LAND OF ITH!?!
THWOCK!!

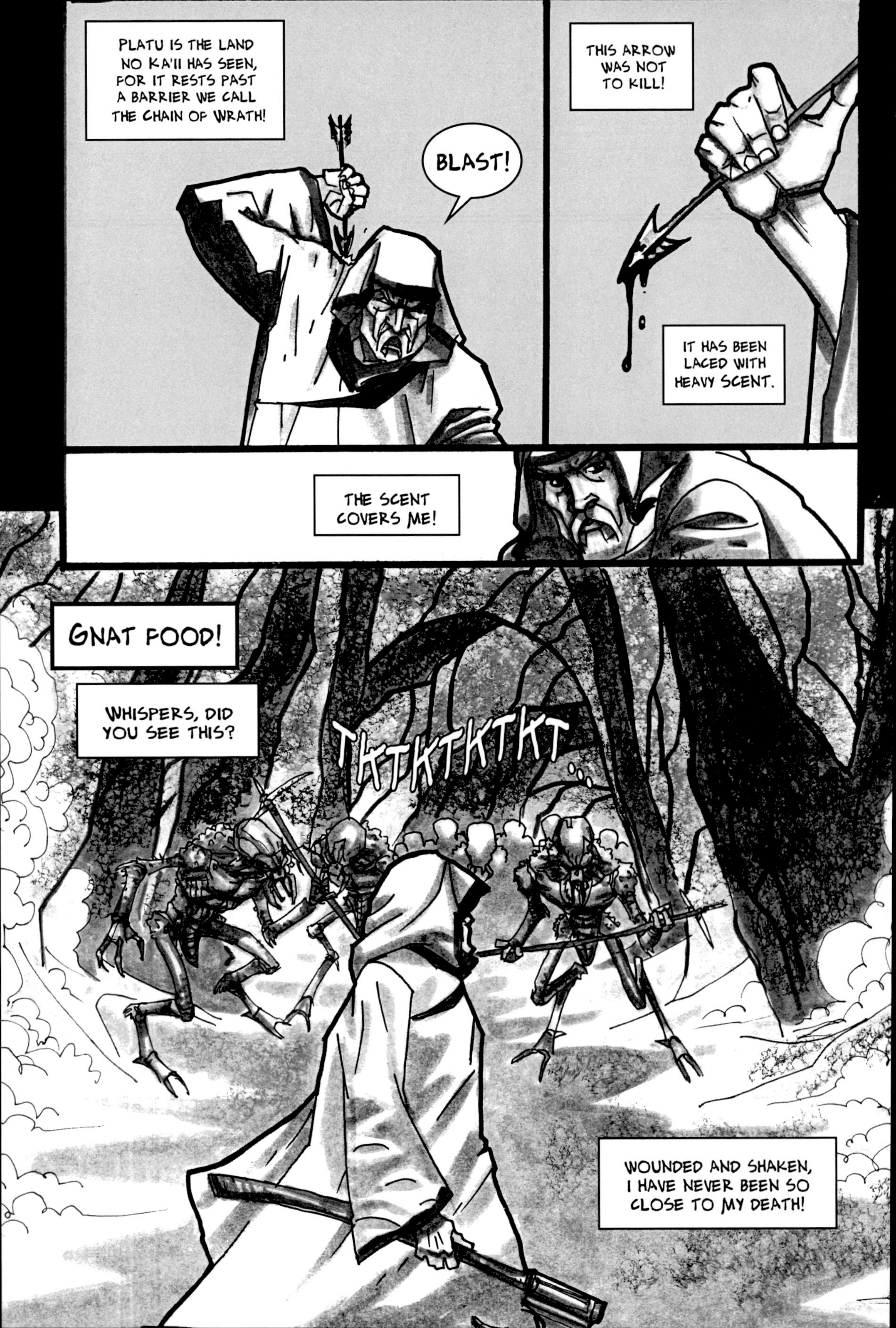
PLATU IS THE LAND NO KA'II HAS SEEN, FOR IT RESTS PAST A BARRIER WE CALL THE CHAIN OF WRATH!
BLAST!
THIS ARROW WAS NOT TO KILL!
IT HAS BEEN LACED WITH HEAVY SCENT.
THE SCENT COVERS ME!
GNAT FOOD!
WHISPERS, DID YOU SEE THIS?
THKTKTKTKT...
WOUNDED AND SHAKEN, I HAVE NEVER BEEN SO CLOSE TO MY DEATH!

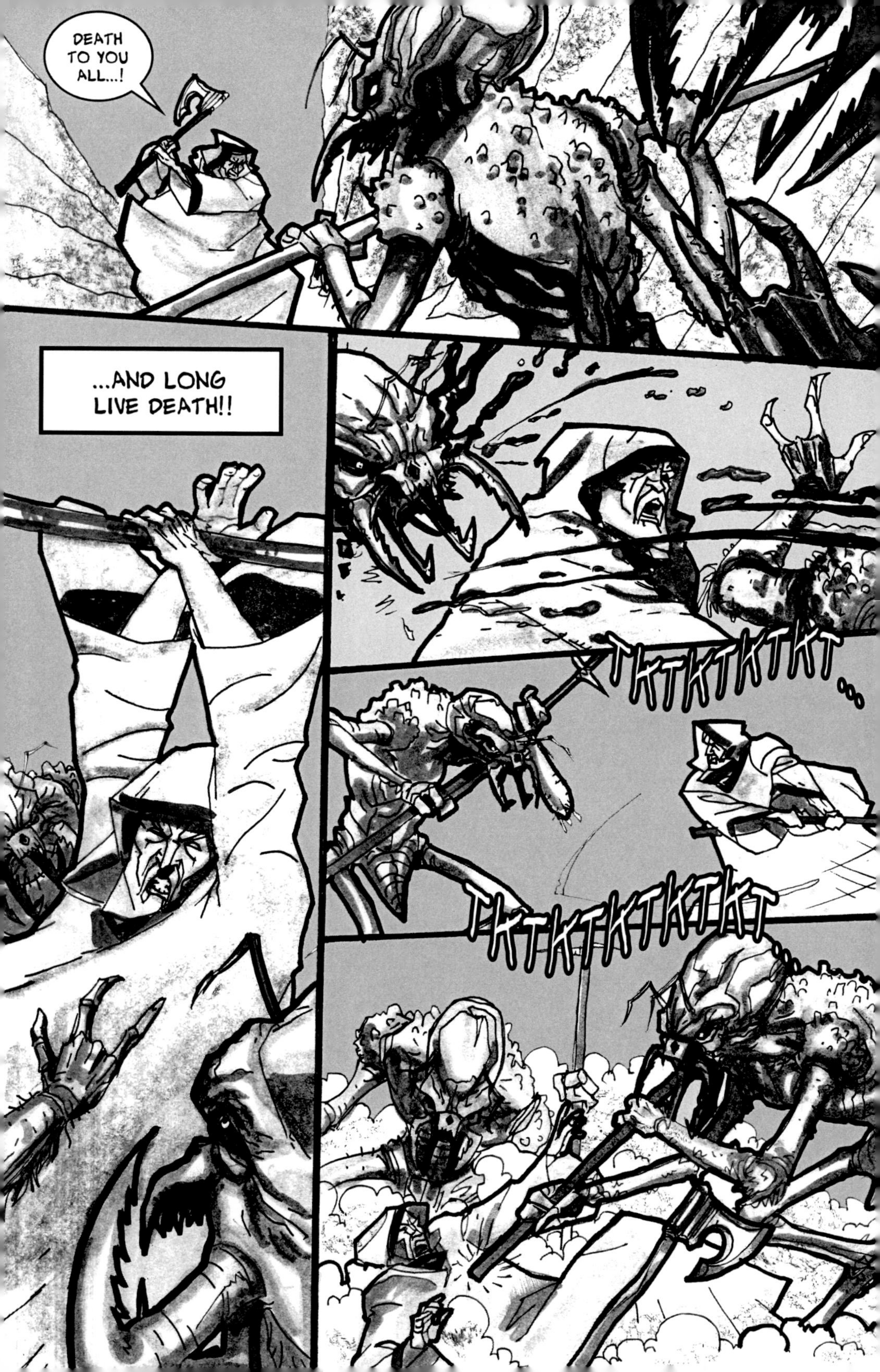
DEATH TO YOU ALL...!
...AND LONG LIVE DEATH!!
TKTKTKTKT...
TKTKTKTKTKT

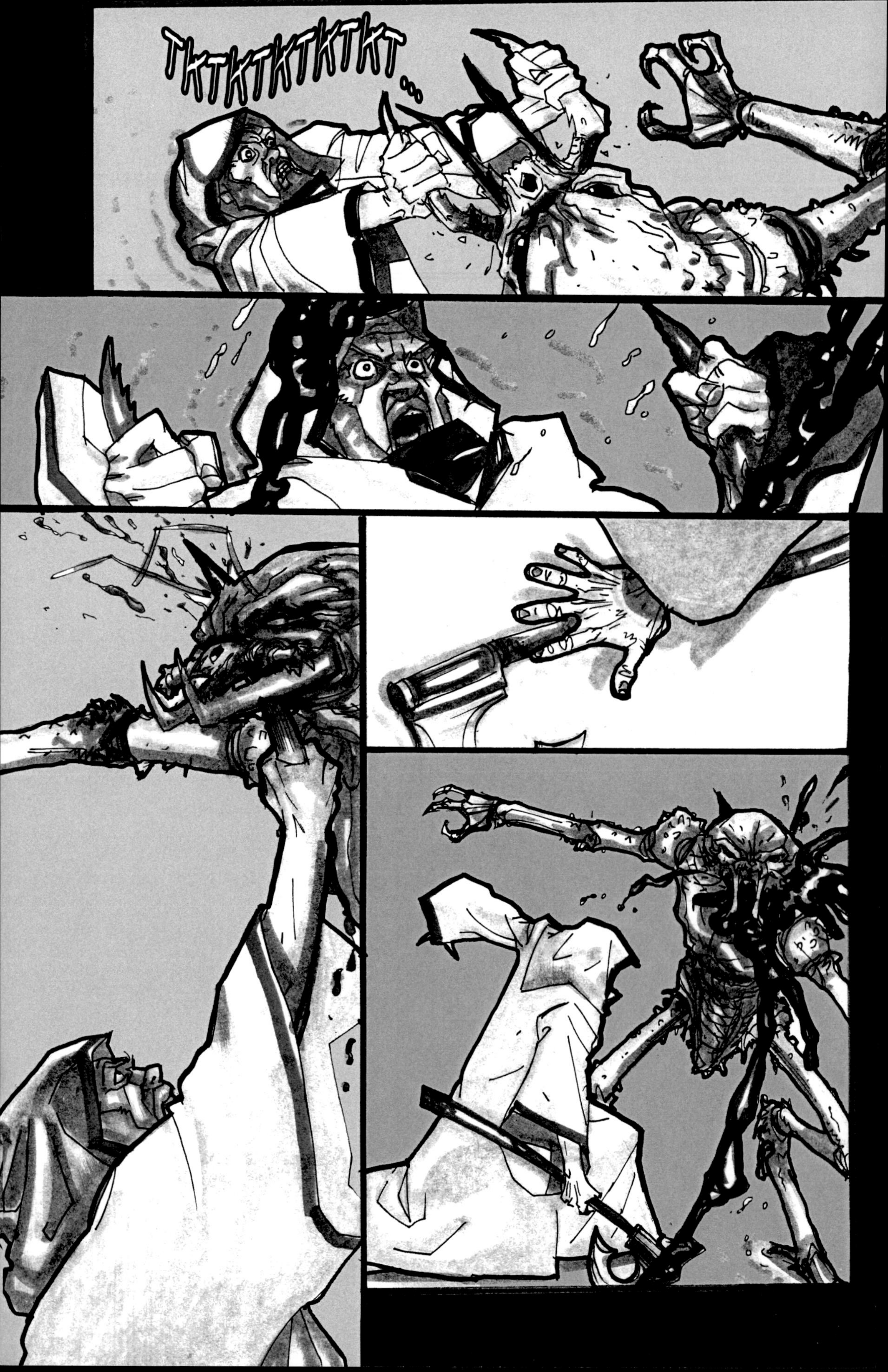
TKTKTKTKTKT...

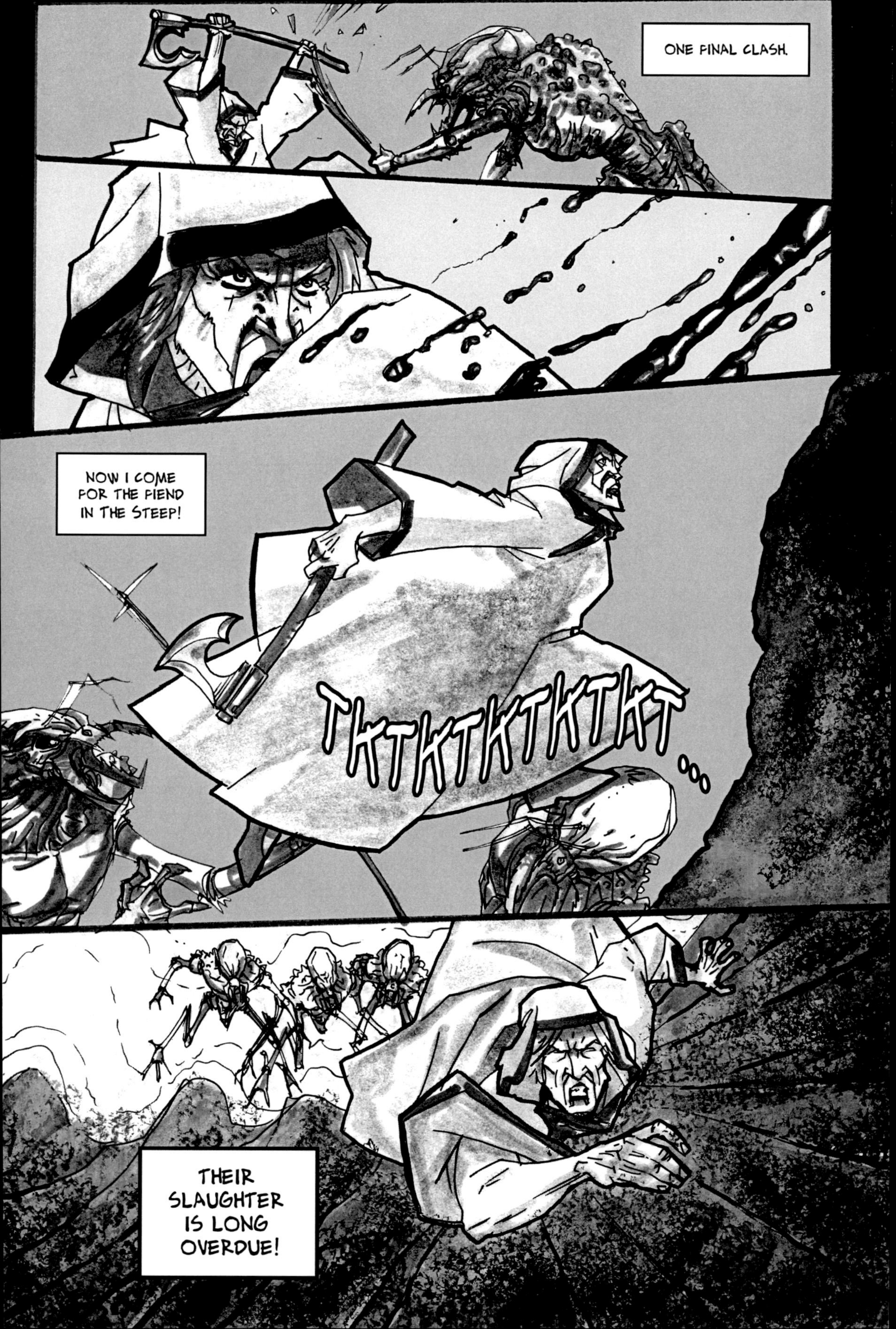
ONE FINAL CLASH.
NOW I COME FOR THE FIEND IN THE STEEP!
THTHTHTHTHT...
THEIR SLAUGHTER IS LONG OVERDUE!

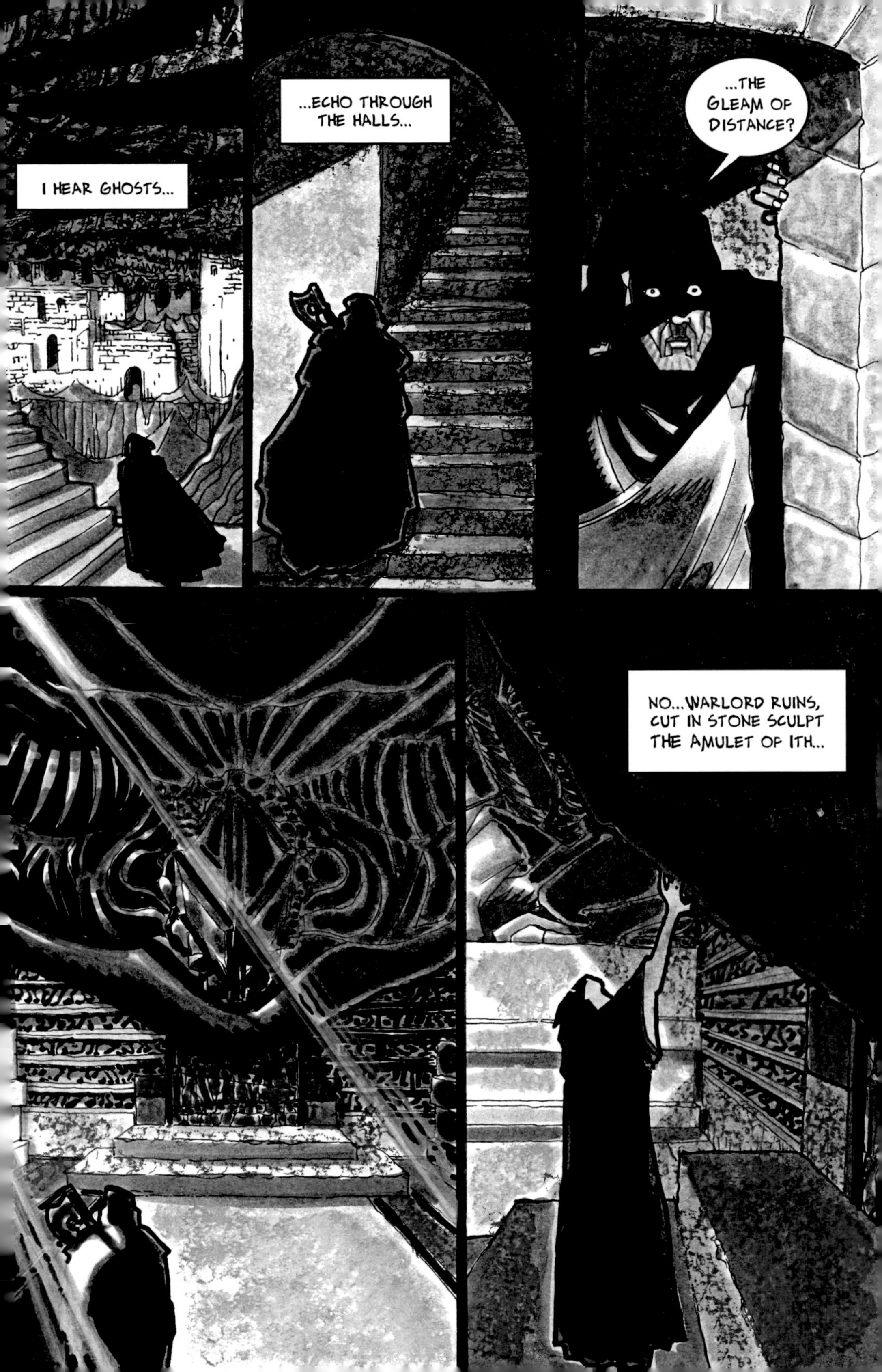
I HEAR GHOSTS...
...ECHO THROUGH THE HALLS...
...THE GLEAM OF DISTANCE?
NO...WARLORD RUINS, CUT IN STONE SCULPT THE AMULET OF ITH...

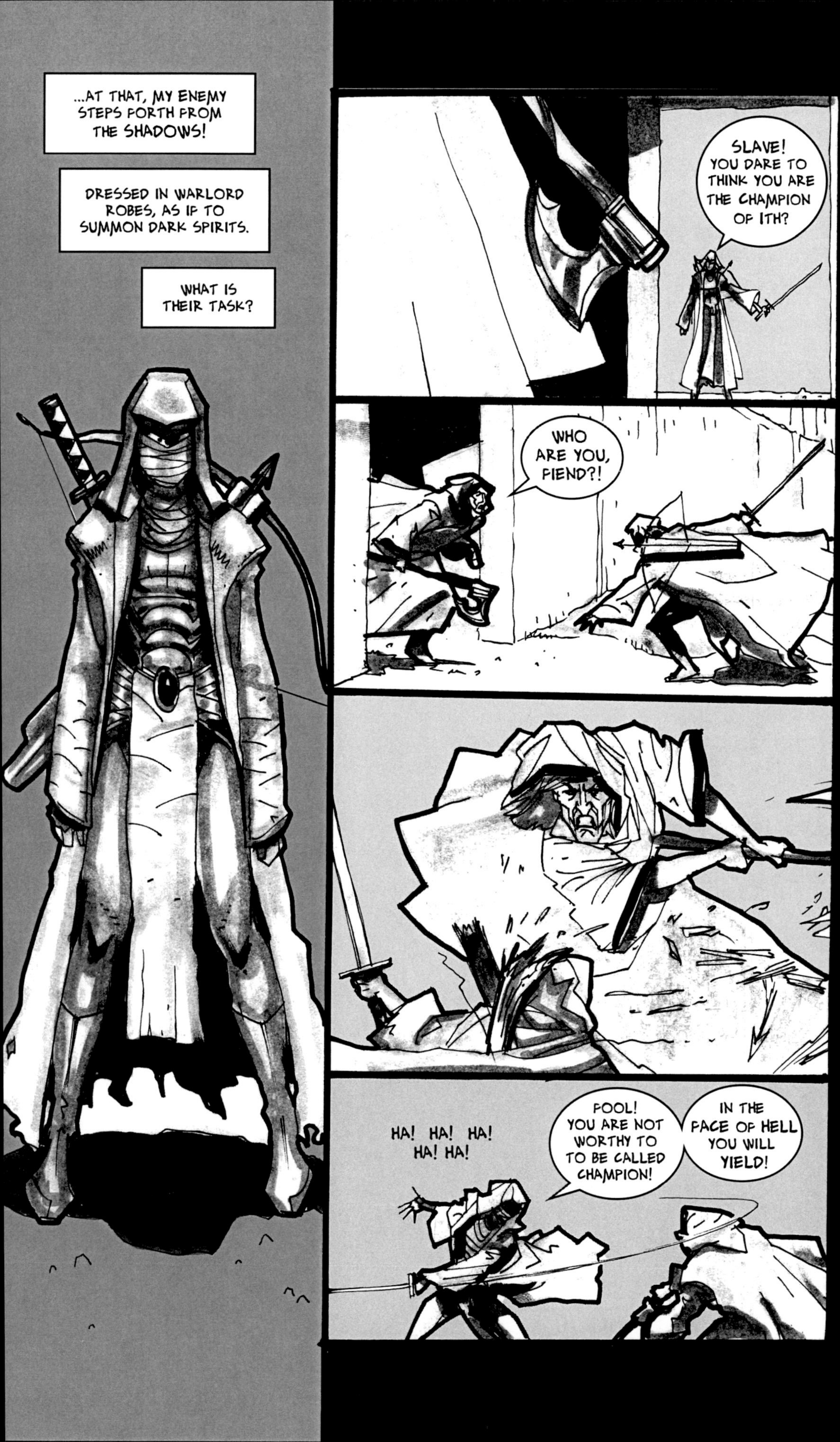
...AT THAT, MY ENEMY STEPS FORTH FROM THE SHADOWS!
DRESSED IN WARLORD ROBES, AS IF TO SUMMON DARK SPIRITS.
WHAT IS THEIR TASK?
SLAVE! YOU DARE TO THINK YOU ARE THE CHAMPION OF ITH?
WHO ARE YOU, FIEND?!
HA! HA! HA! HA! HA!
FOOL! YOU ARE NOT WORTHY TO BE CALLED CHAMPION!
IN THE FACE OF HELL YOU WILL YIELD!

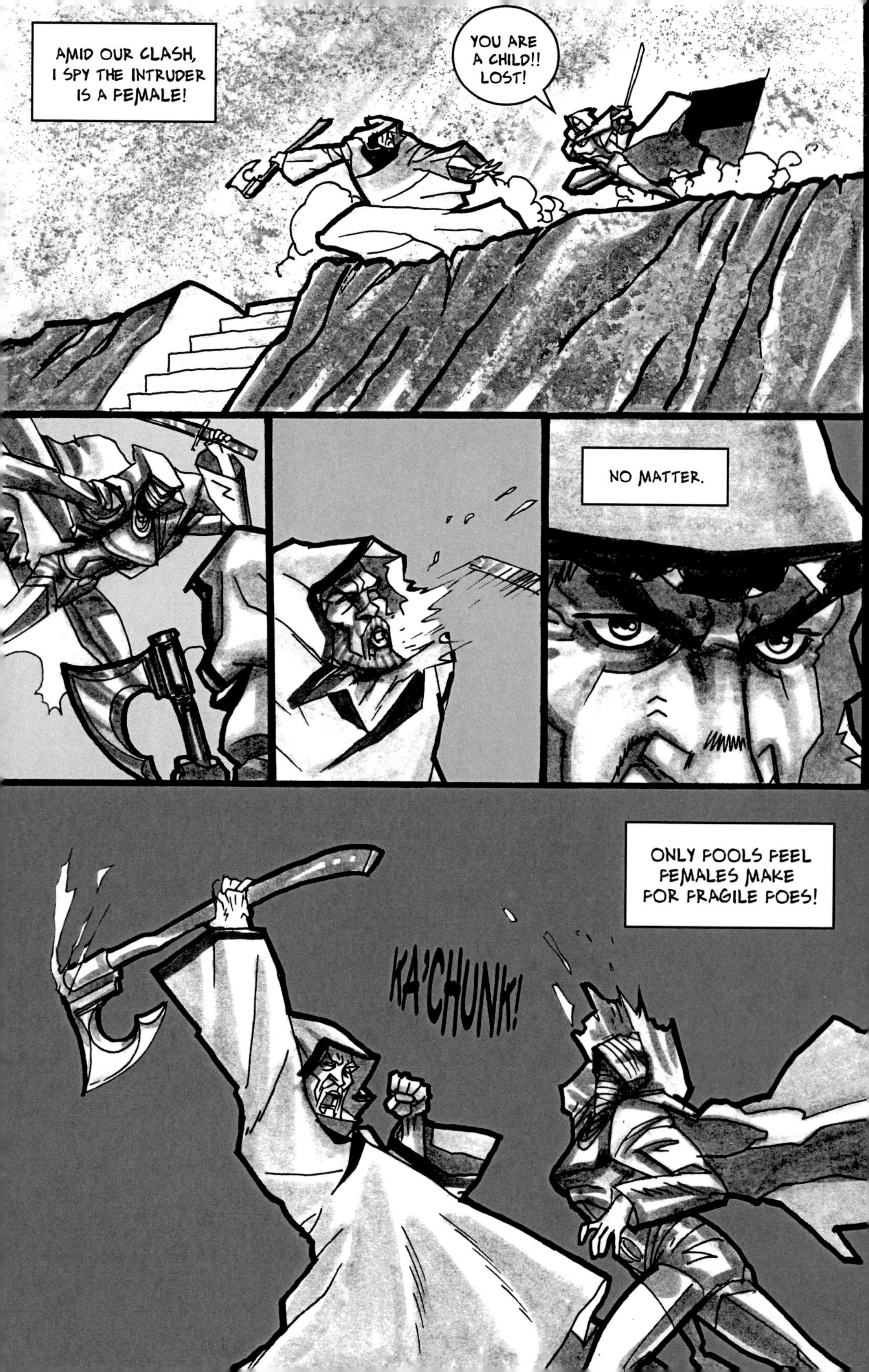
AMID OUR CLASH, I SPY THE INTRUDER IS A FEMALE!
YOU ARE A CHILD!! LOST!
NO MATTER.
ONLY FOOLS FEEL FEMALES MAKE FOR FRAGILE FOES!
KA'CHUNK!

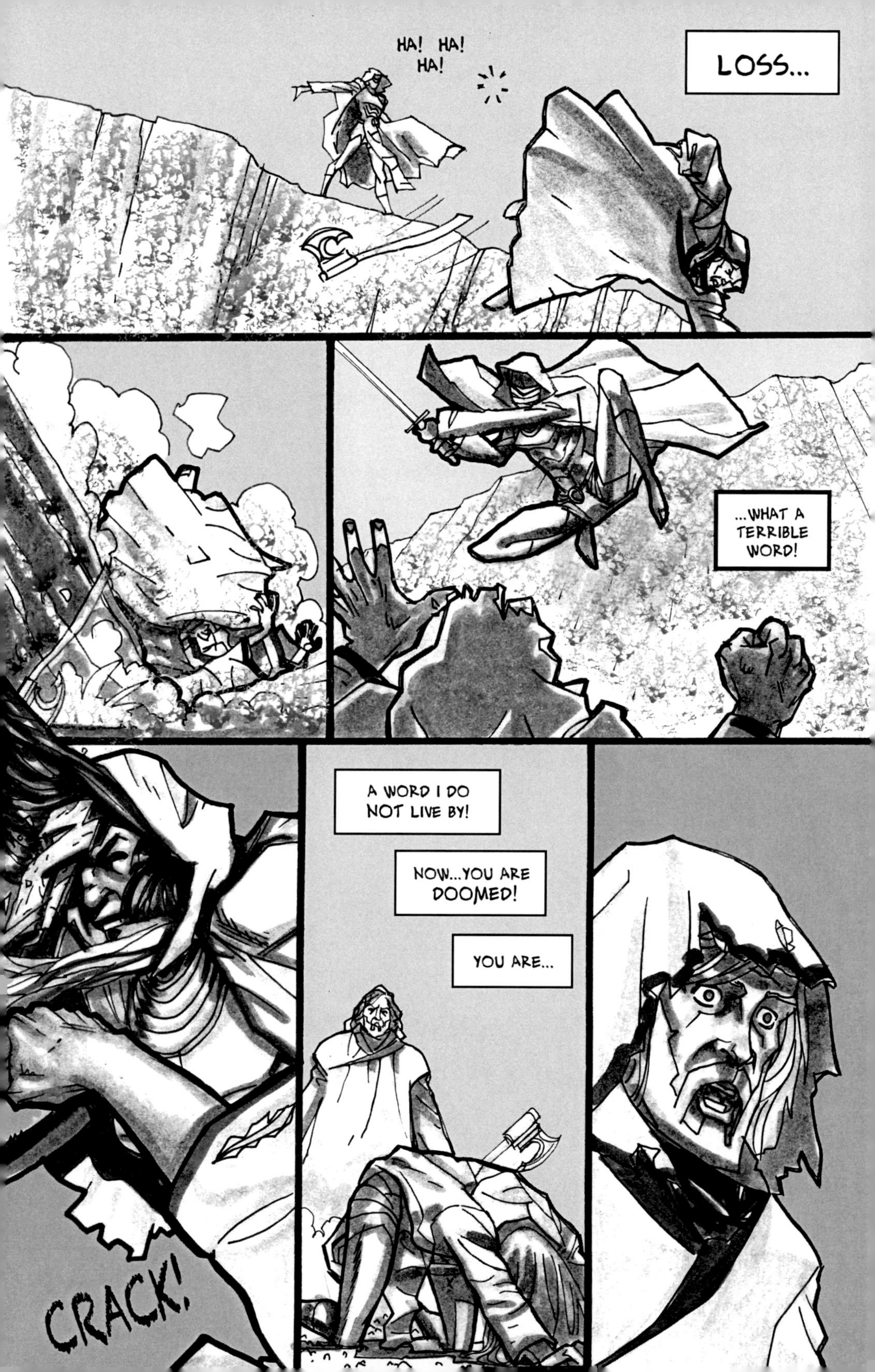
HA! HA!
HA!
LOSS...
...WHAT A TERRIBLE WORD!
CRACK!
A WORD I DO NOT LIVE BY!
NOW...YOU ARE DOOMED!
YOU ARE...

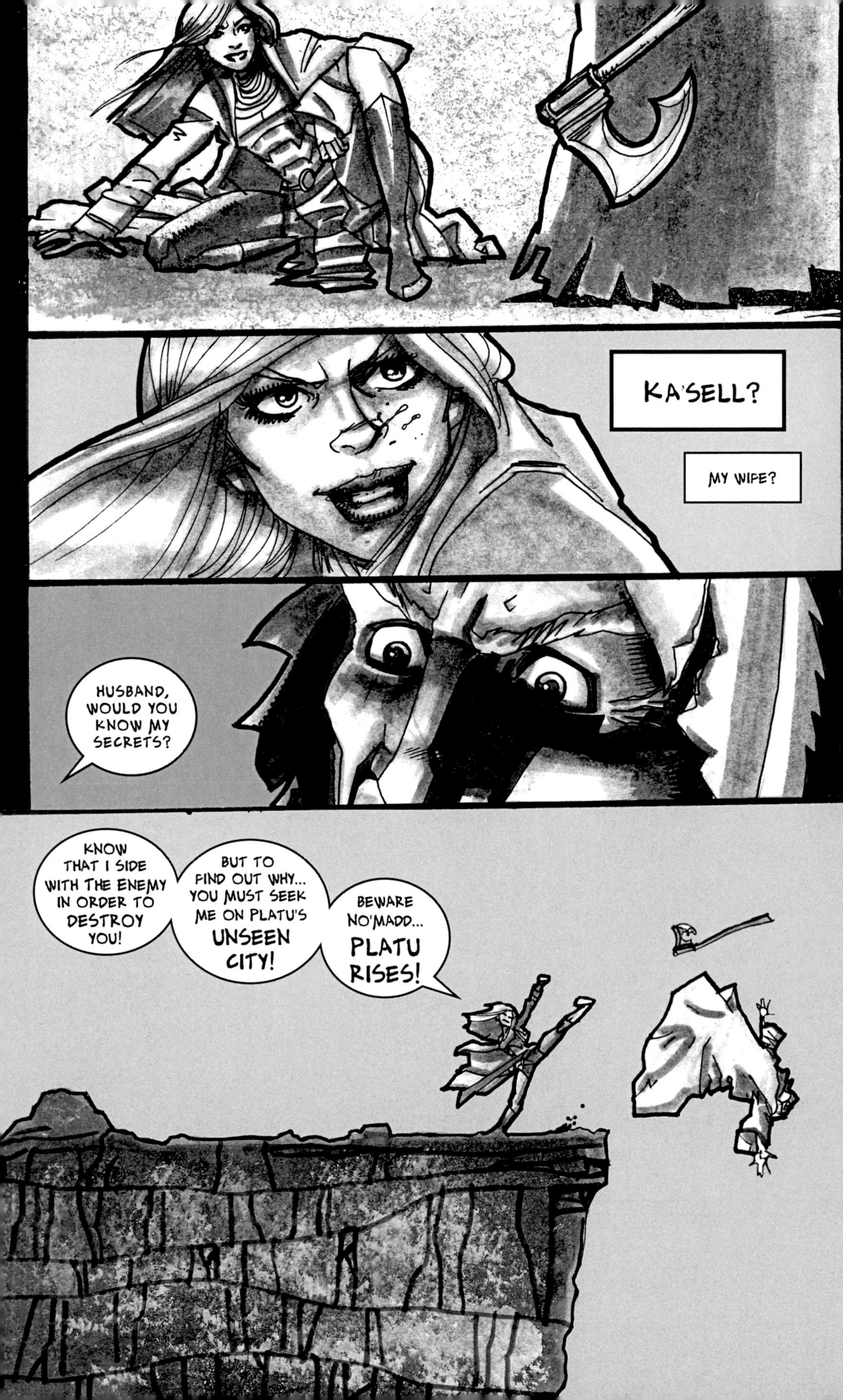
KA'SELL?
MY WIFE?
HUSBAND, WOULD YOU KNOW MY SECRETS?
KNOW THAT I SIDE WITH THE ENEMY IN ORDER TO DESTROY YOU!
BUT TO FIND OUT WHY... YOU MUST SEEK ME ON PLATU'S UNSEEN CITY!
BEWARE NO'MADD... PLATU RISES!

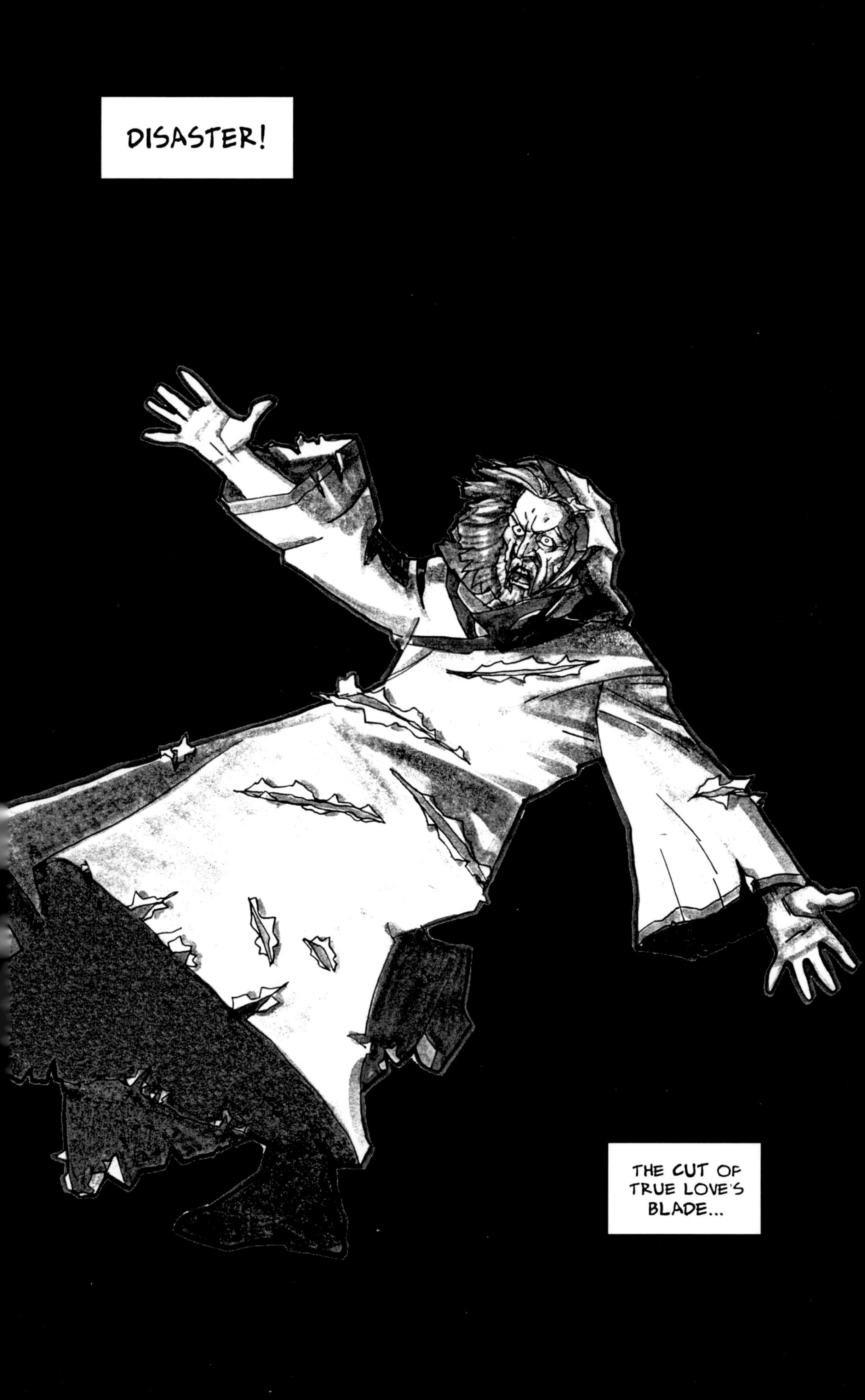
DISASTER!
THE CUT OF TRUE LOVE'S BLADE...

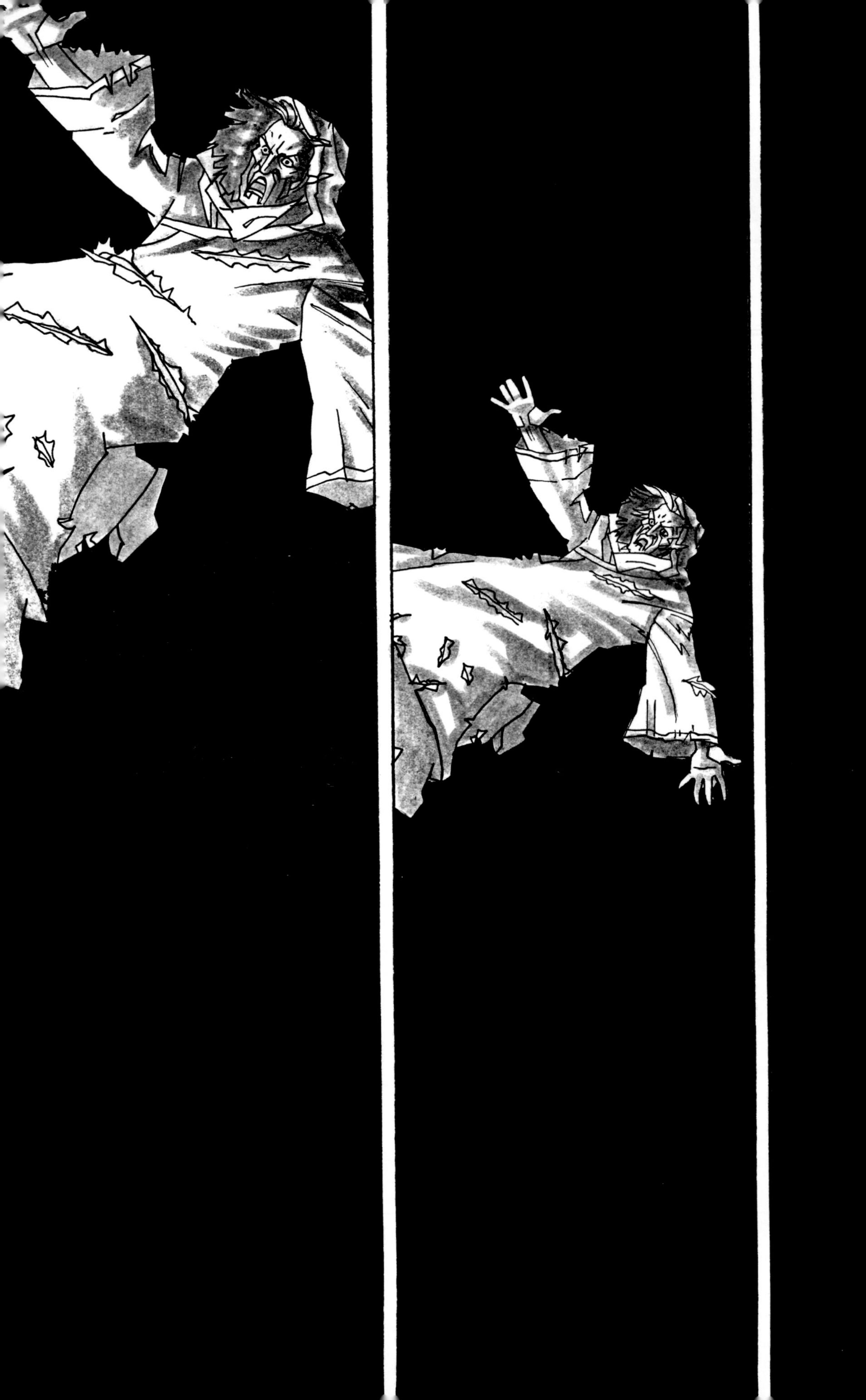

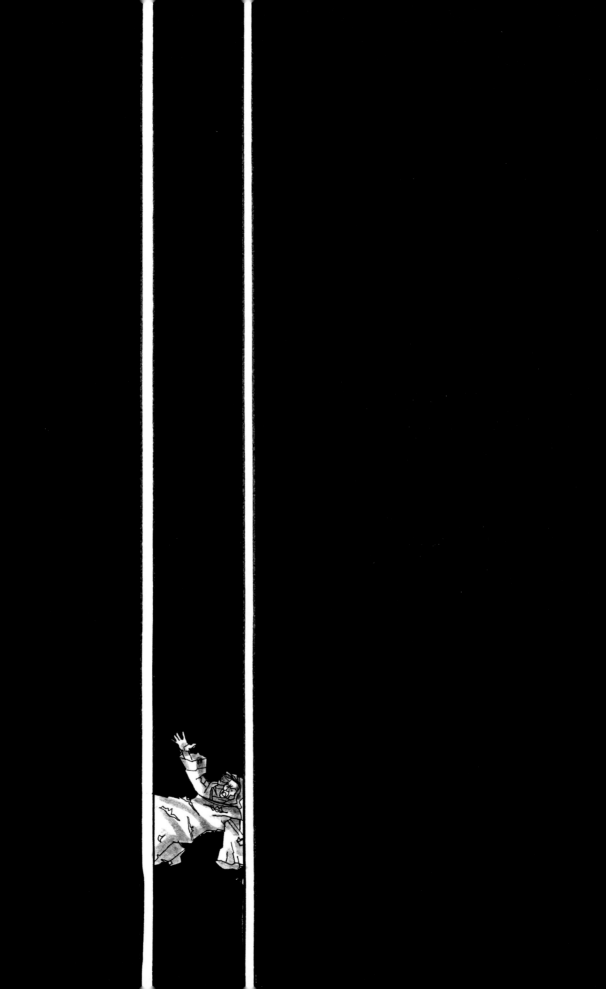

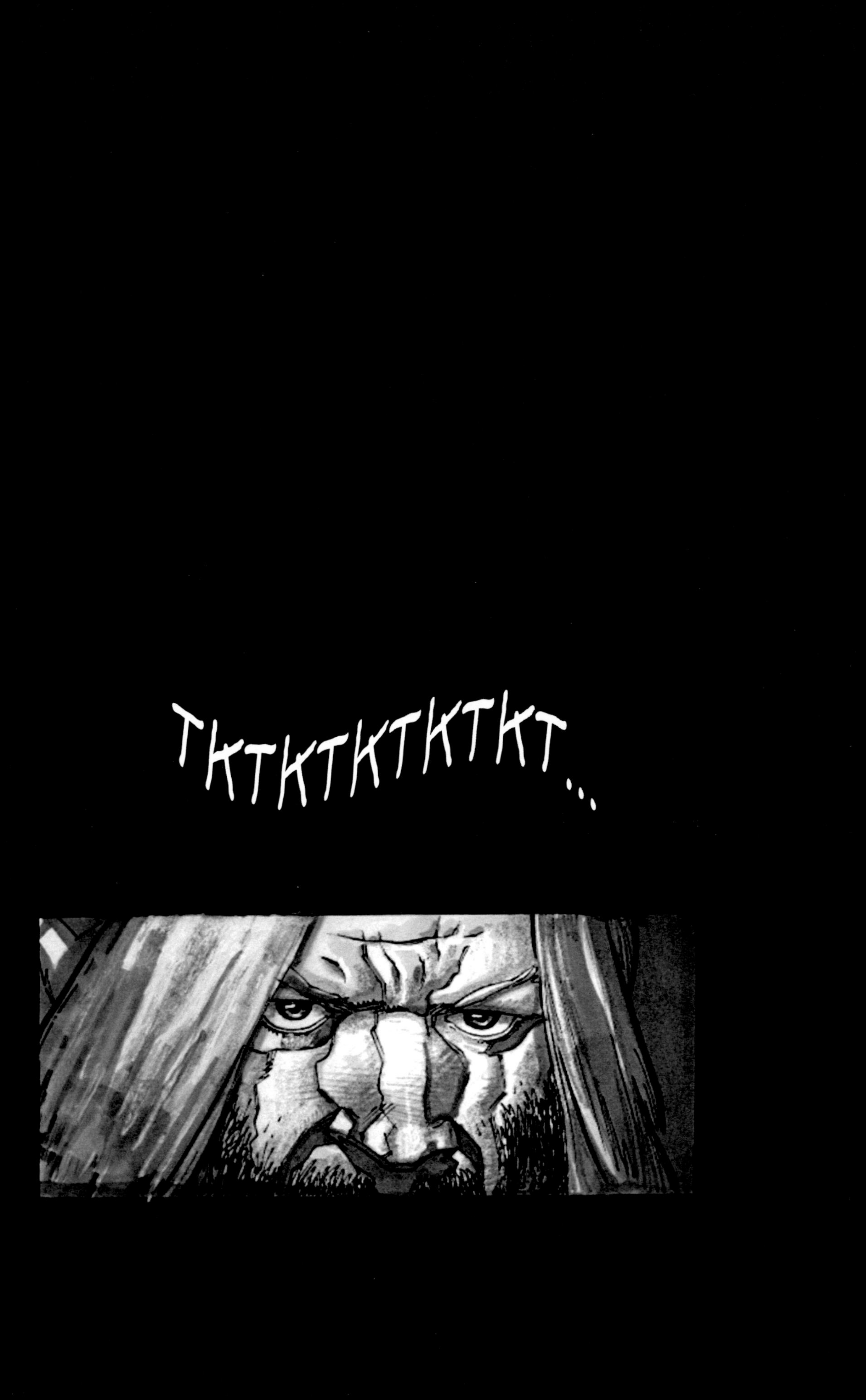
TKTKTKTKTKT...

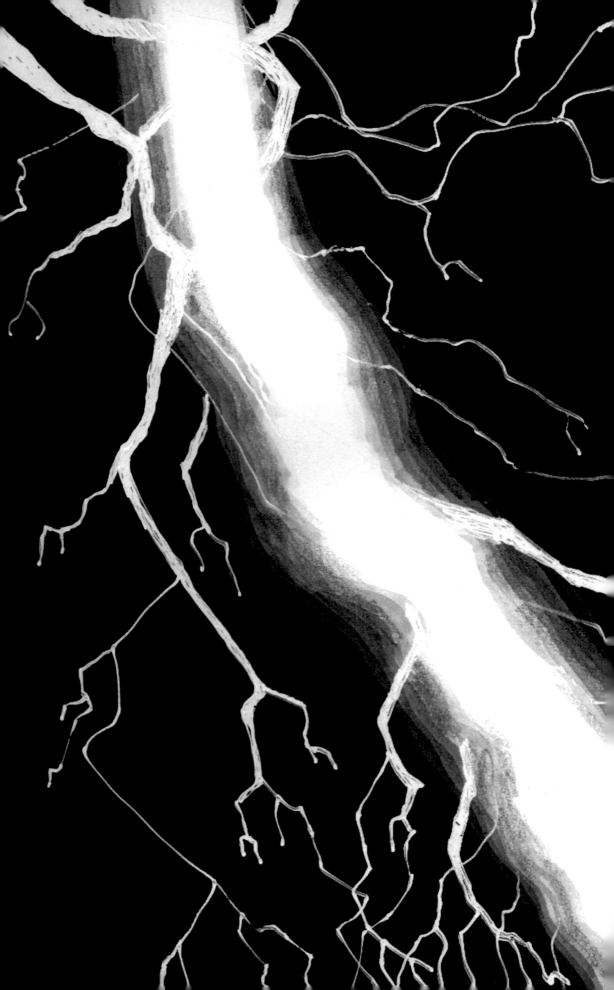

CHAPTER TWO

KA'SELL

"BETRAYED...

...I ROAM TO
THE ROAR OF WAVES."

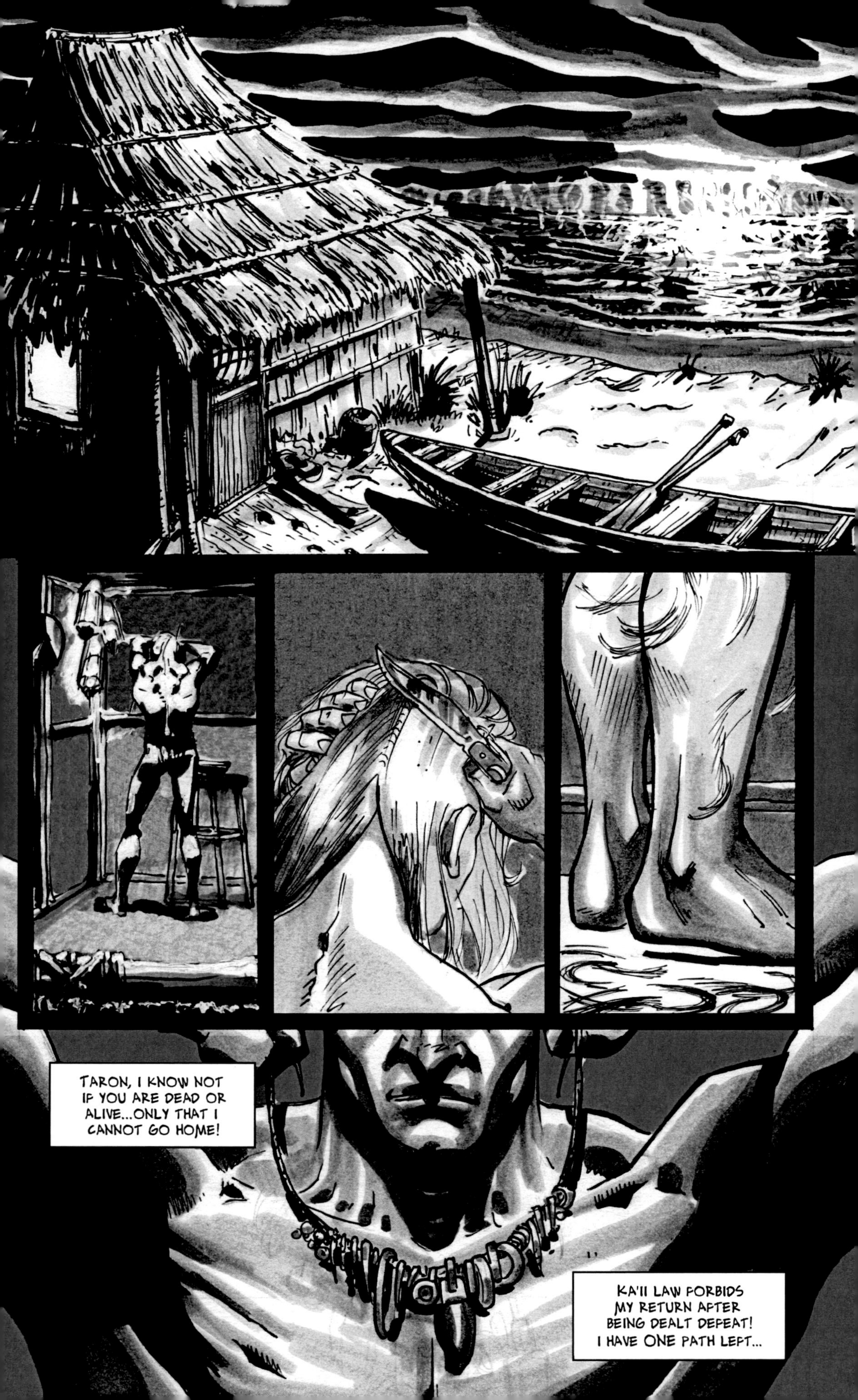
TARON, I KNOW NOT IF YOU ARE DEAD OR ALIVE...ONLY THAT I CANNOT GO HOME!
KA'II LAW FORBIDS MY RETURN AFTER BEING DEALT DEFEAT! I HAVE ONE PATH LEFT...

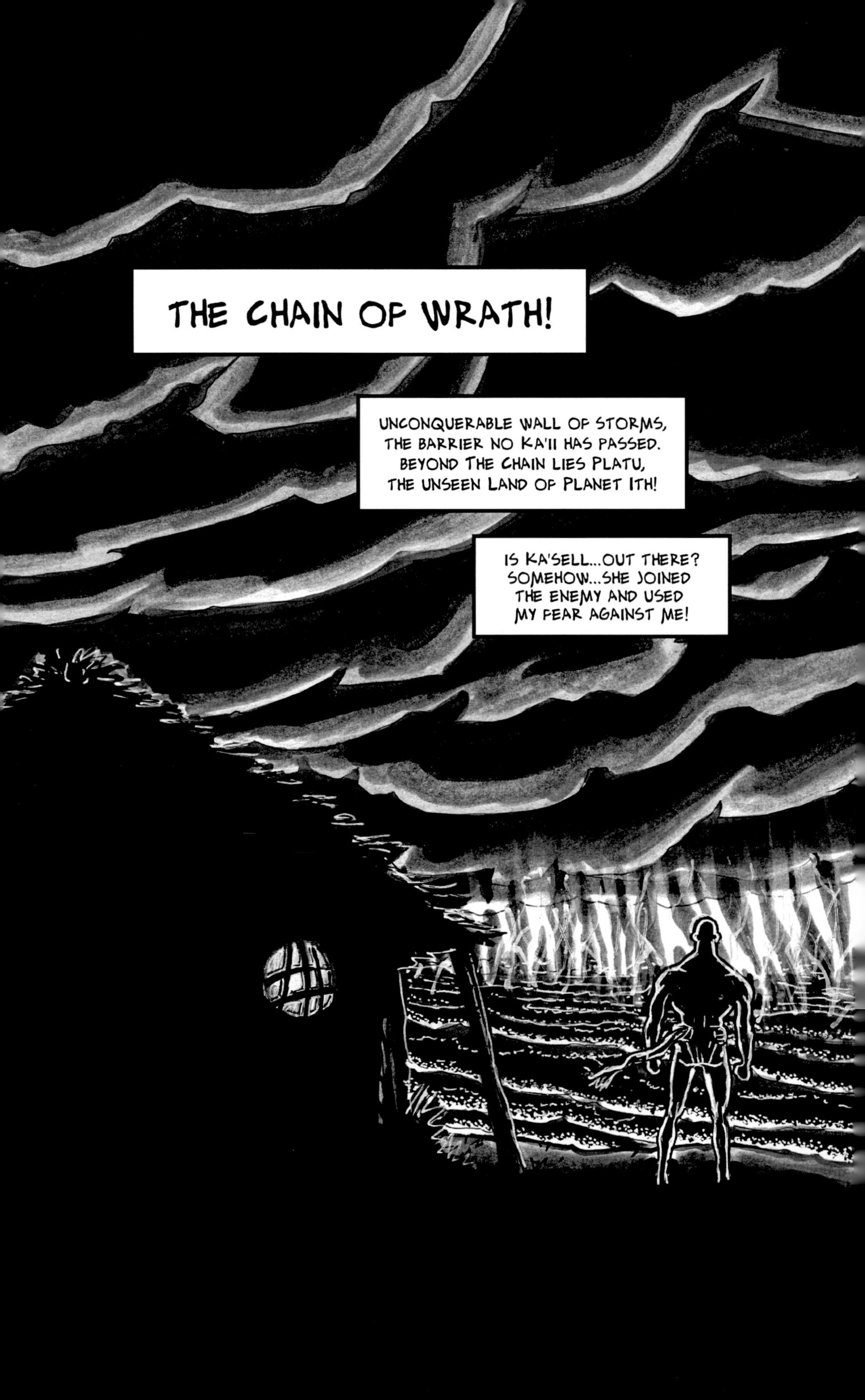
THE CHAIN OF WRATH!
UNCONQUERABLE WALL OF STORMS, THE BARRIER NO KA'II HAS PASSED. BEYOND THE CHAIN LIES PLATU, THE UNSEEN LAND OF PLANET ITH!
IS KA'SELL...OUT THERE? SOMEHOW...SHE JOINED THE ENEMY AND USED MY FEAR AGAINST ME!

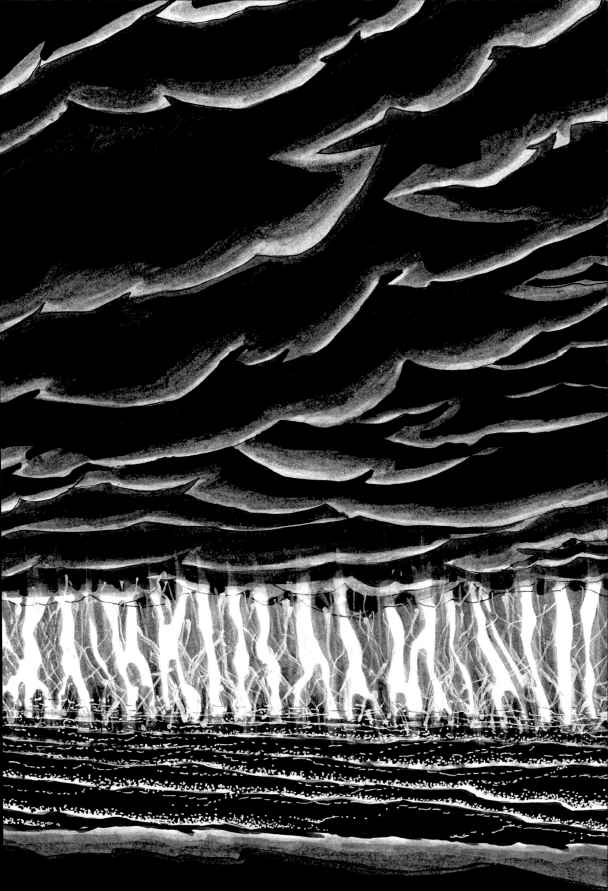

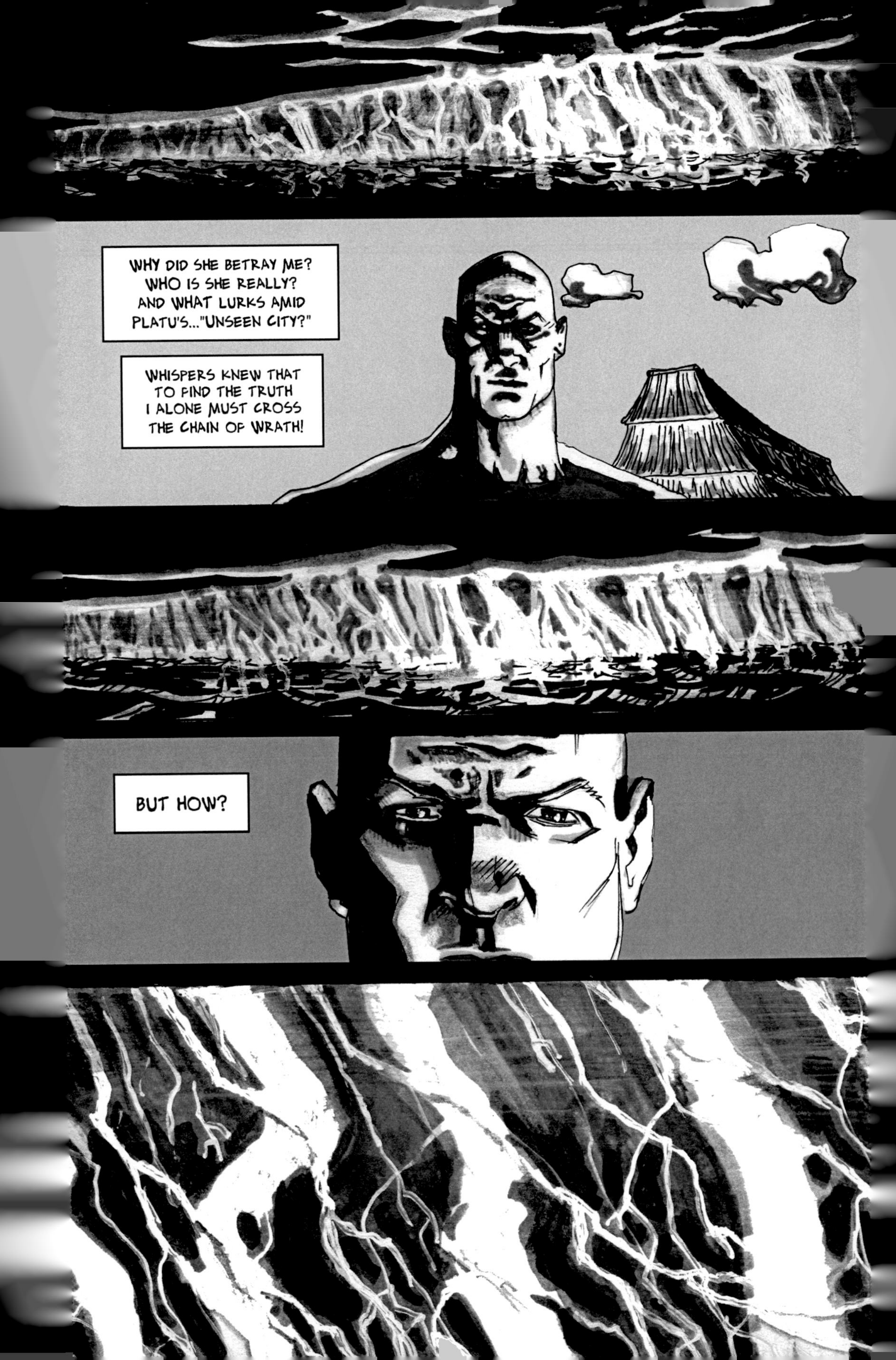
WHY DID SHE BETRAY ME? WHO IS SHE REALLY? AND WHAT LURKS AMID PLATU'S..."UNSEEN CITY?"
WHISPERS KNEW THAT TO FIND THE TRUTH I ALONE MUST CROSS THE CHAIN OF WRATH!
BUT HOW?

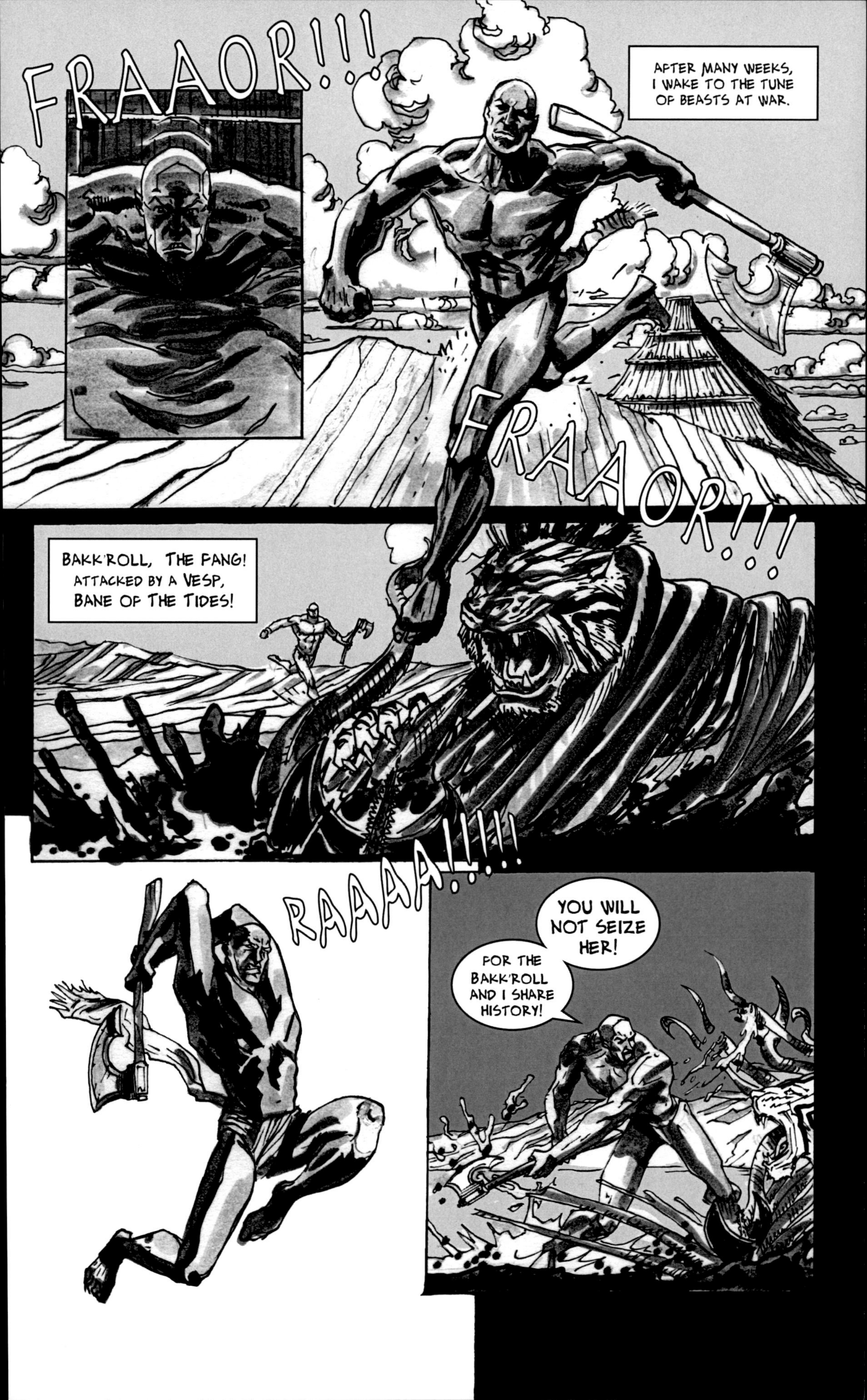
FRAAOR!!!
AFTER MANY WEEKS, I WAKE TO THE TUNE OF BEASTS AT WAR.
FRAAOR!!!
BAKK'ROLL, THE FANG! ATTACKED BY A VESP, BANE OF THE TIDES!
RAAAA!!!!
YOU WILL NOT SEIZE HER!
FOR THE BAKK'ROLL AND I SHARE HISTORY!

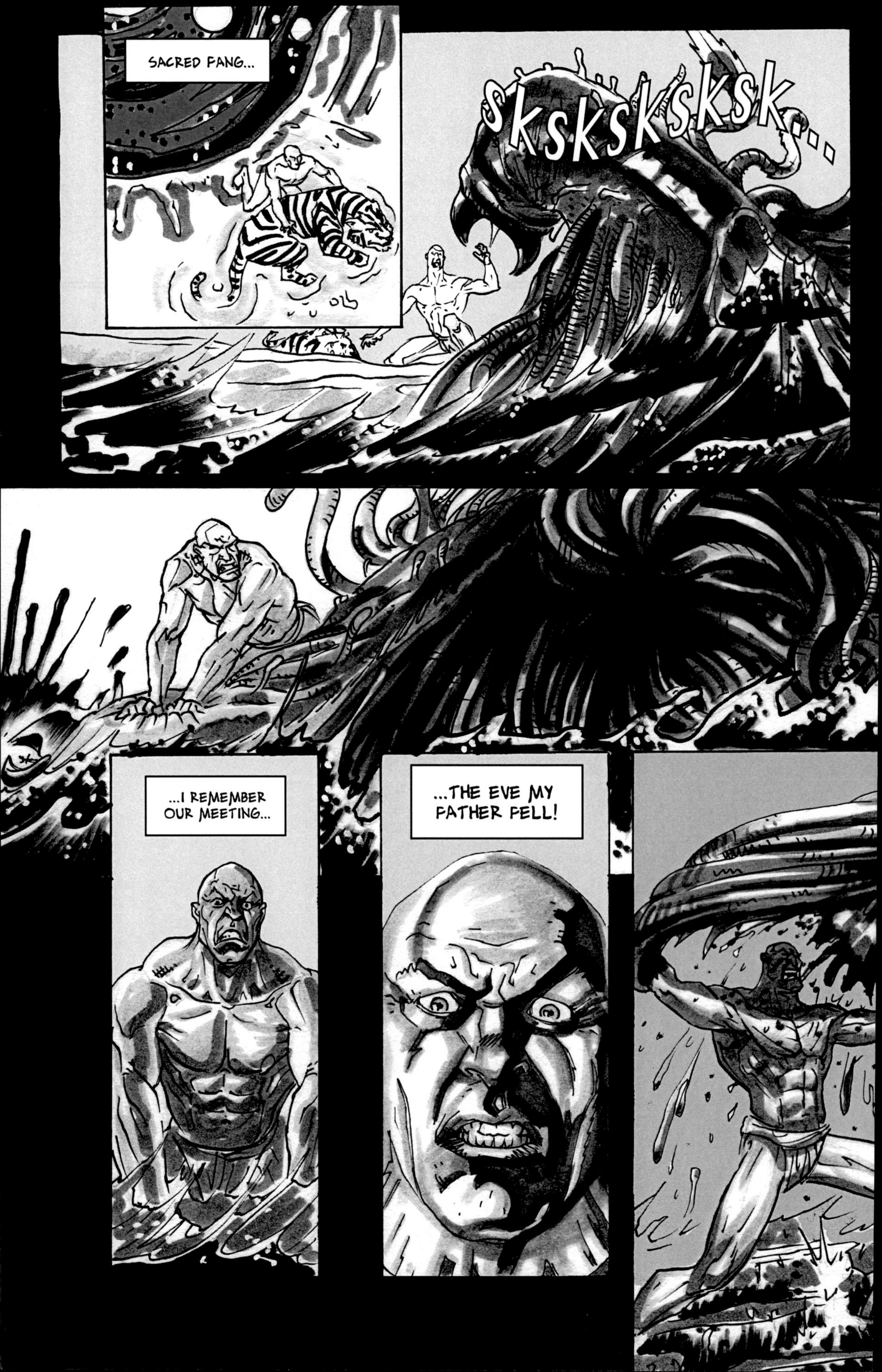
SACRED FANG...
SKSKSKSKSK...
...I REMEMBER OUR MEETING...
...THE EVE MY FATHER FELL!

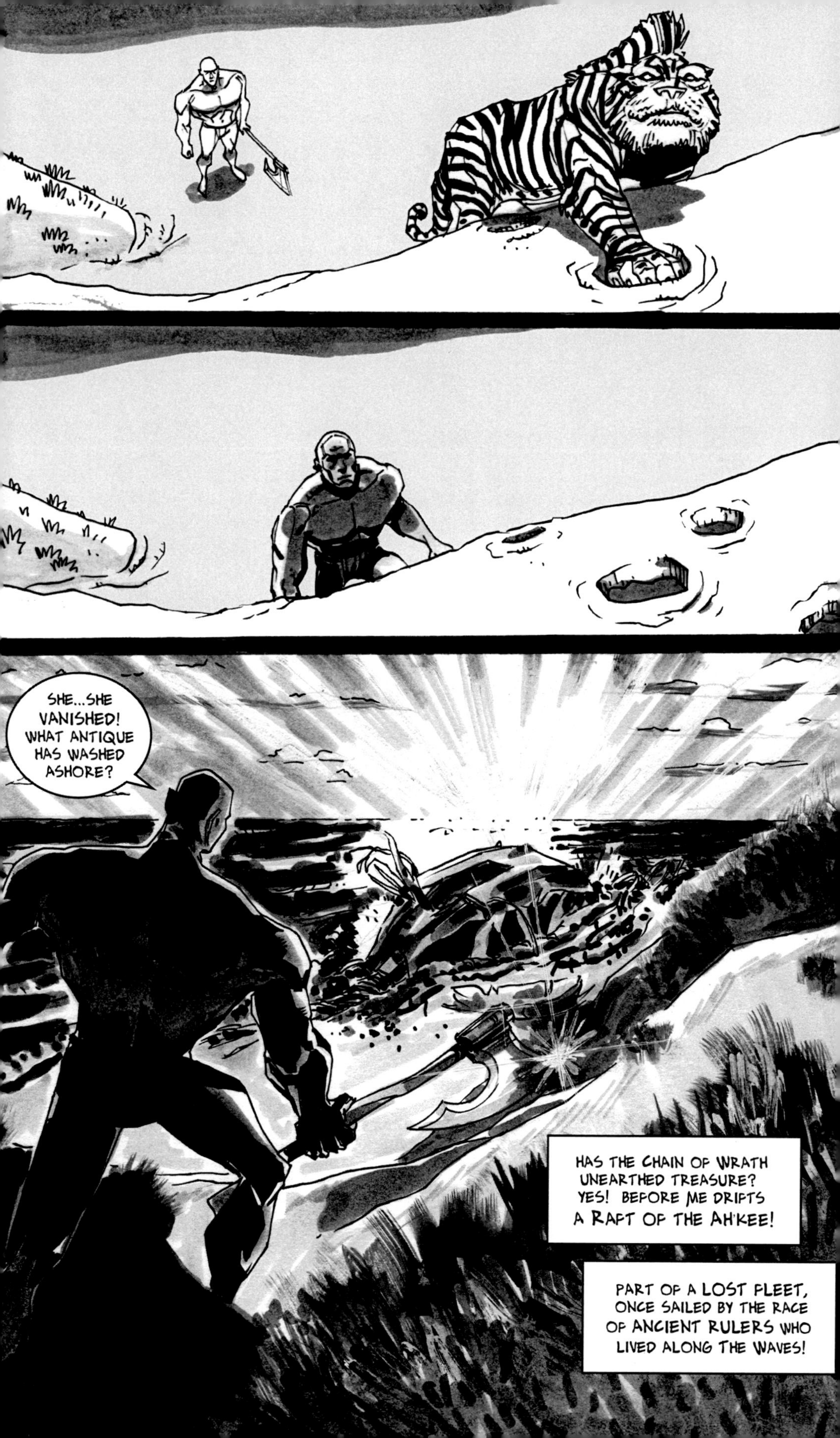
SHE...SHE VANISHED! WHAT ANTIQUE HAS WASHED ASHORE?
HAS THE CHAIN OF WRATH UNEARTHED TREASURE? YES! BEFORE ME DRIFTS A RAFT OF THE AH'KEE!
PART OF A LOST FLEET, ONCE SAILED BY THE RACE OF ANCIENT RULERS WHO LIVED ALONG THE WAVES!

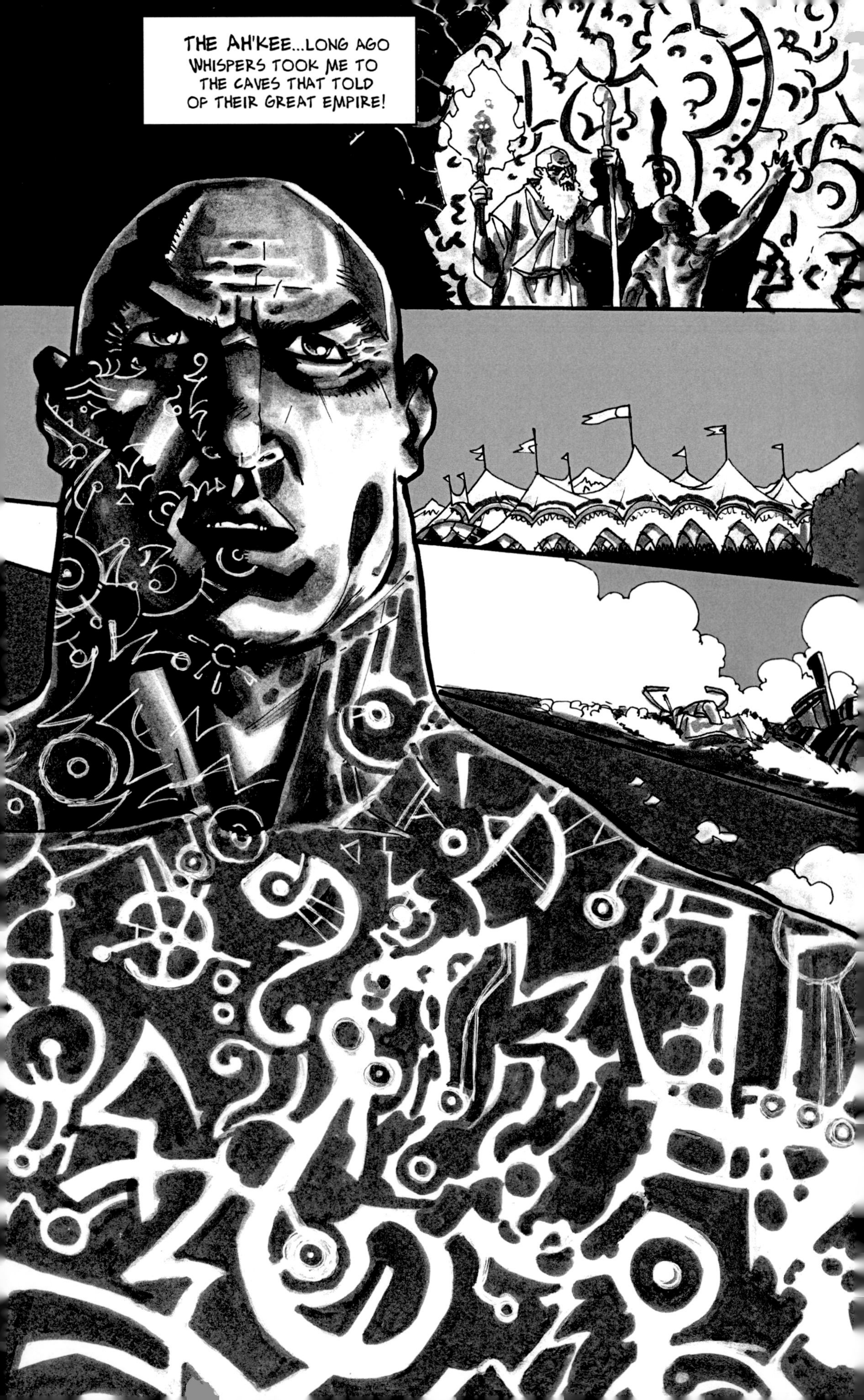
THE AH'KEE...LONG AGO WHISPERS TOOK ME TO THE CAVES THAT TOLD OF THEIR GREAT EMPIRE!

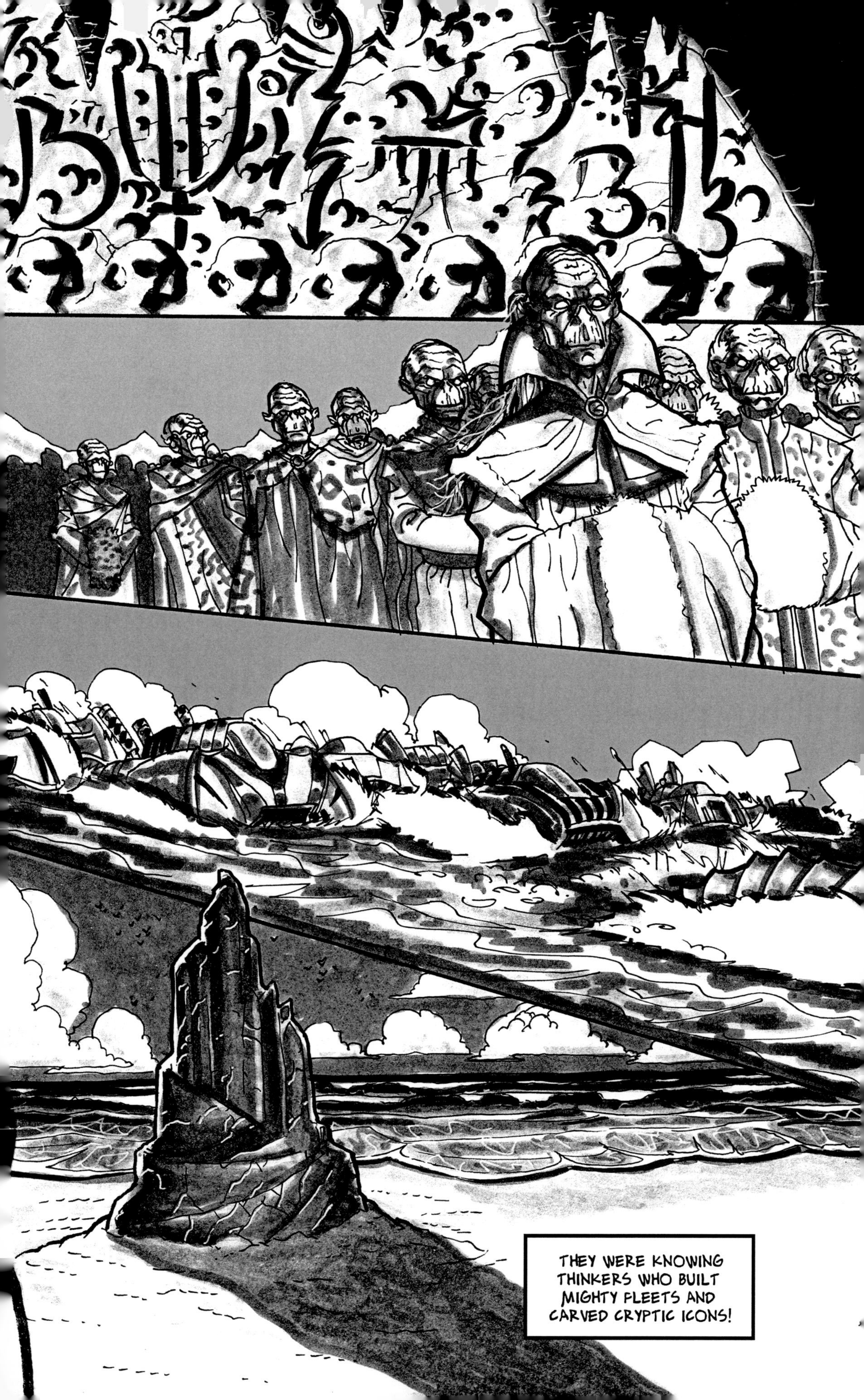
THEY WERE KNOWING THINKERS WHO BUILT MIGHTY FLEETS AND CARVED CRYPTIC ICONS!

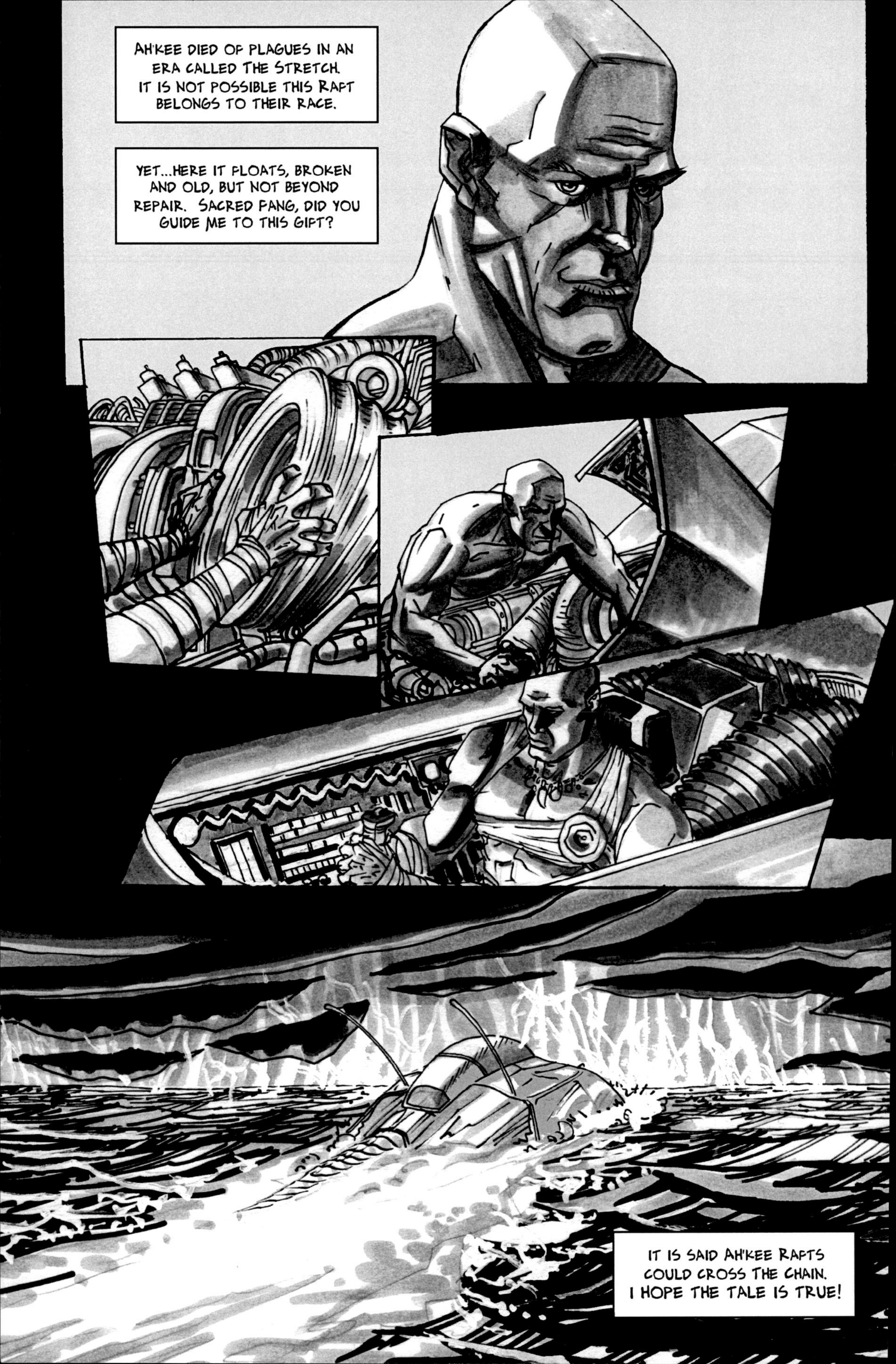
AH'KEE DIED OF PLAGUES IN AN ERA CALLED THE STRETCH. IT IS NOT POSSIBLE THIS RAFT BELONGS TO THEIR RACE.
YET...HERE IT FLOATS, BROKEN AND OLD, BUT NOT BEYOND REPAIR. SACRED FANG, DID YOU GUIDE ME TO THIS GIFT?
IT IS SAID AH'KEE RAFTS COULD CROSS THE CHAIN. I HOPE THE TALE IS TRUE!

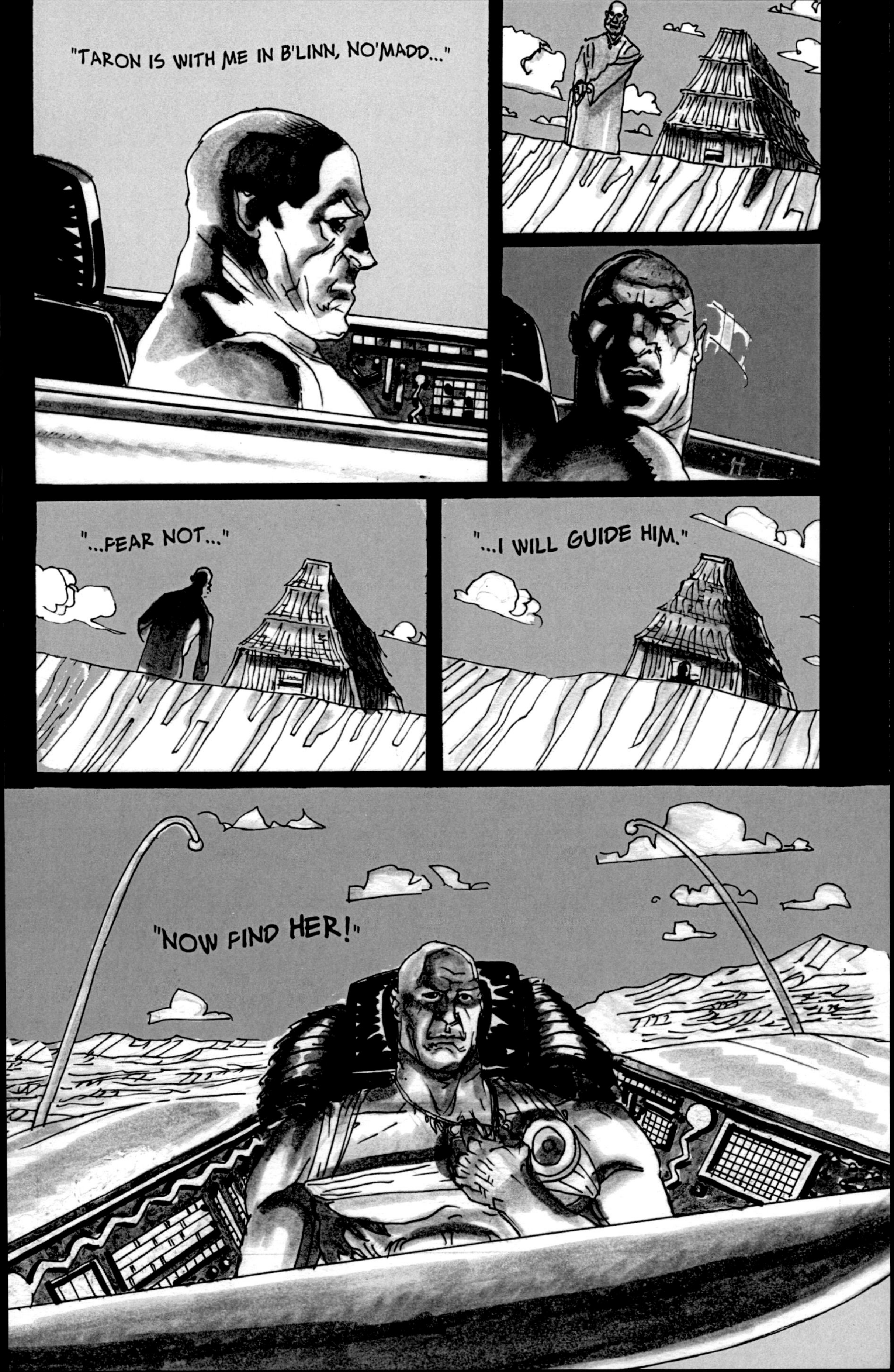
"TARON IS WITH ME IN B'LINN, NO'MADD..."
"...FEAR NOT..."
"...I WILL GUIDE HIM."
"NOW FIND HER!"

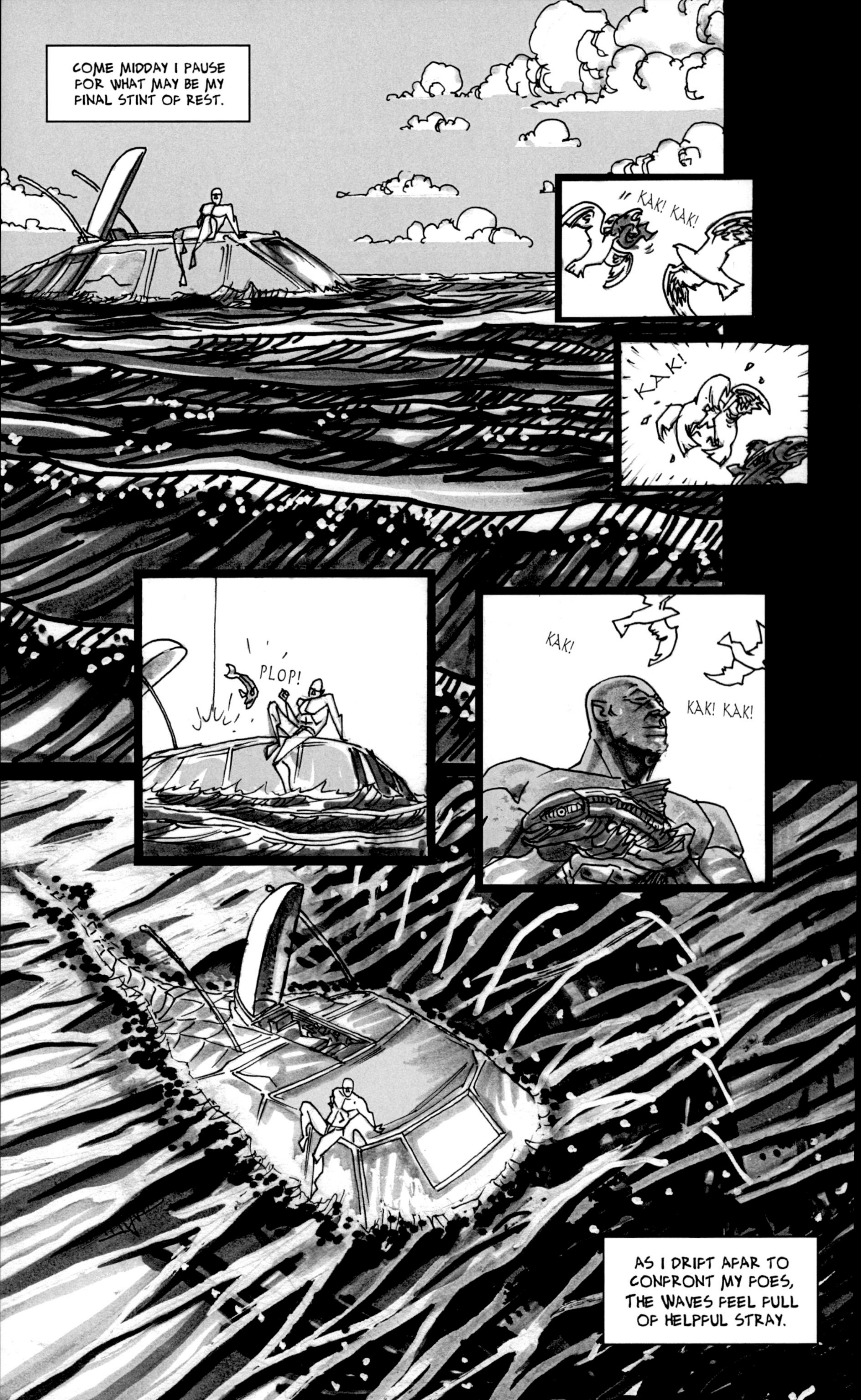
COME MIDDAY I PAUSE FOR WHAT MAY BE MY FINAL STINT OF REST.
KAK! KAK!
KAK!
PLOP!
KAK!
KAK! KAK!
AS I DRIFT AFAR TO CONFRONT MY FOES, THE WAVES FEEL FULL OF HELPFUL STRAY.

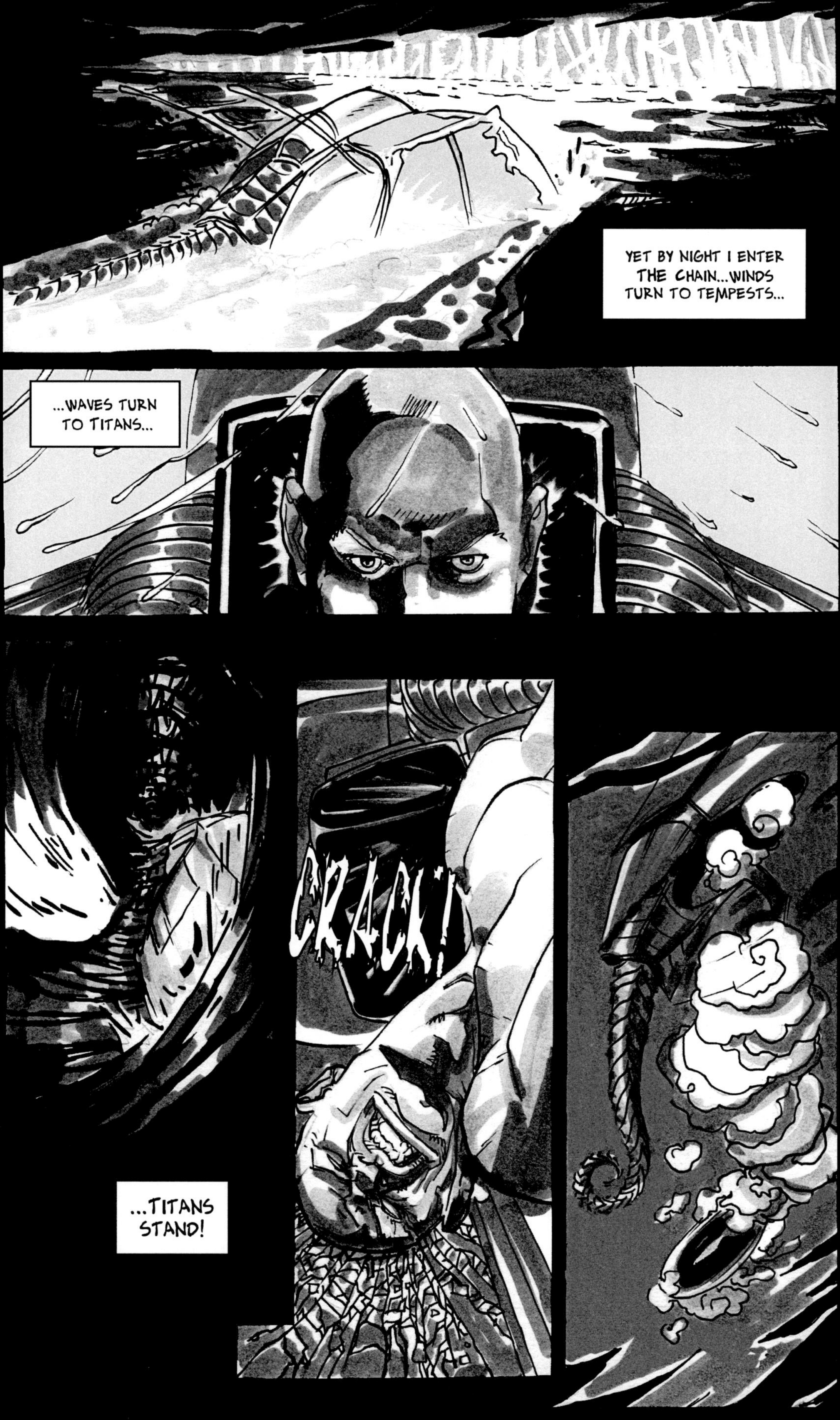

YET BY NIGHT I ENTER THE CHAIN...WINDS TURN TO TEMPESTS...
...WAVES TURN TO TITANS...
CRACK!
...TITANS STAND!

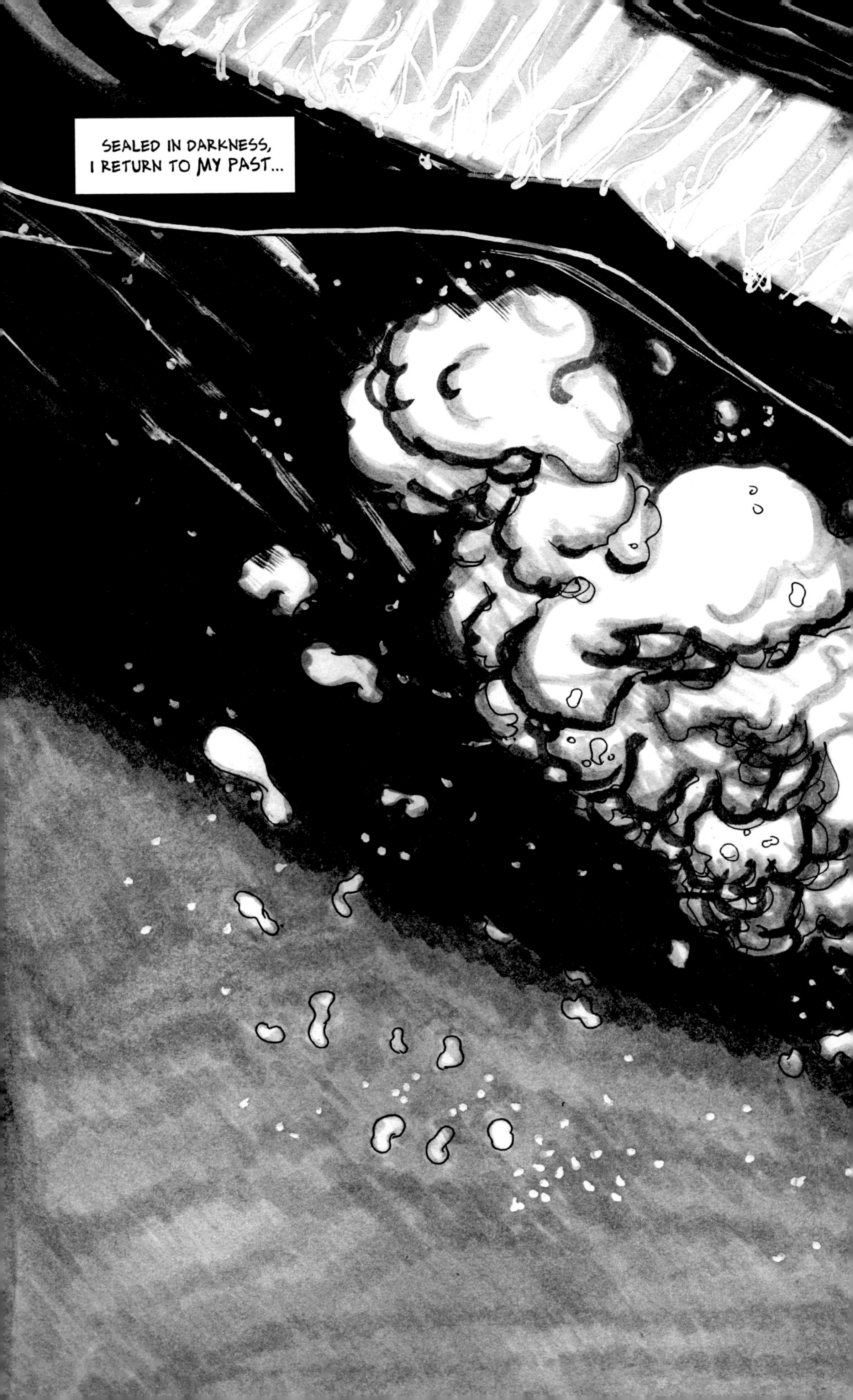
SEALED IN DARKNESS,
I RETURN TO MY PAST...

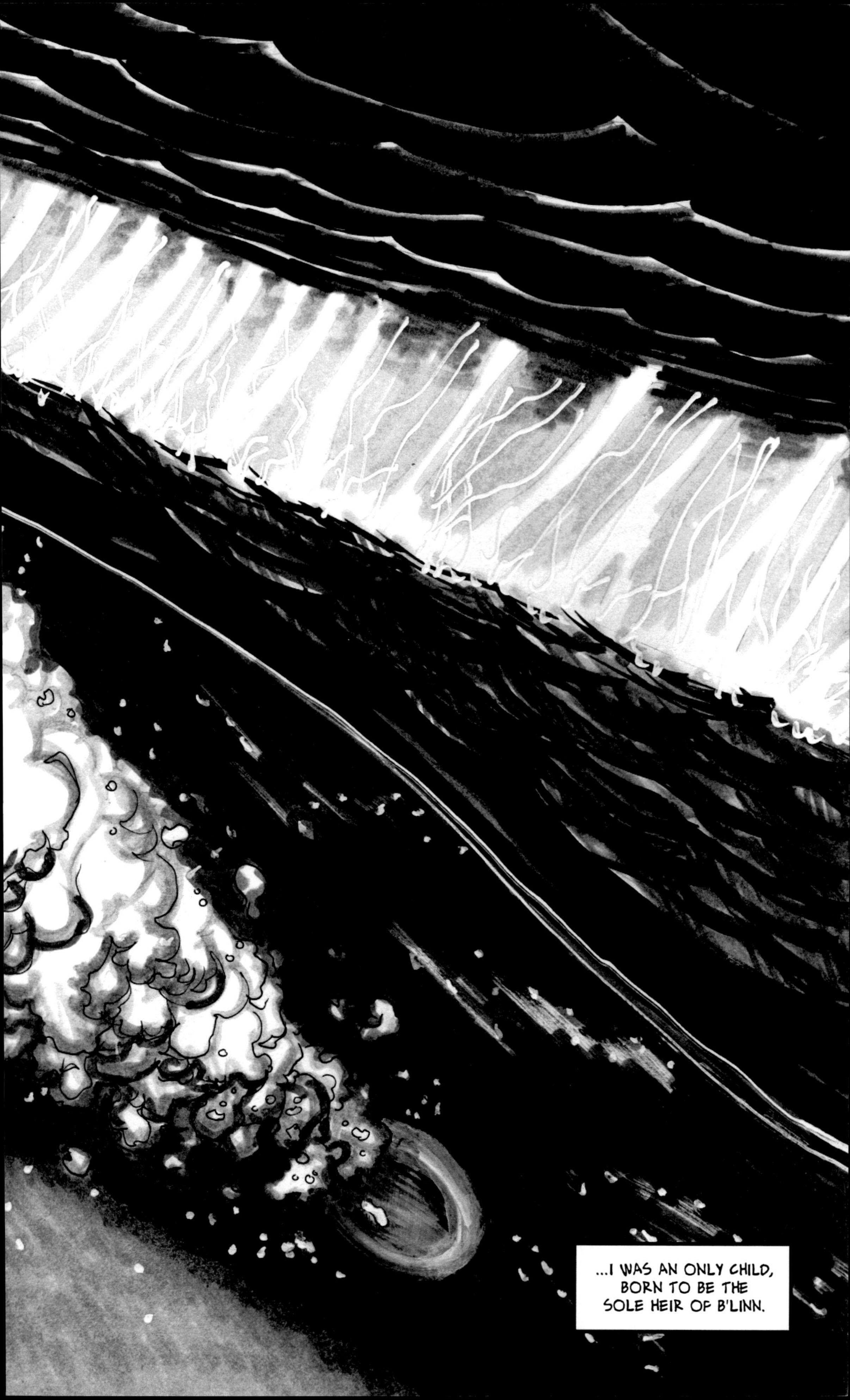
...I WAS AN ONLY CHILD,
BORN TO BE THE
SOLE HEIR OF B'LINN.

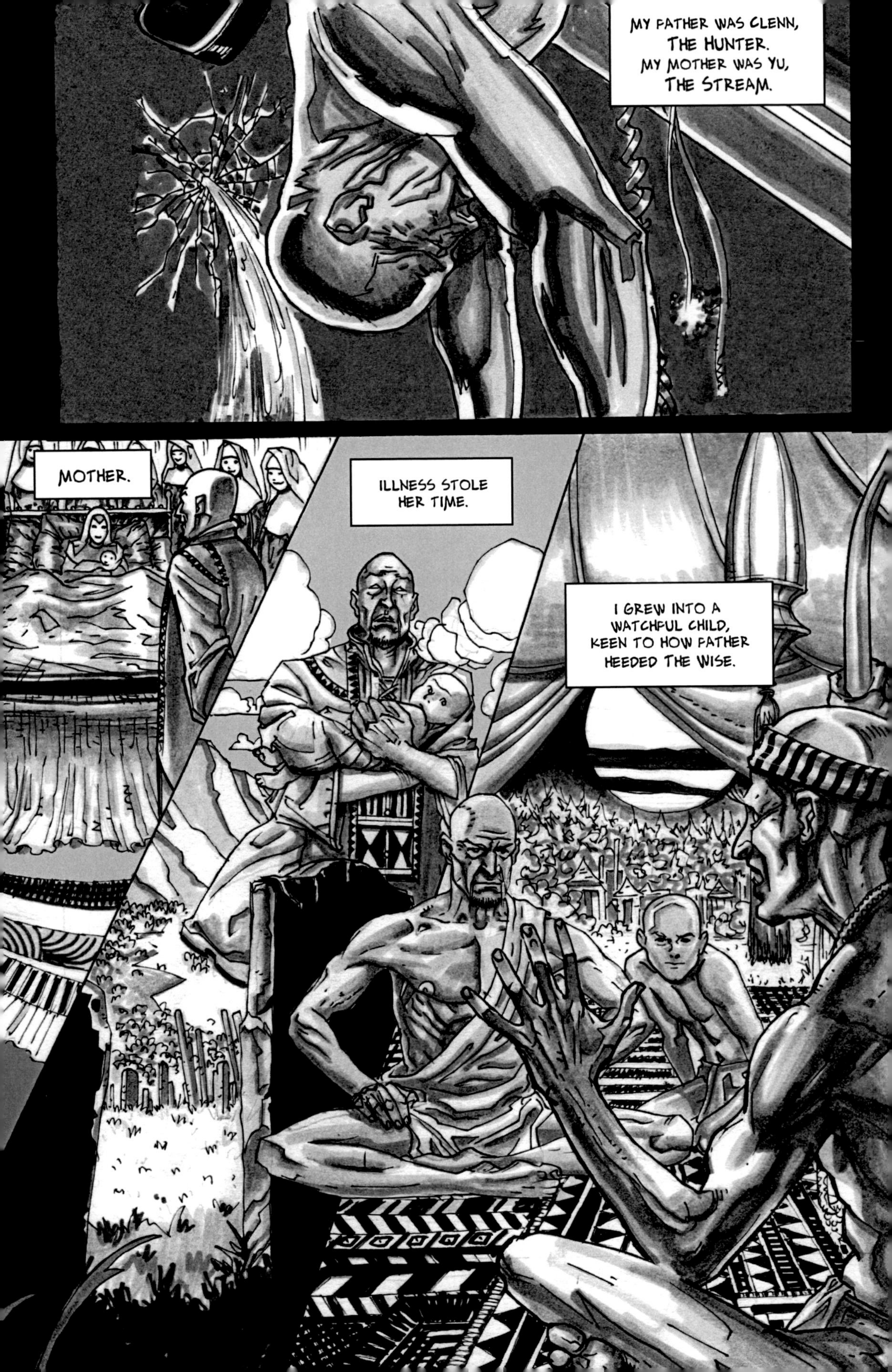
MY FATHER WAS CLENN, THE HUNTER.
MY MOTHER WAS YU, THE STREAM.
MOTHER.
ILLNESS STOLE HER TIME.
I GREW INTO A WATCHFUL CHILD, KEEN TO HOW FATHER HEEDED THE WISE.

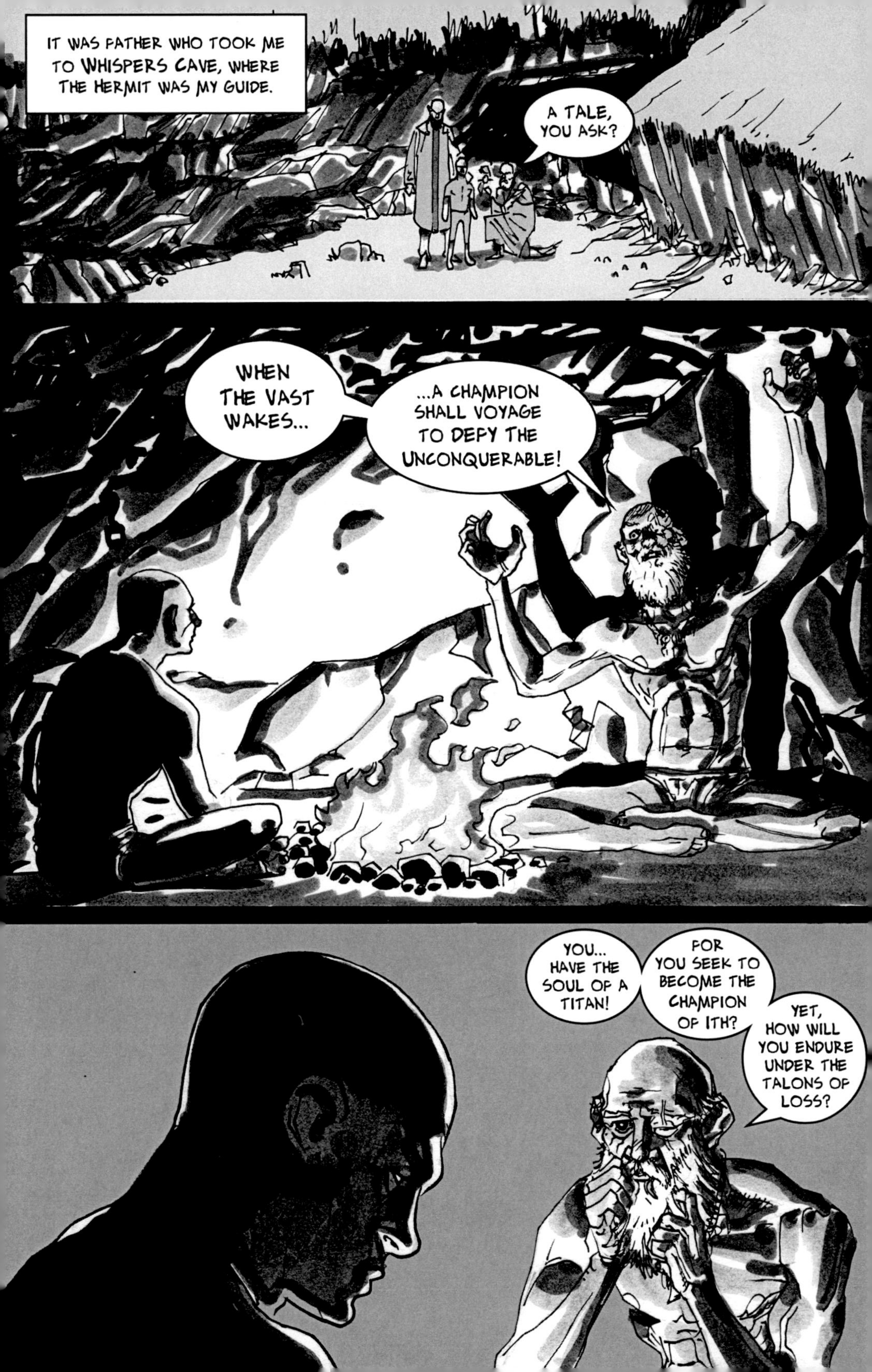
IT WAS FATHER WHO TOOK ME TO WHISPERS CAVE, WHERE THE HERMIT WAS MY GUIDE.
A TALE, YOU ASK?
WHEN THE VAST WAKES...
...A CHAMPION SHALL VOYAGE TO DEFY THE UNCONQUERABLE!
YOU... HAVE THE SOUL OF A TITAN!
FOR YOU SEEK TO BECOME THE CHAMPION OF ITH?
YET, HOW WILL YOU ENDURE UNDER THE TALONS OF LOSS?

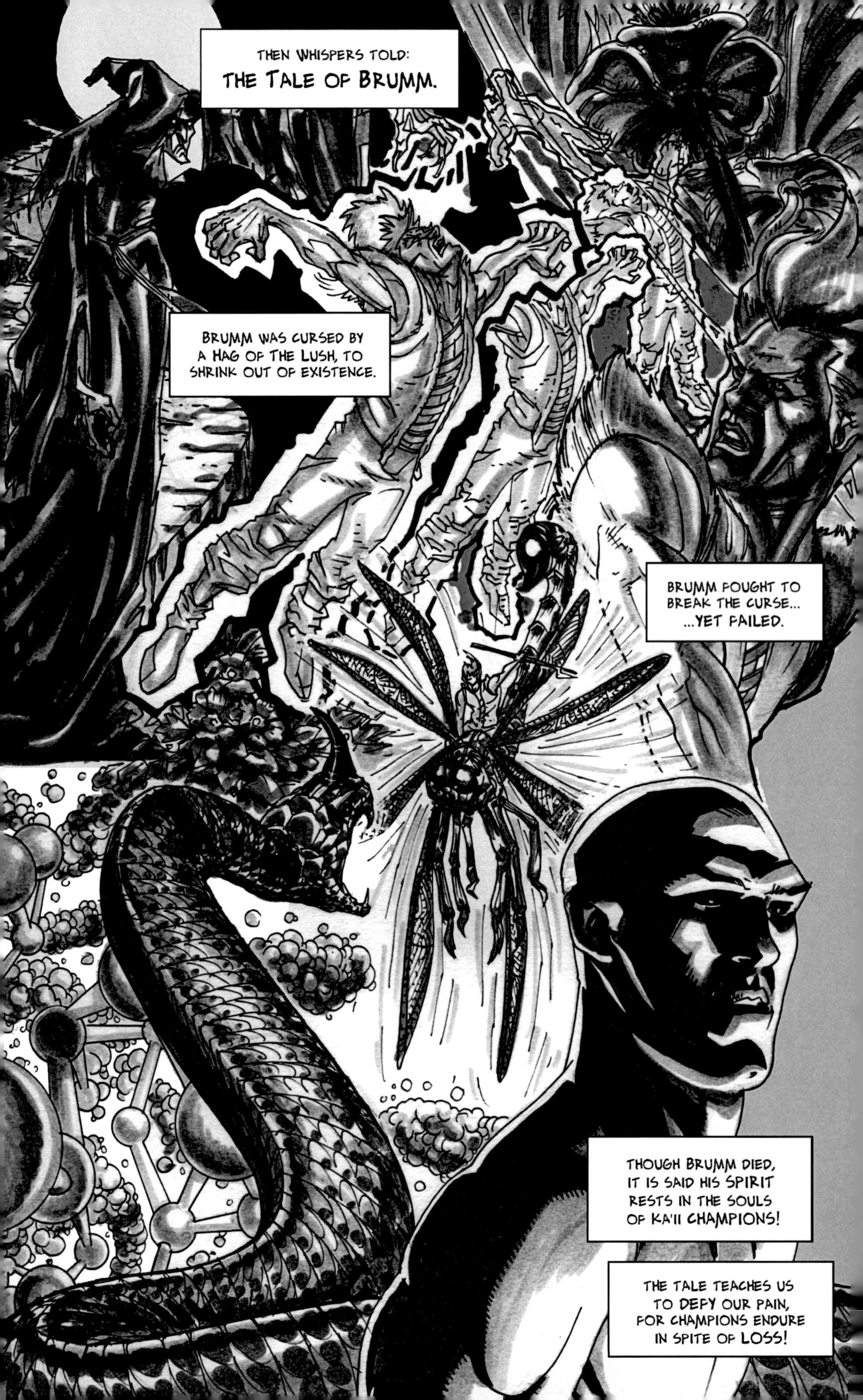
THEN WHISPERS TOLD:
THE TALE OF BRUMM.
BRUMM WAS CURSED BY A HAG OF THE LUSH, TO SHRINK OUT OF EXISTENCE.
BRUMM FOUGHT TO BREAK THE CURSE... ...YET FAILED.
THOUGH BRUMM DIED, IT IS SAID HIS SPIRIT RESTS IN THE SOULS OF KA'II CHAMPIONS!
THE TALE TEACHES US TO DEFY OUR PAIN, FOR CHAMPIONS ENDURE IN SPITE OF LOSS!

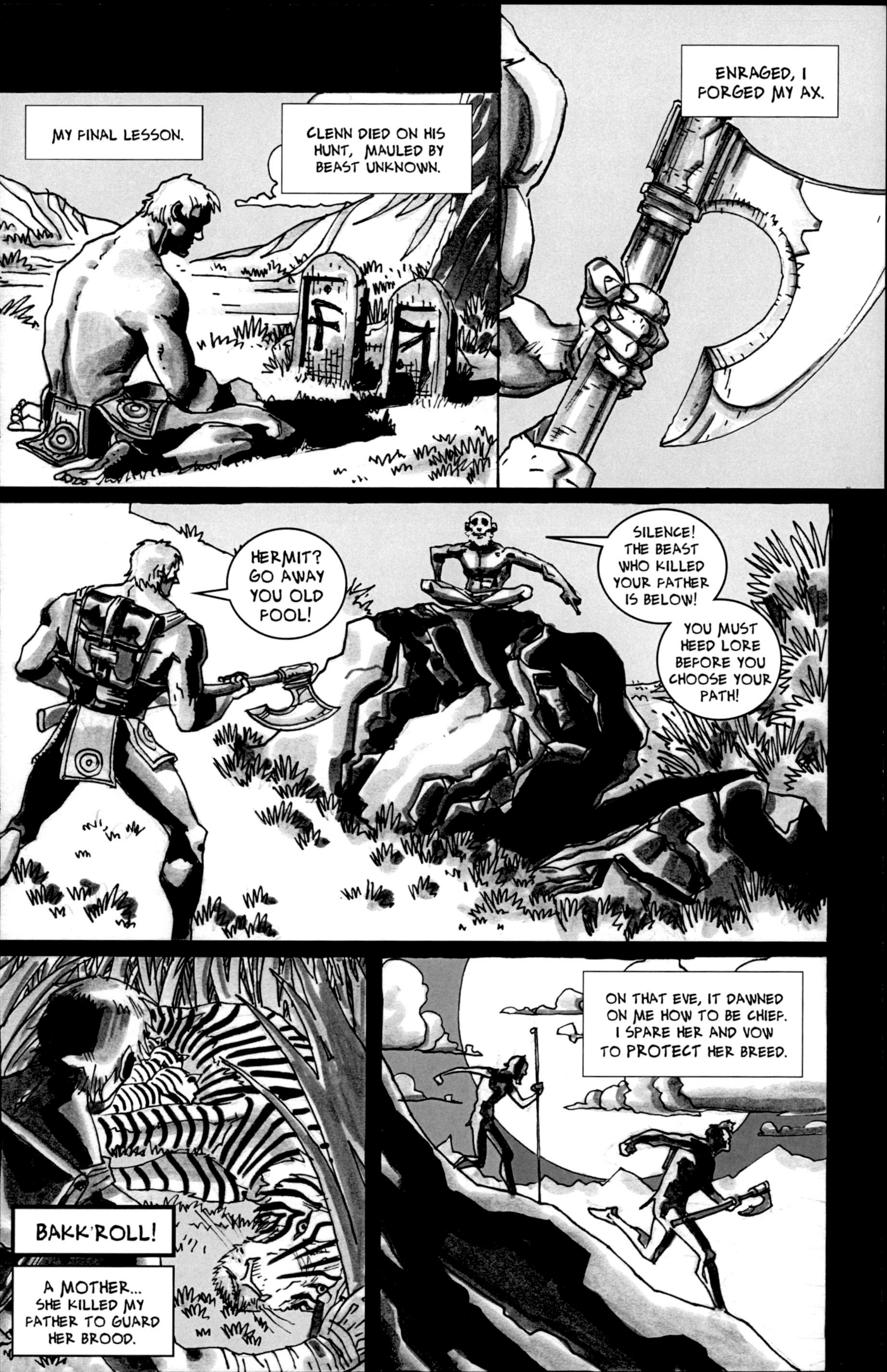
MY FINAL LESSON.
CLENN DIED ON HIS HUNT, MAULED BY BEAST UNKNOWN.
ENRAGED, I FORGED MY AX.
HERMIT? GO AWAY YOU OLD FOOL!
SILENCE! THE BEAST WHO KILLED YOUR FATHER IS BELOW!
YOU MUST HEED LORE BEFORE YOU CHOOSE YOUR PATH!
BAKK'ROLL!
A MOTHER... SHE KILLED MY FATHER TO GUARD HER BROOD.
ON THAT EVE, IT DAWNED ON ME HOW TO BE CHIEF. I SPARE HER AND VOW TO PROTECT HER BREED.

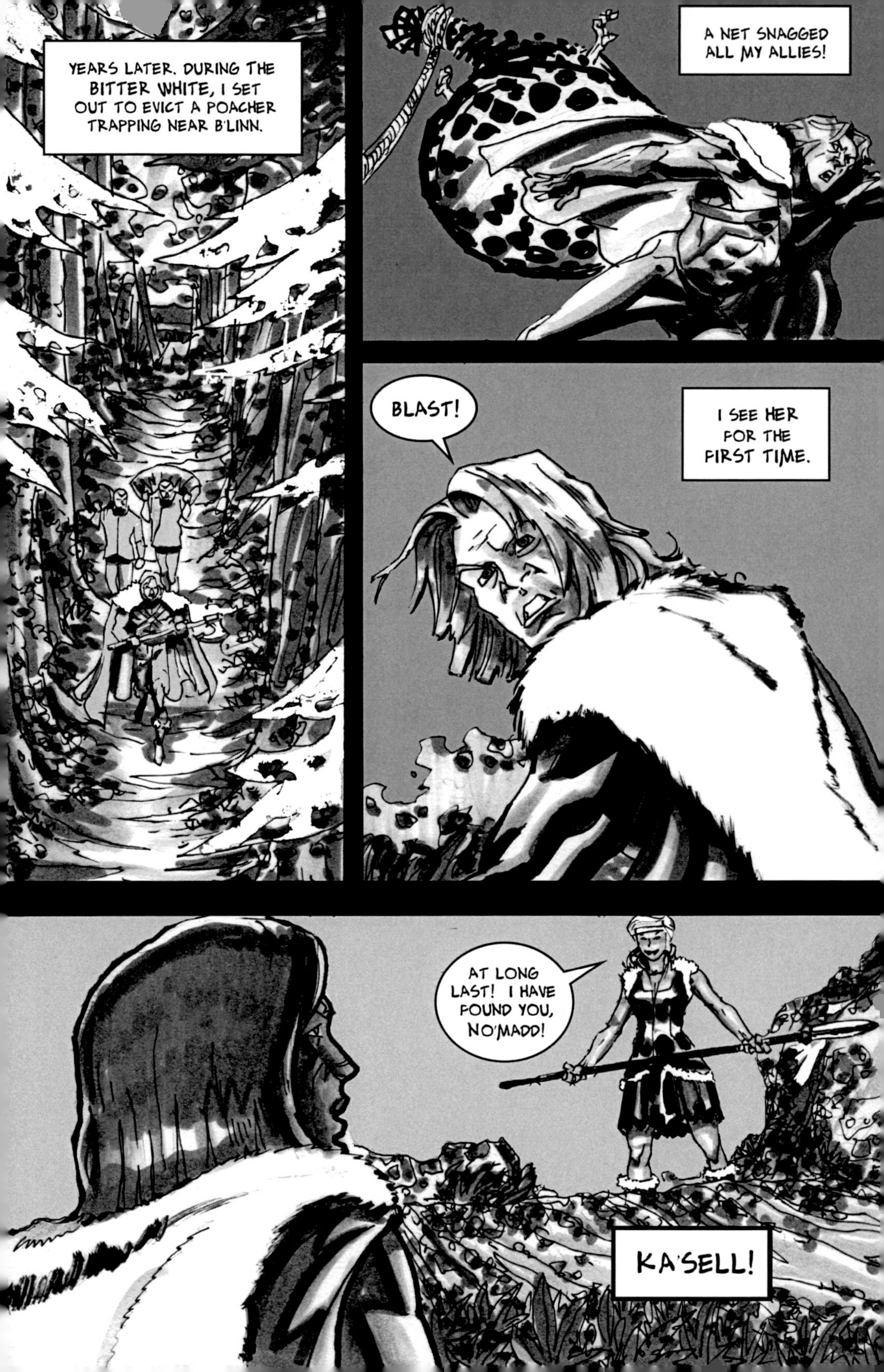
YEARS LATER. DURING THE BITTER WHITE, I SET OUT TO EVICT A POACHER TRAPPING NEAR B'LINN.
A NET SNAGGED ALL MY ALLIES!
BLAST!
I SEE HER FOR THE FIRST TIME.
AT LONG LAST! I HAVE FOUND YOU, NO'MADD!
KA'SELL!

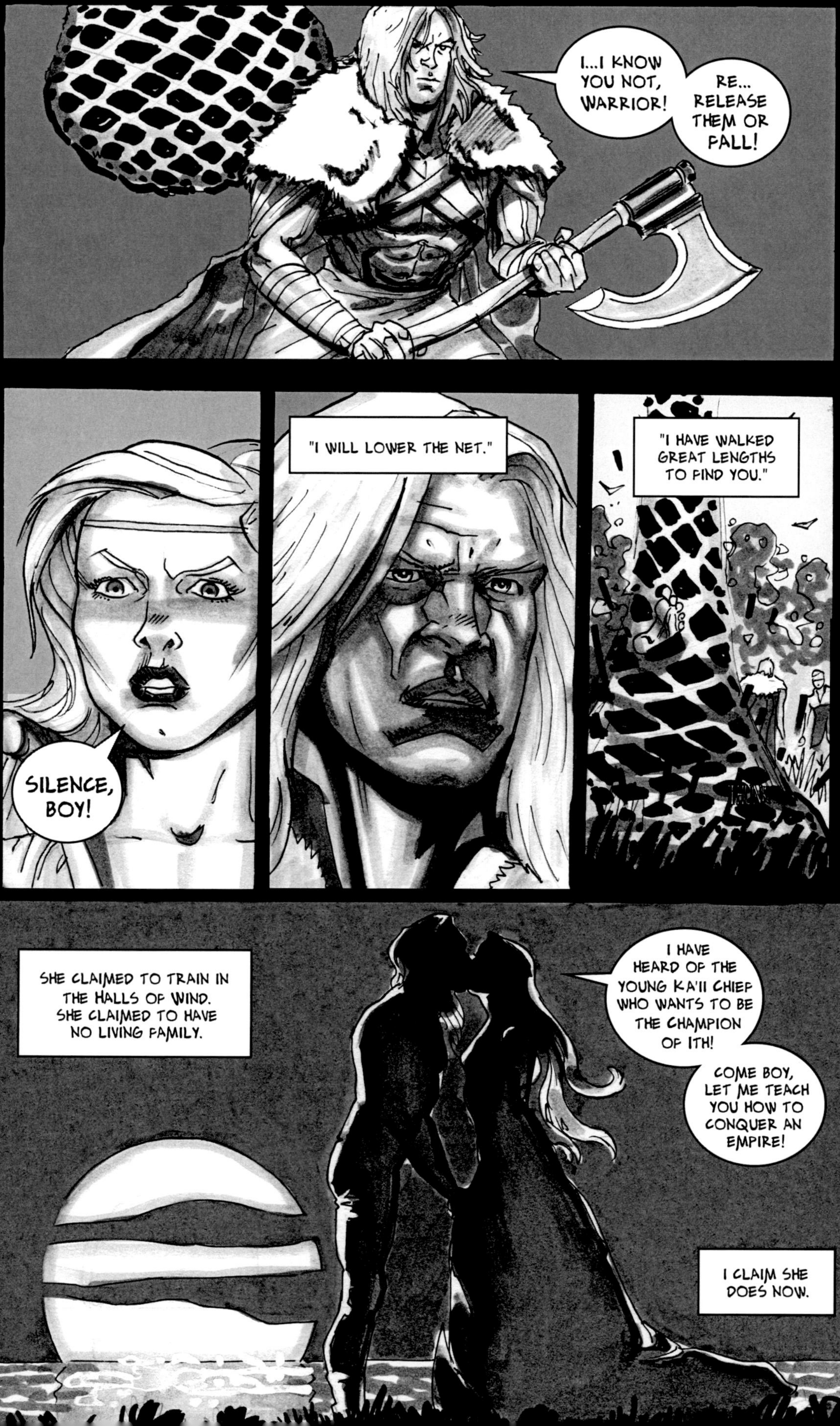
I...I KNOW YOU NOT, WARRIOR!
RE... RELEASE THEM OR FALL!
SILENCE, BOY!
"I WILL LOWER THE NET."
"I HAVE WALKED GREAT LENGTHS TO FIND YOU."
SHE CLAIMED TO TRAIN IN THE HALLS OF WIND. SHE CLAIMED TO HAVE NO LIVING FAMILY.
I HAVE HEARD OF THE YOUNG KA'II CHIEF WHO WANTS TO BE THE CHAMPION OF ITH!
COME BOY, LET ME TEACH YOU HOW TO CONQUER AN EMPIRE!
I CLAIM SHE DOES NOW.

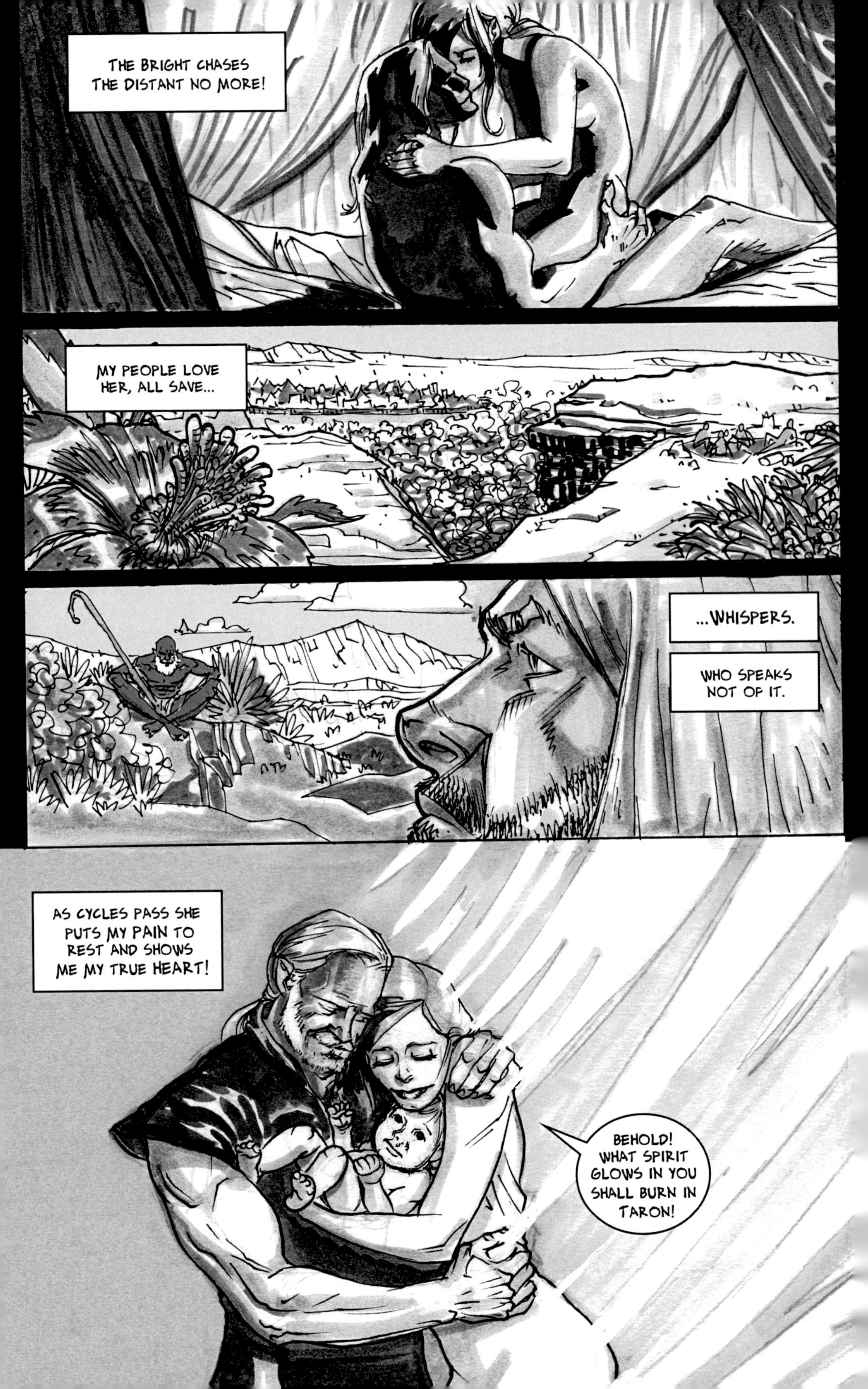
THE BRIGHT CHASES THE DISTANT NO MORE!
MY PEOPLE LOVE HER, ALL SAVE...
...WHISPERS.
WHO SPEAKS NOT OF IT.
AS CYCLES PASS SHE PUTS MY PAIN TO REST AND SHOWS ME MY TRUE HEART!
BEHOLD! WHAT SPIRIT GLOWS IN YOU SHALL BURN IN TARON!

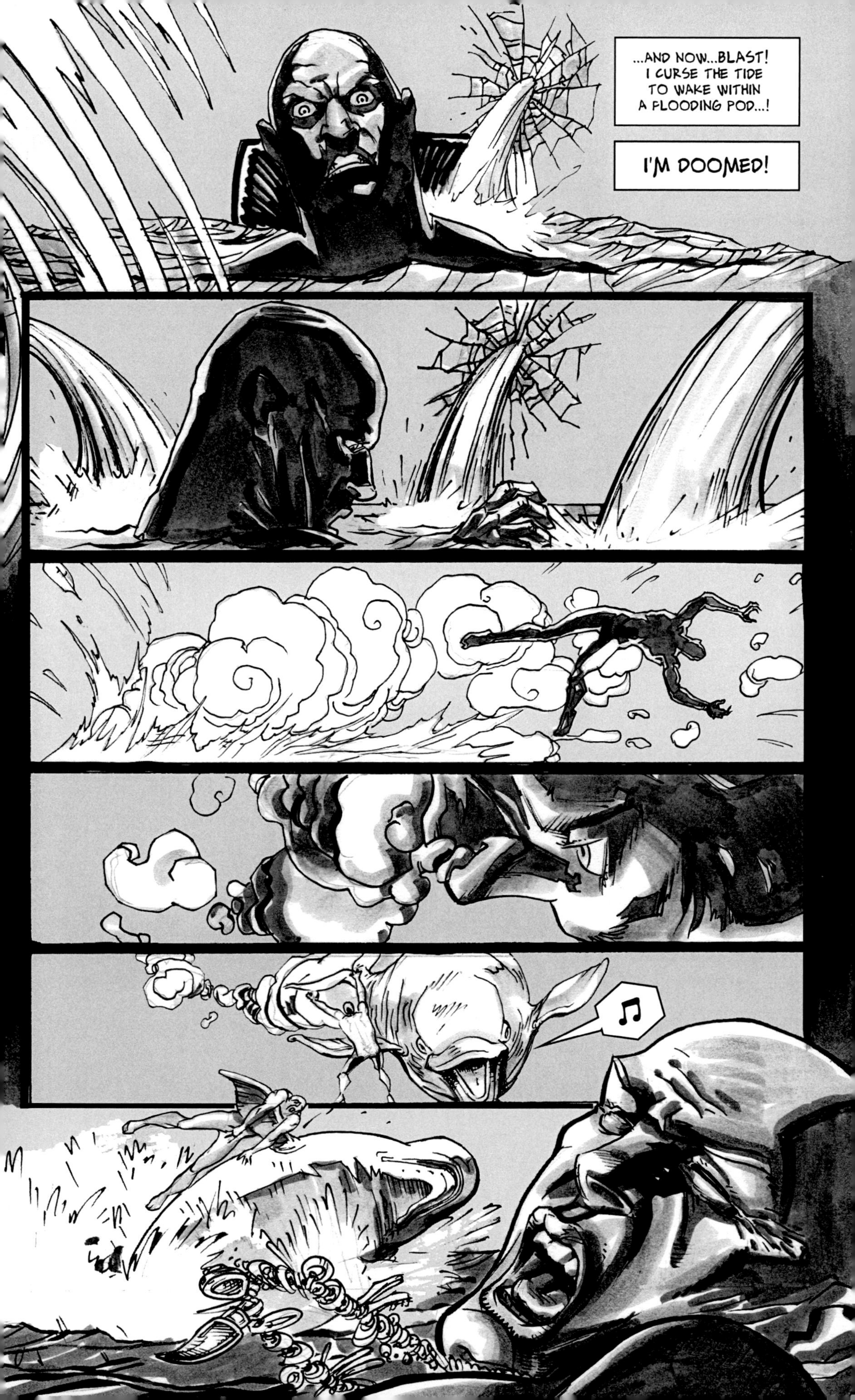
...AND NOW...BLAST! I CURSE THE TIDE TO WAKE WITHIN A FLOODING POD...!
I'M DOOMED!
♫

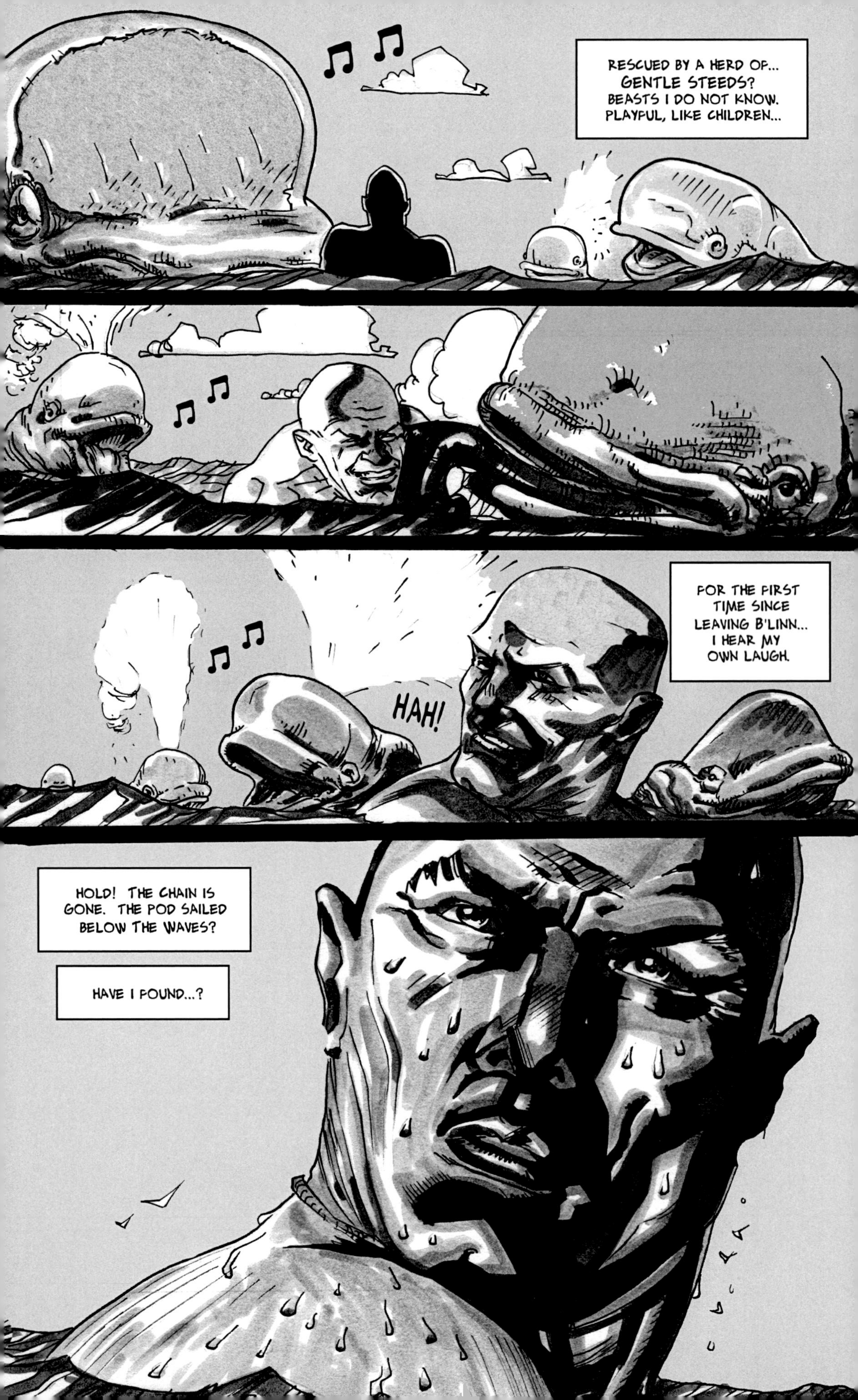
RESCUED BY A HERD OF... GENTLE STEEDS? BEASTS I DO NOT KNOW. PLAYFUL, LIKE CHILDREN...
FOR THE FIRST TIME SINCE LEAVING B'LINN... I HEAR MY OWN LAUGH.
HAH!
HOLD! THE CHAIN IS GONE. THE POD SAILED BELOW THE WAVES?
HAVE I FOUND...?

CHAPTER THREE

PLATU

"MOSS AND CARRION MY FOOD...

WITHERED SKIN MY CLOCK...

I AGE ALONE AMID THE TOWERS..."

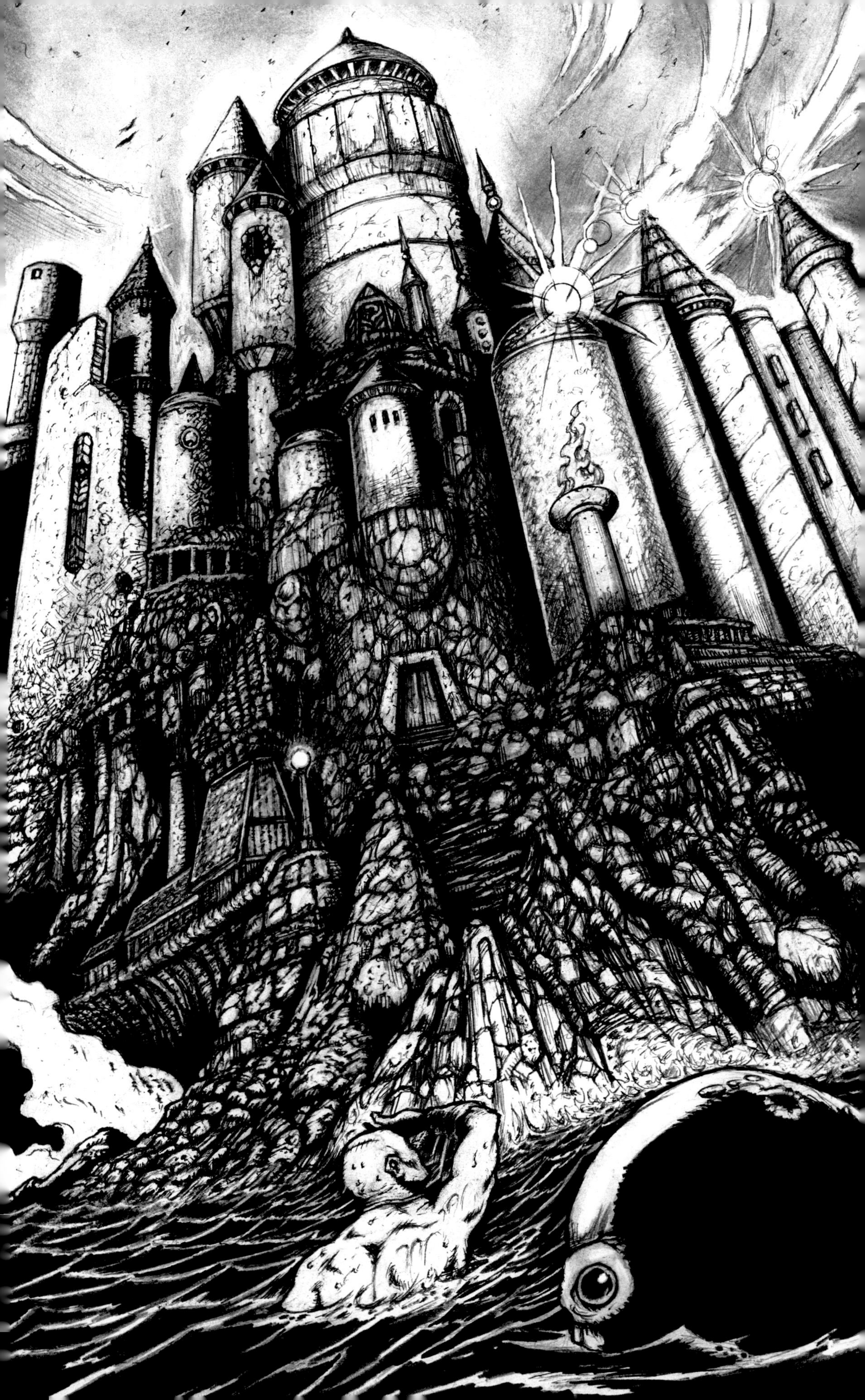

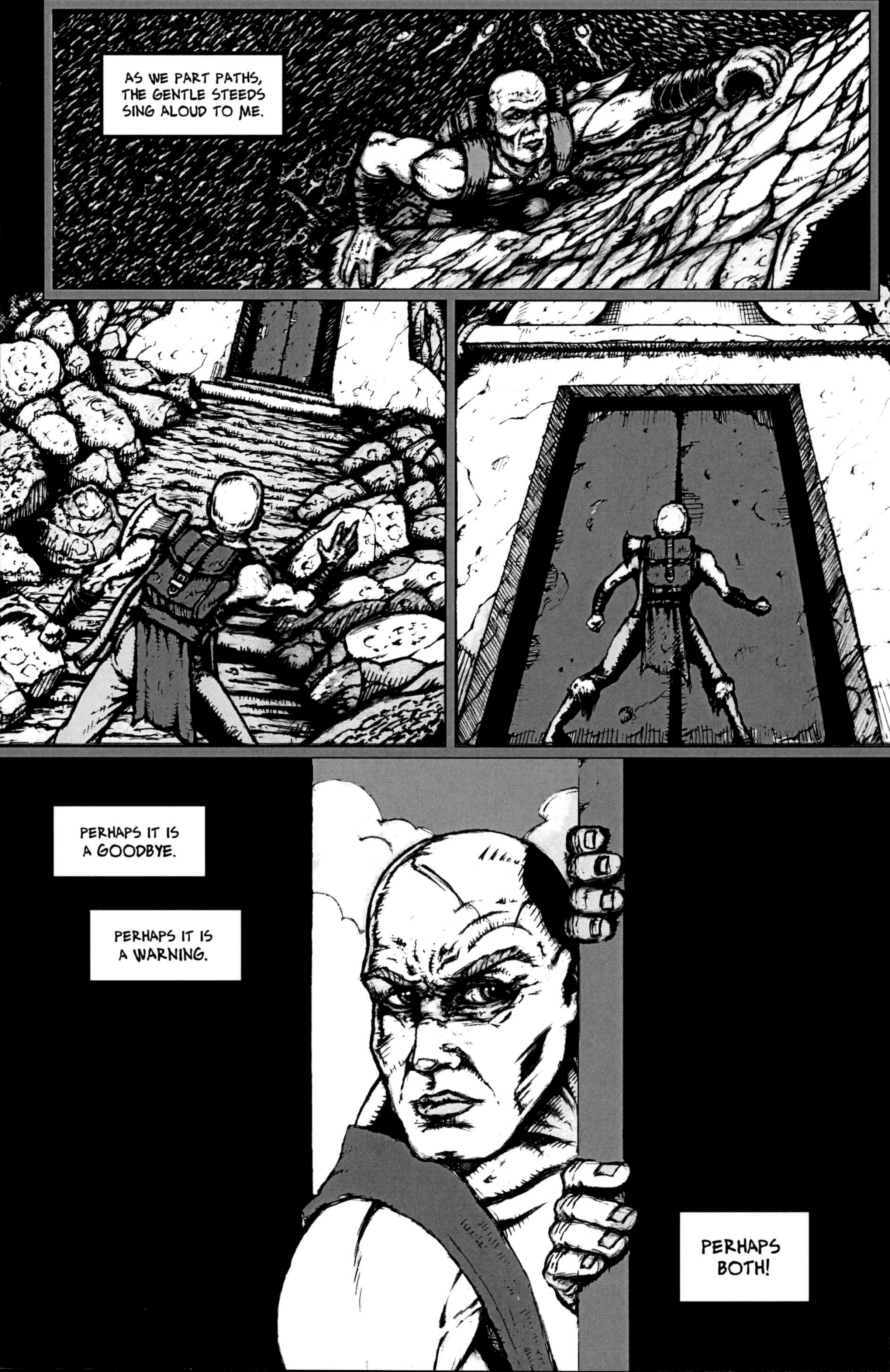
AS WE PART PATHS, THE GENTLE STEEDS SING ALOUD TO ME.
PERHAPS IT IS A GOODBYE.
PERHAPS IT IS A WARNING.
PERHAPS BOTH!

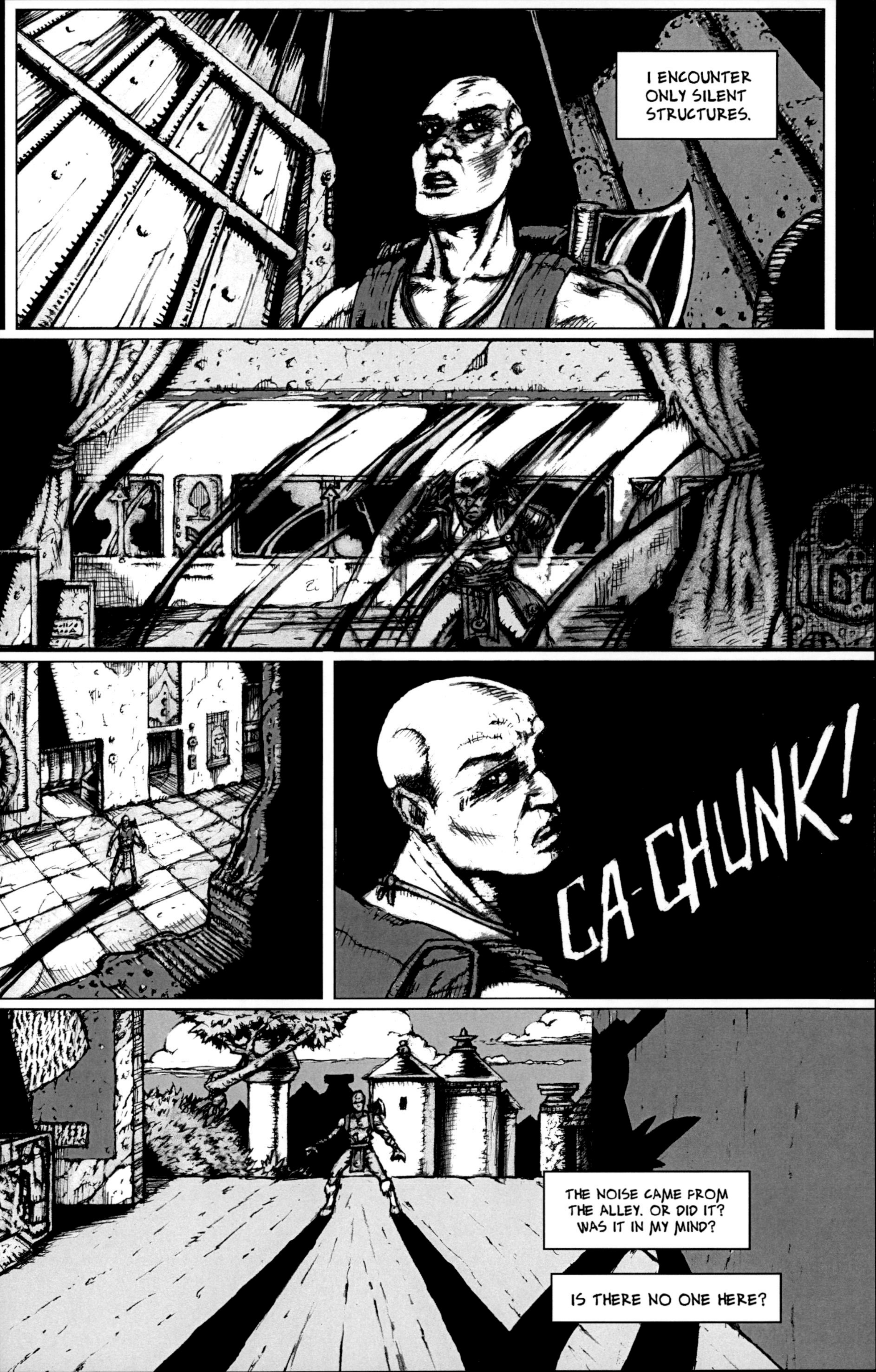
I ENCOUNTER ONLY SILENT STRUCTURES.
CA-CHUNK!
THE NOISE CAME FROM THE ALLEY. OR DID IT? WAS IT IN MY MIND?
IS THERE NO ONE HERE?

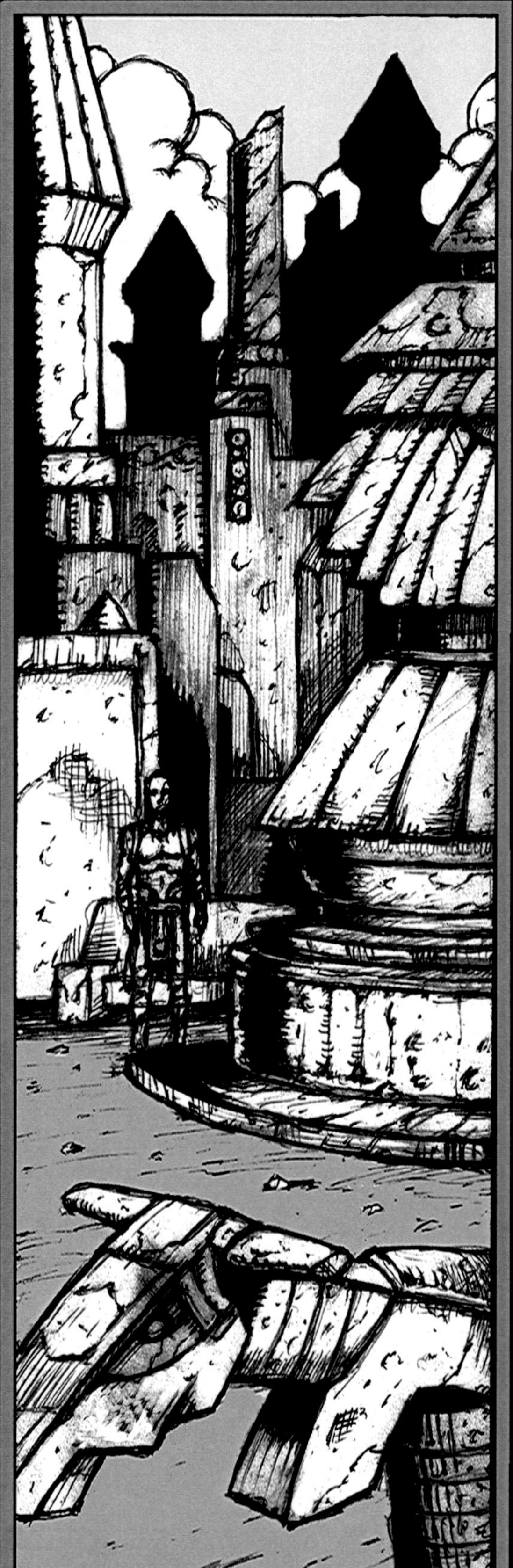
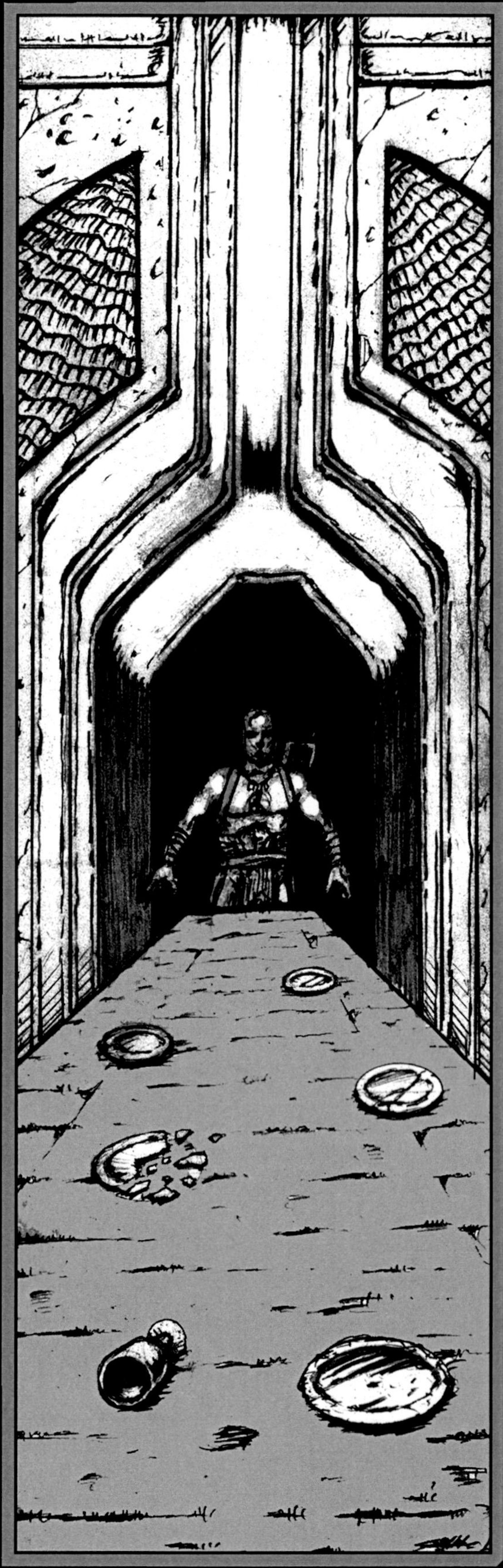

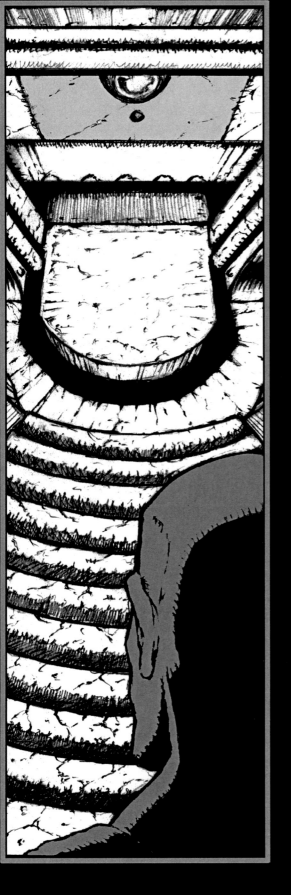

NO! IT CANNOT BE! HAVE I BEEN MISLED? OR, AM I A PRISONER DOOMED TO DIE ALONE?

NOW I HEAR KA'SELL LAUGH ATOP THE STEEP. "IN THE FACE OF HELL... YOU WILL YIELD!"

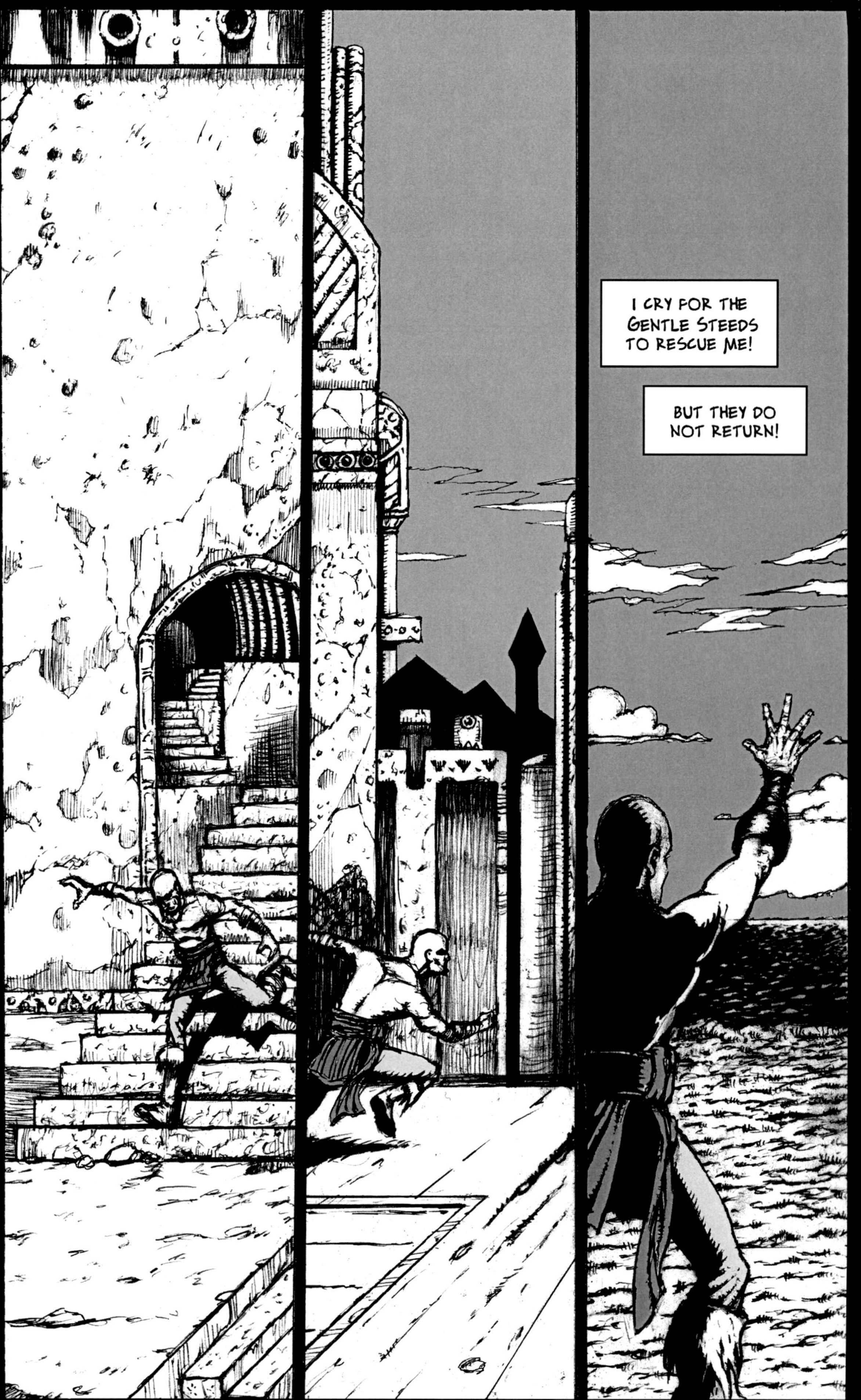
I CRY FOR THE GENTLE STEEDS TO RESCUE ME!
BUT THEY DO NOT RETURN!

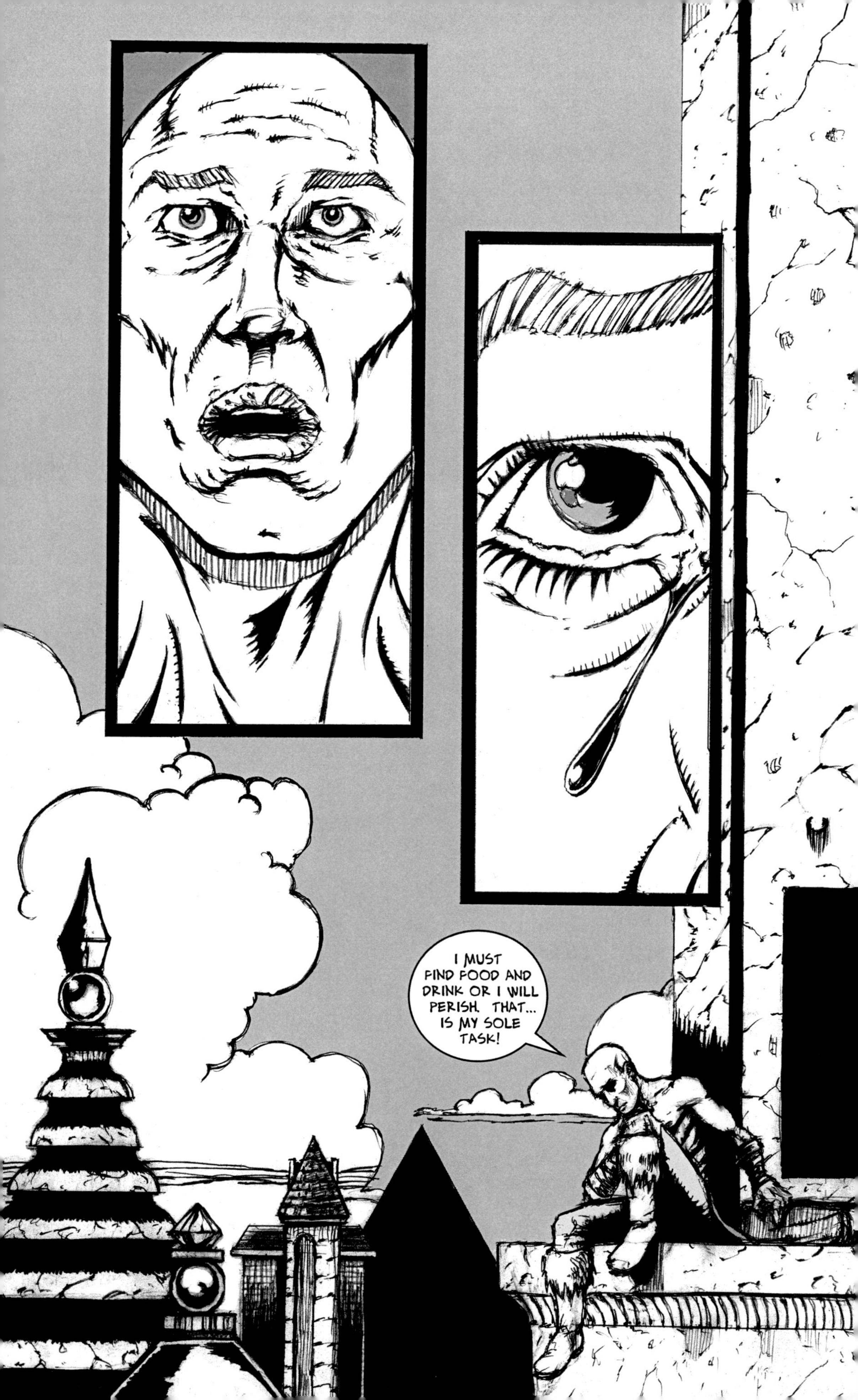
I MUST FIND FOOD AND DRINK OR I WILL PERISH. THAT... IS MY SOLE TASK!

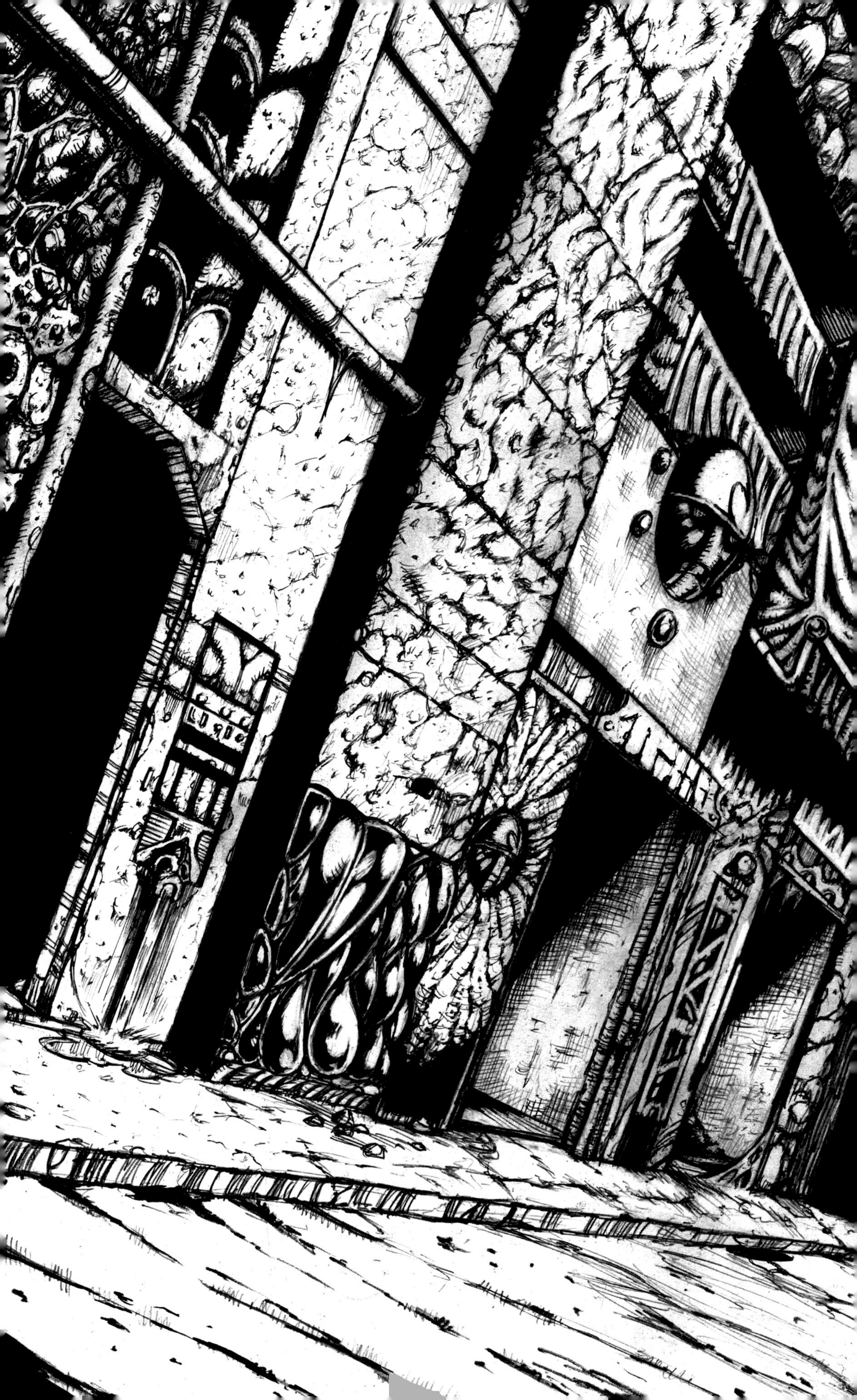

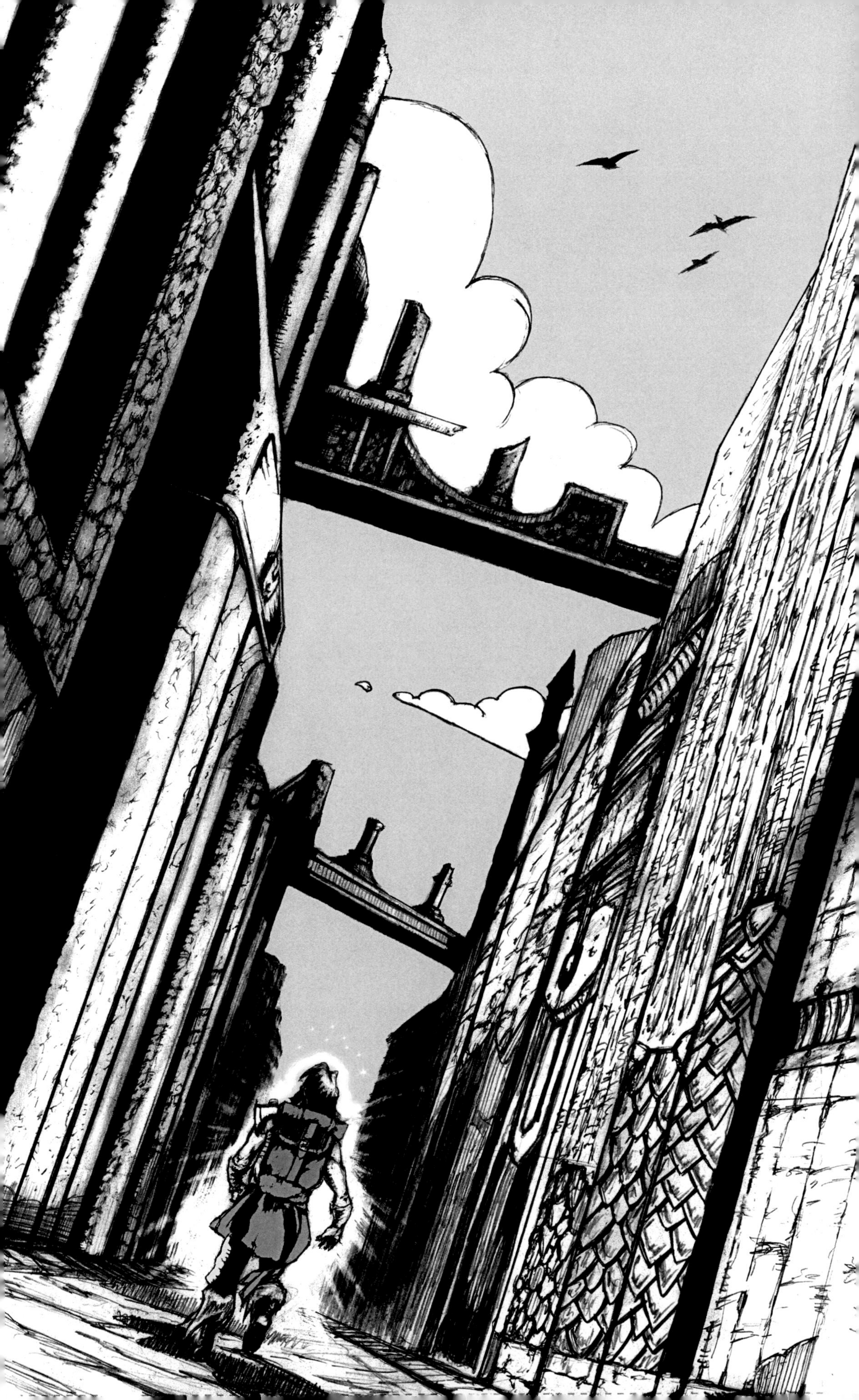

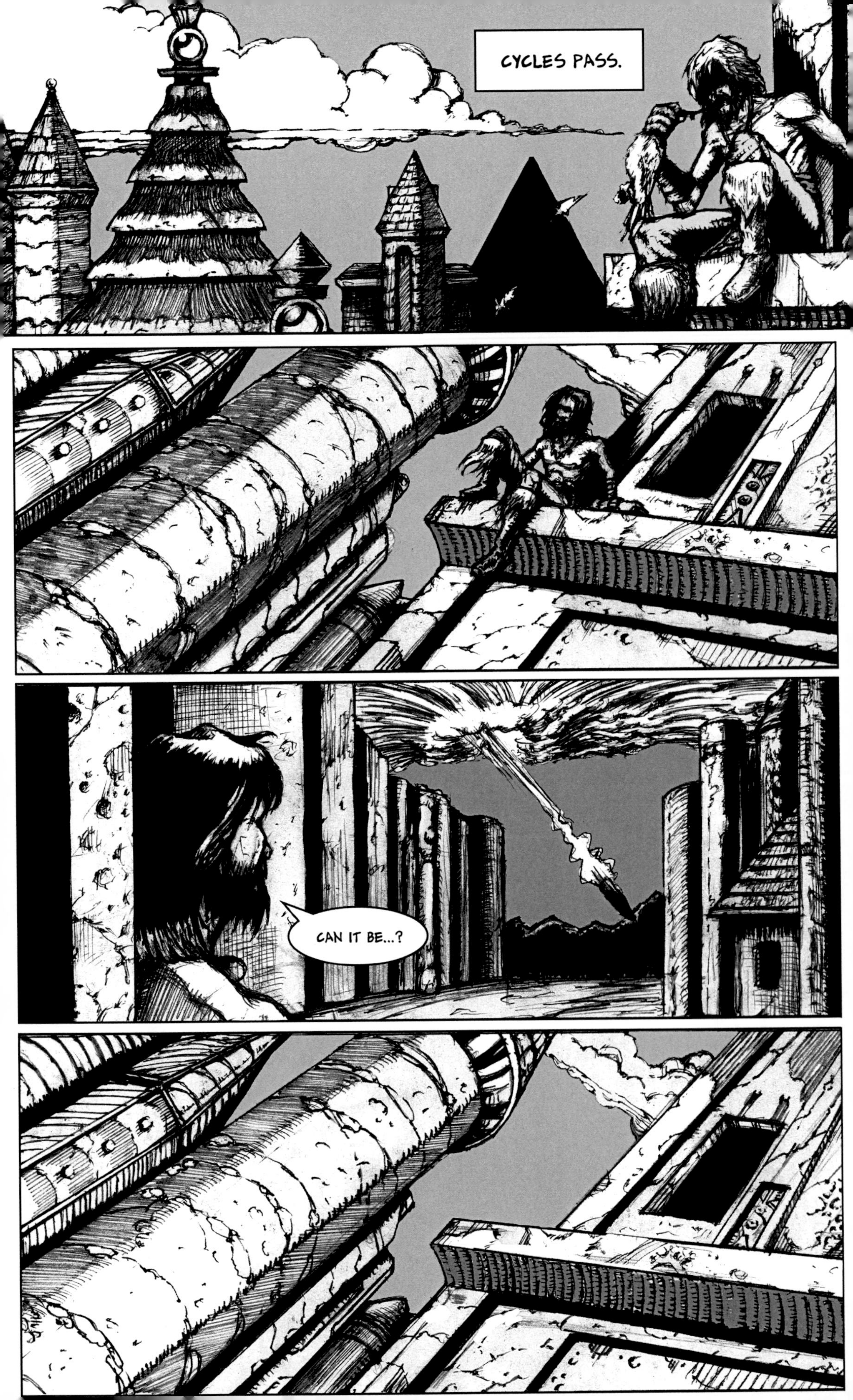
CYCLES PASS.
CAN IT BE...?

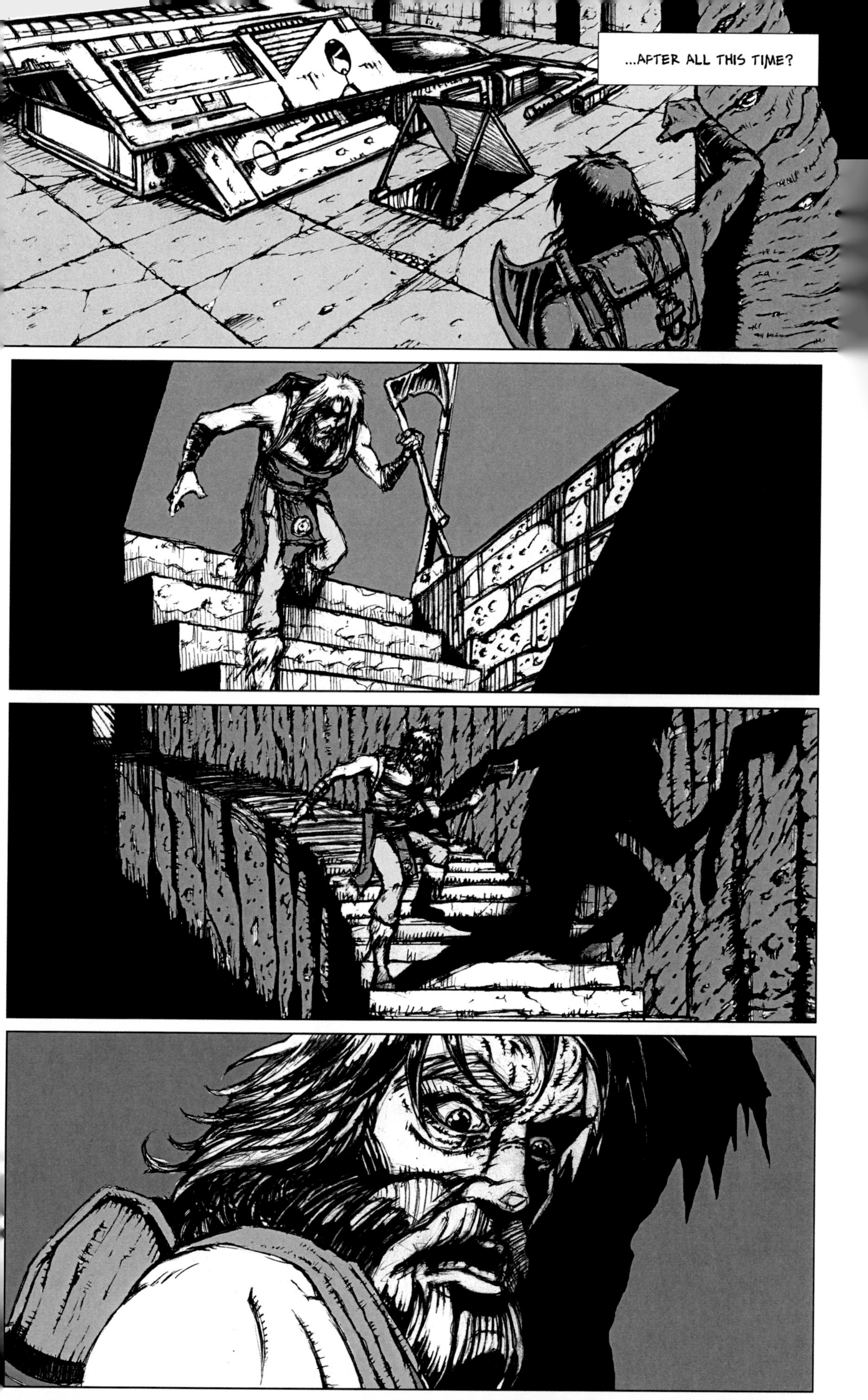
...AFTER ALL THIS TIME?

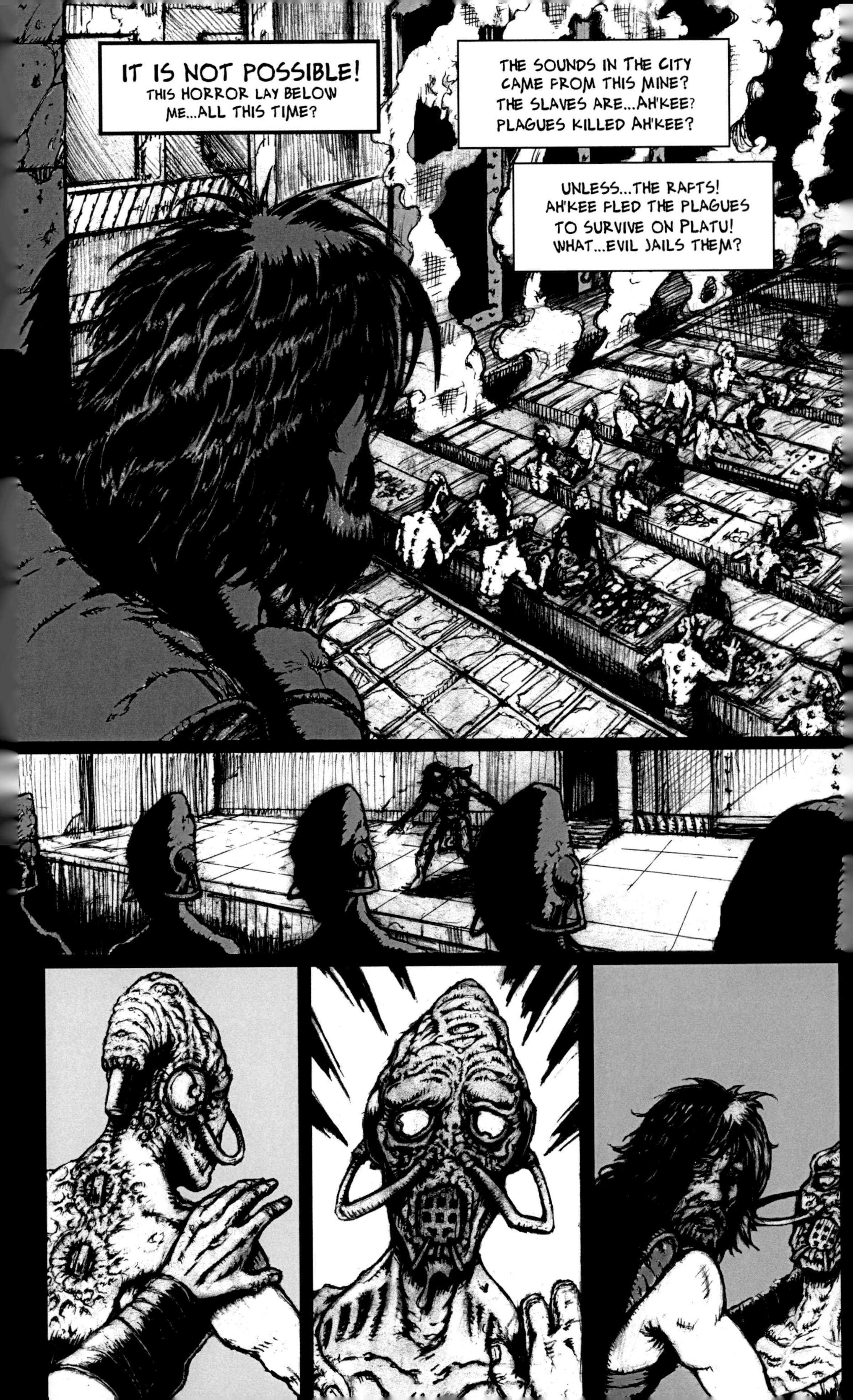
IT IS NOT POSSIBLE!
THIS HORROR LAY BELOW ME...ALL THIS TIME?
THE SOUNDS IN THE CITY CAME FROM THIS MINE? THE SLAVES ARE...AH'KEE? PLAGUES KILLED AH'KEE?
UNLESS...THE RAFTS! AH'KEE FLED THE PLAGUES TO SURVIVE ON PLATU! WHAT...EVIL JAILS THEM?

UNLIVING OVERLORD!
I...I CANNOT STOP IT!
OR HURT IT!!

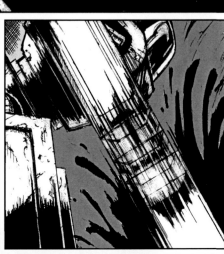

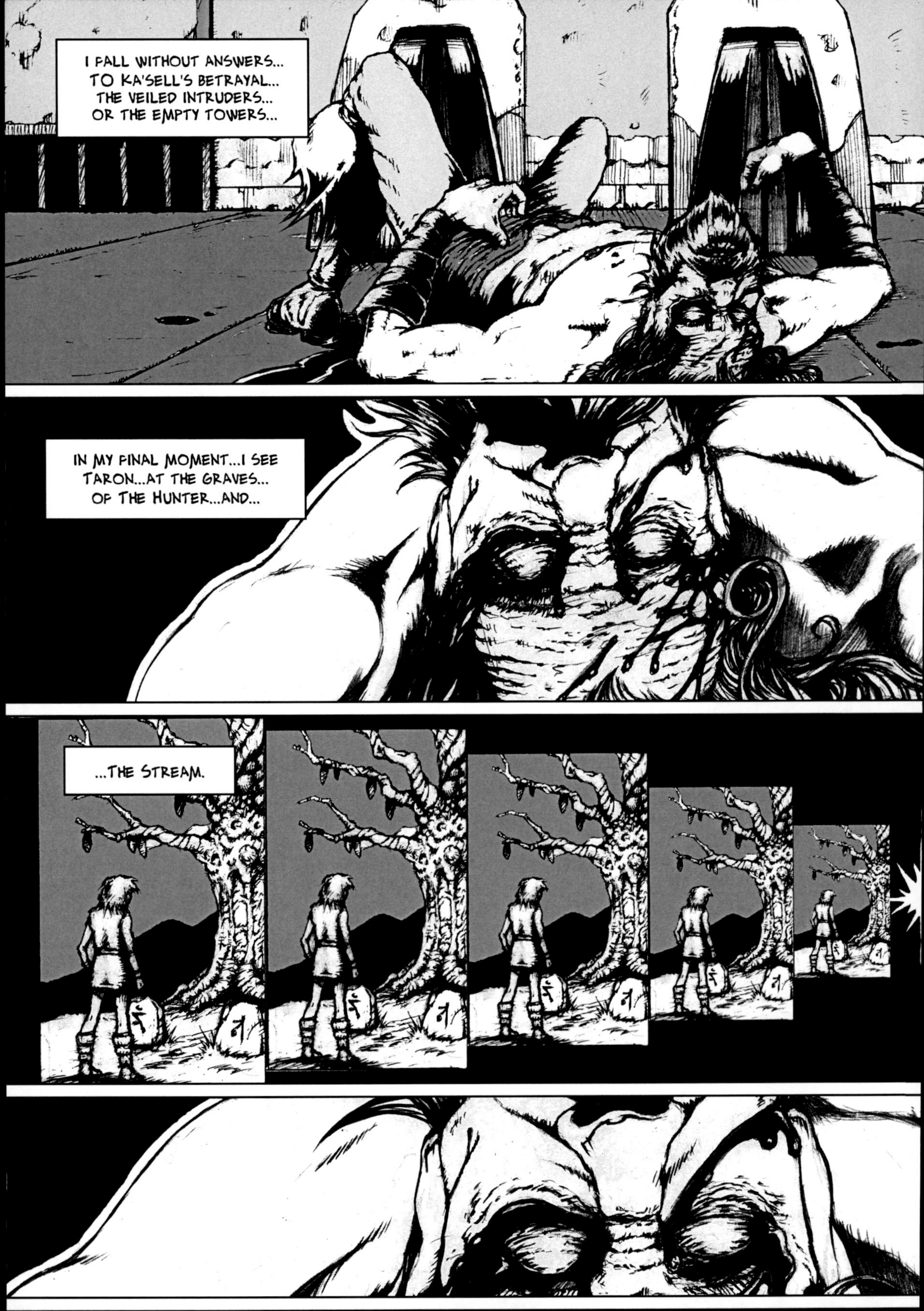
I FALL WITHOUT ANSWERS... TO KA'SELL'S BETRAYAL... THE VEILED INTRUDERS... OR THE EMPTY TOWERS...
IN MY FINAL MOMENT...I SEE TARON...AT THE GRAVES... OF THE HUNTER...AND...
...THE STREAM.

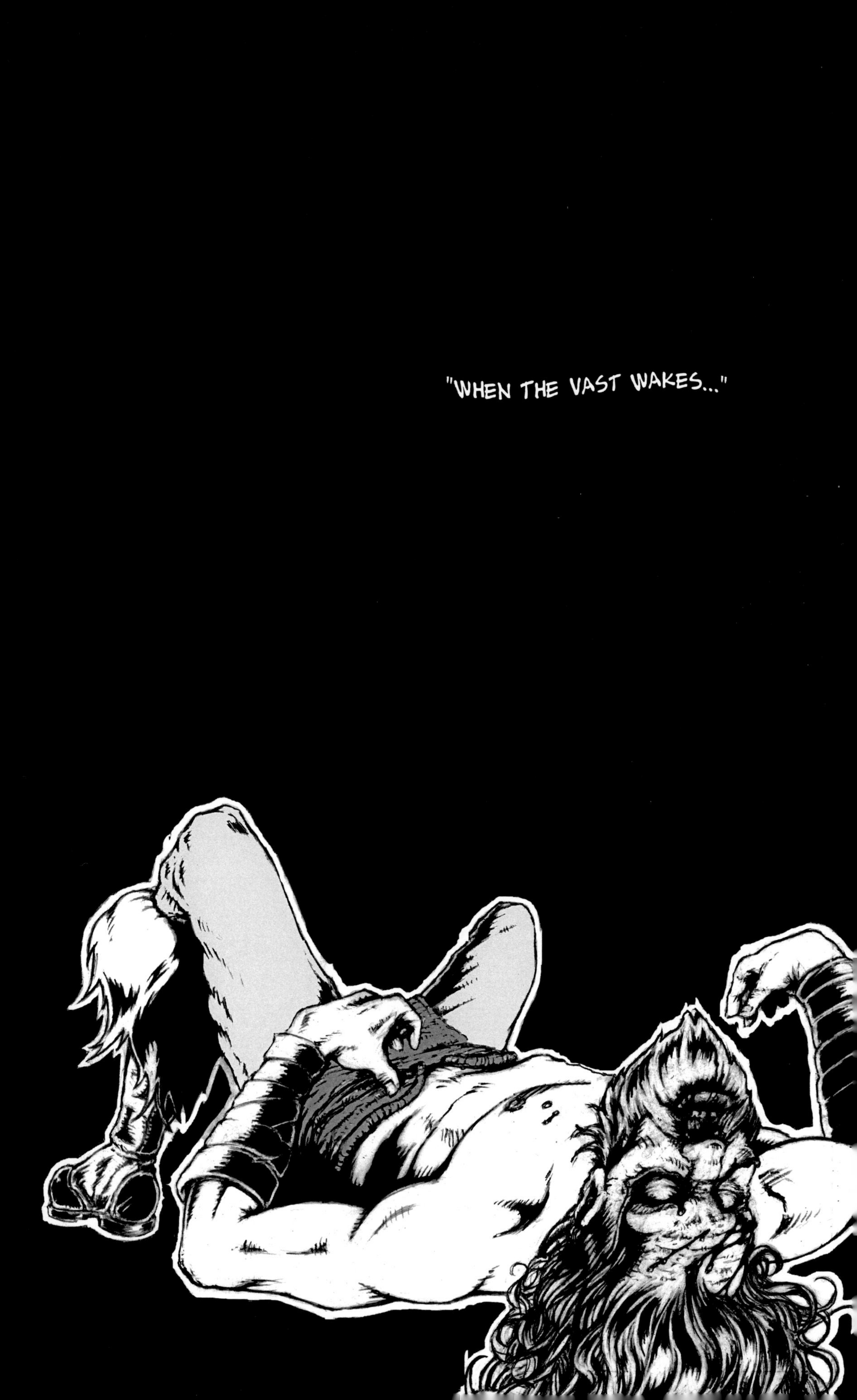
"WHEN THE VAST WAKES..."

"...A CHAMPION SHALL VOYAGE..."

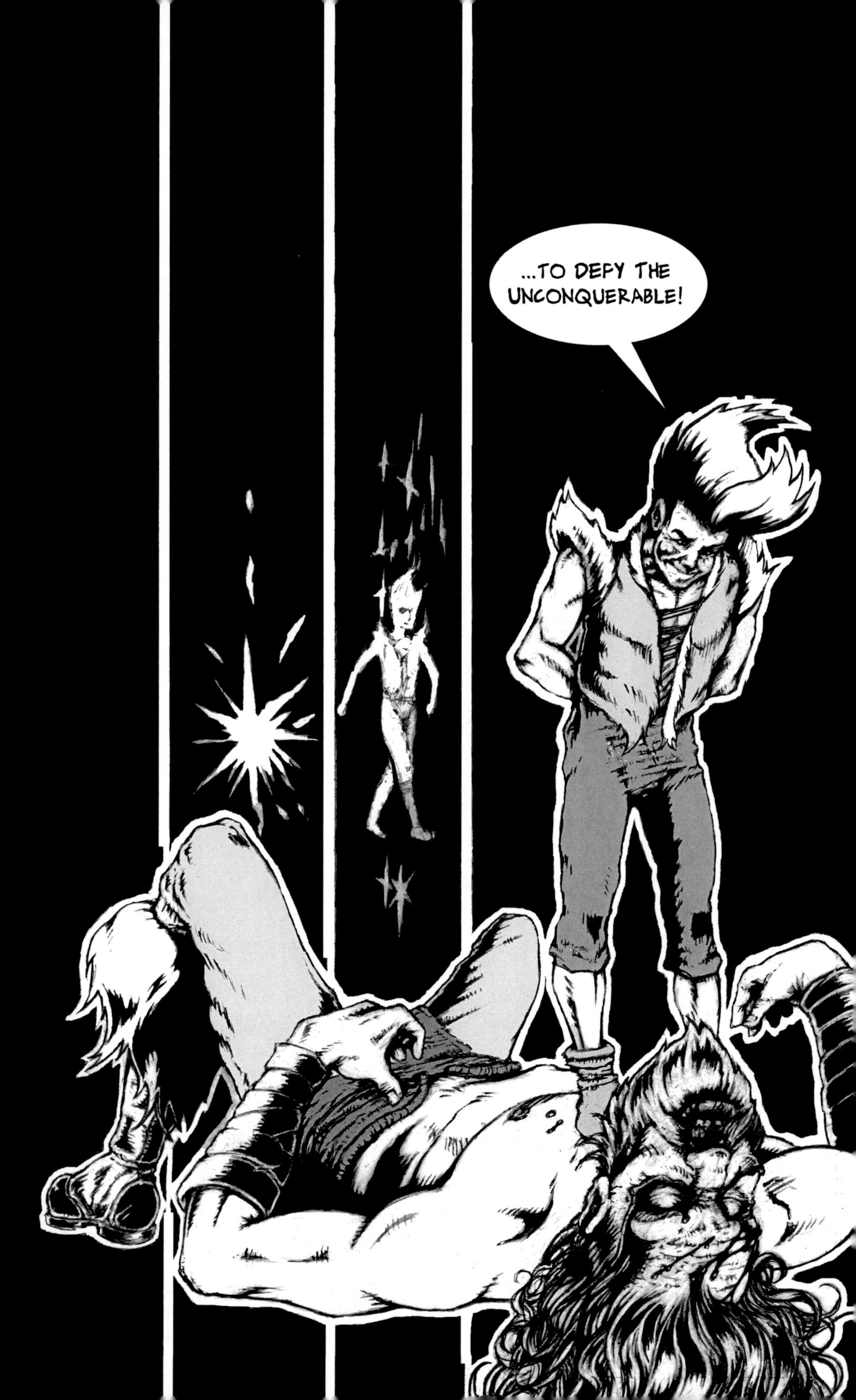
...TO DEFY THE UNCONQUERABLE!

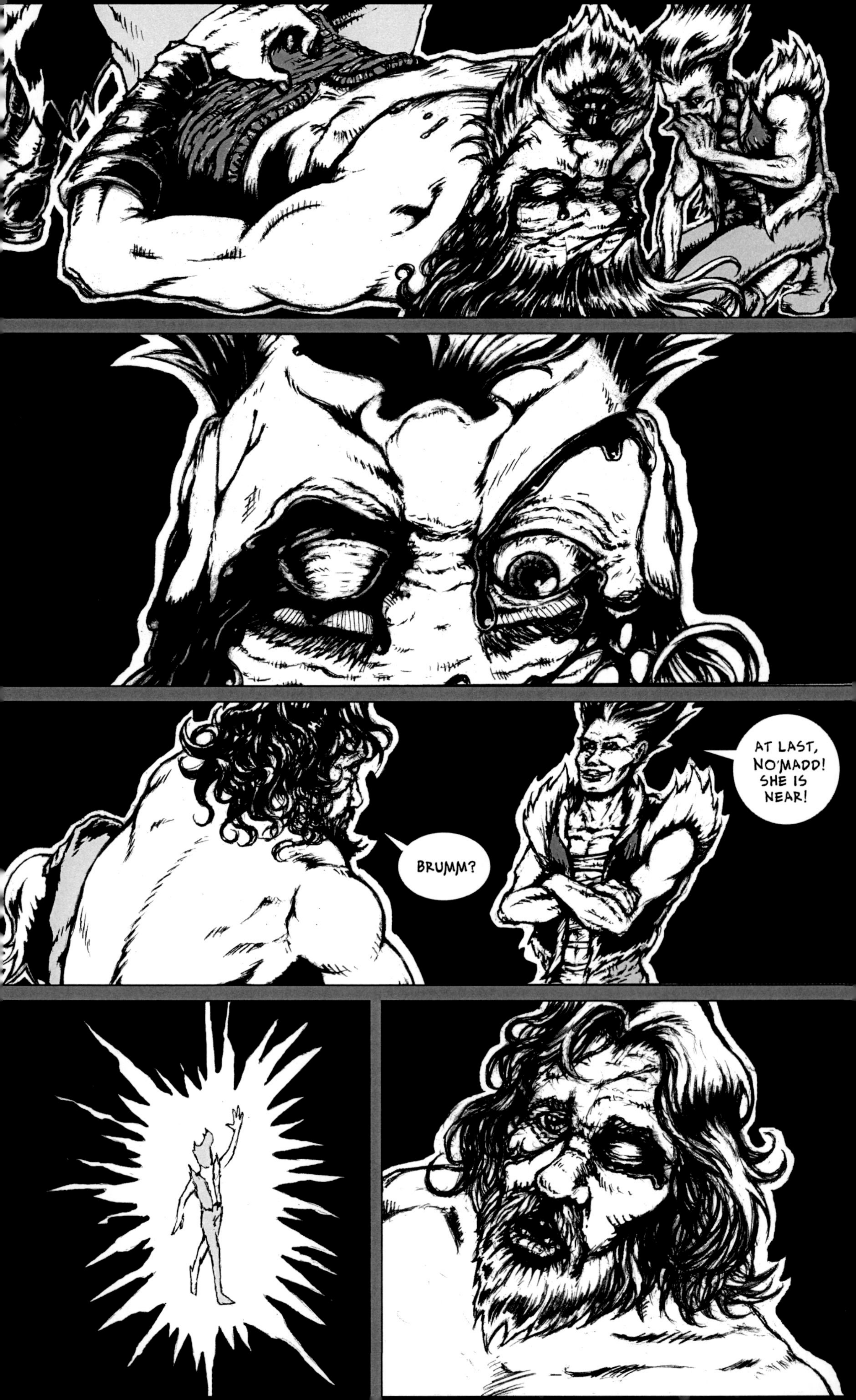
BRUMM?
AT LAST, NO'MADD! SHE IS NEAR!

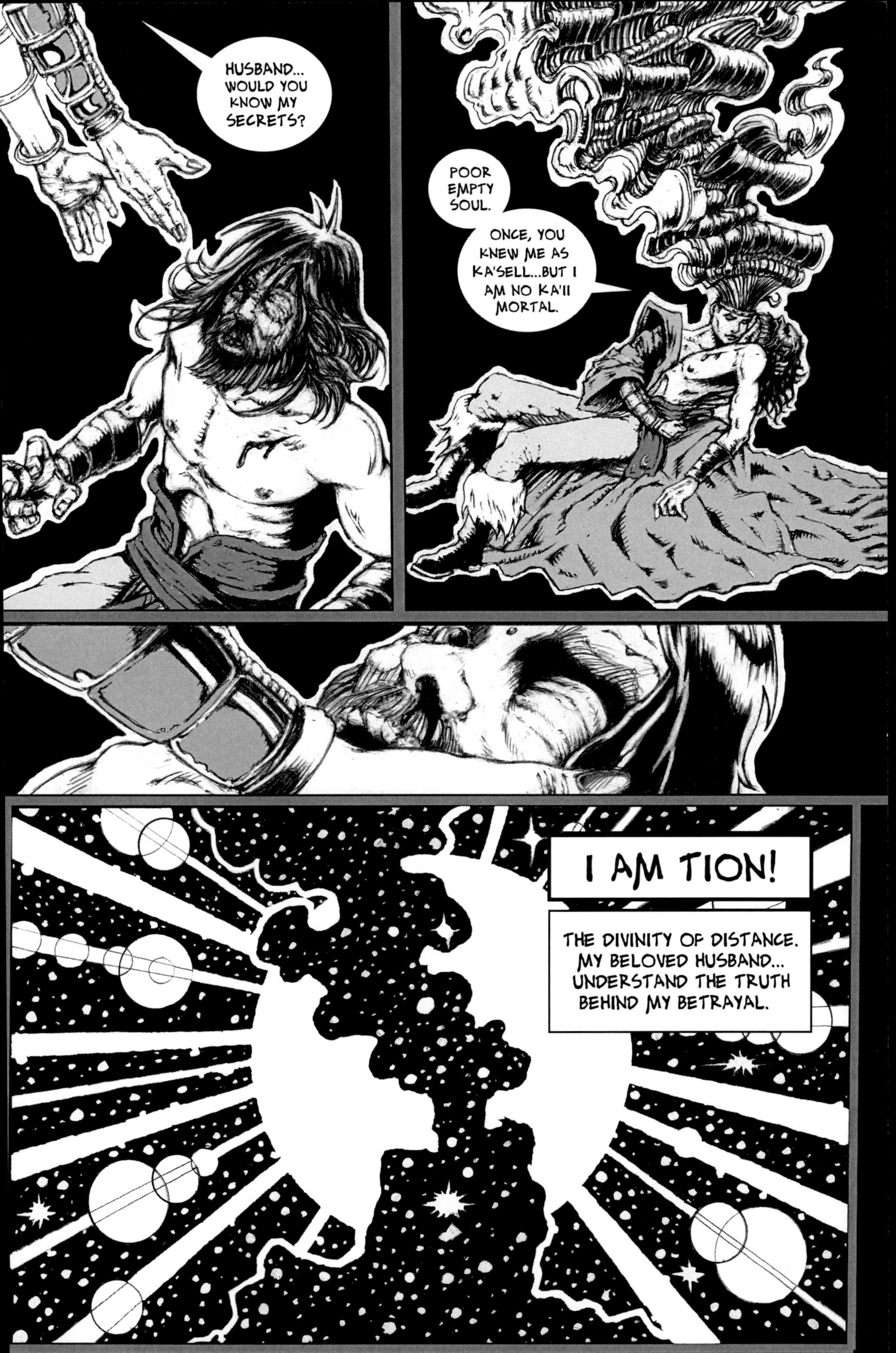
HUSBAND... WOULD YOU KNOW MY SECRETS?
POOR EMPTY SOUL.
ONCE, YOU KNEW ME AS KA'SELL...BUT I AM NO KA'II MORTAL.
I AM TION!
THE DIVINITY OF DISTANCE. MY BELOVED HUSBAND... UNDERSTAND THE TRUTH BEHIND MY BETRAYAL.

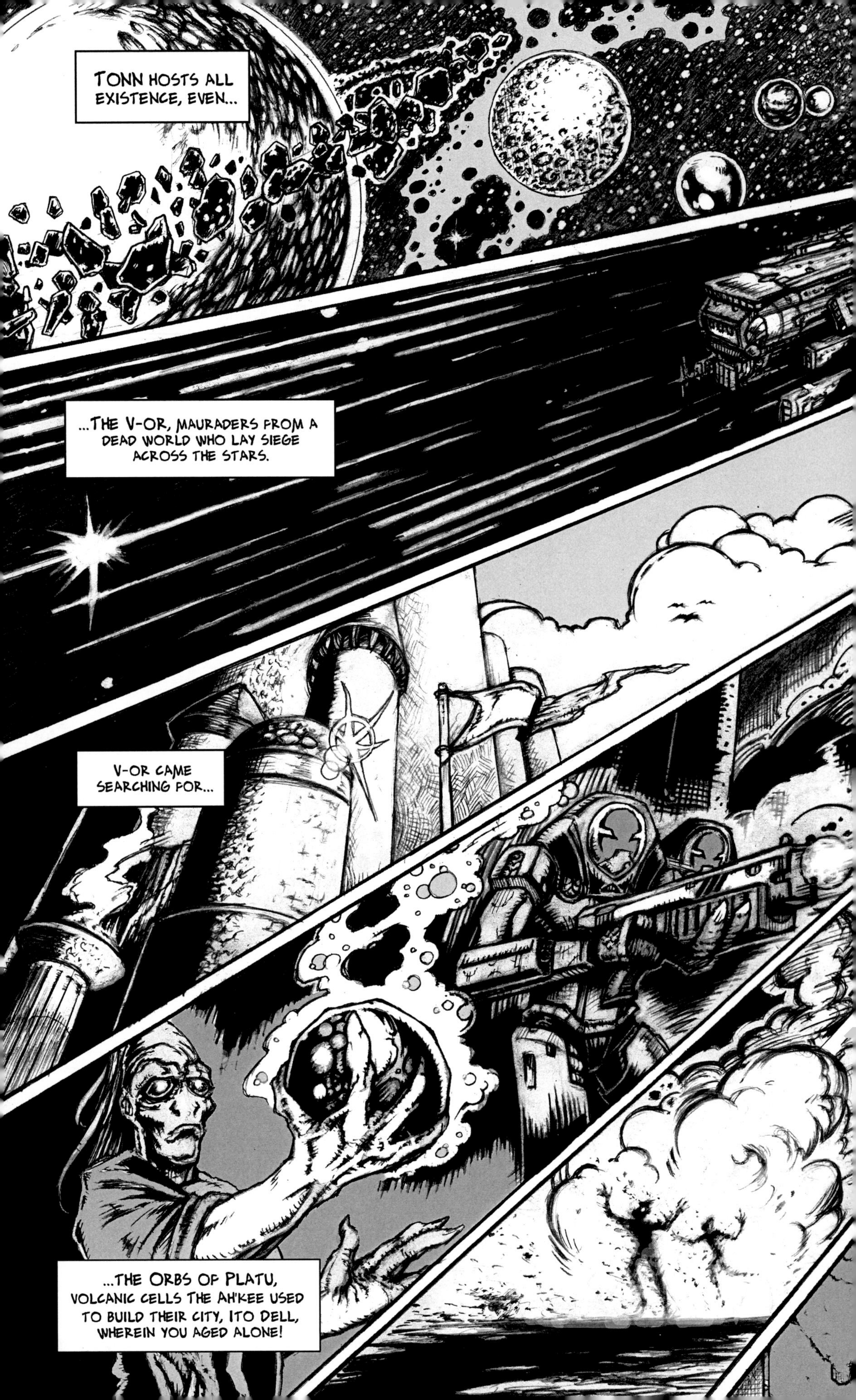
TONN HOSTS ALL EXISTENCE, EVEN...
...THE V-OR, MAURADERS FROM A DEAD WORLD WHO LAY SIEGE ACROSS THE STARS.
V-OR CAME SEARCHING FOR...
...THE ORBS OF PLATU, VOLCANIC CELLS THE AH'KEE USED TO BUILD THEIR CITY, ITO DELL, WHEREIN YOU AGED ALONE!

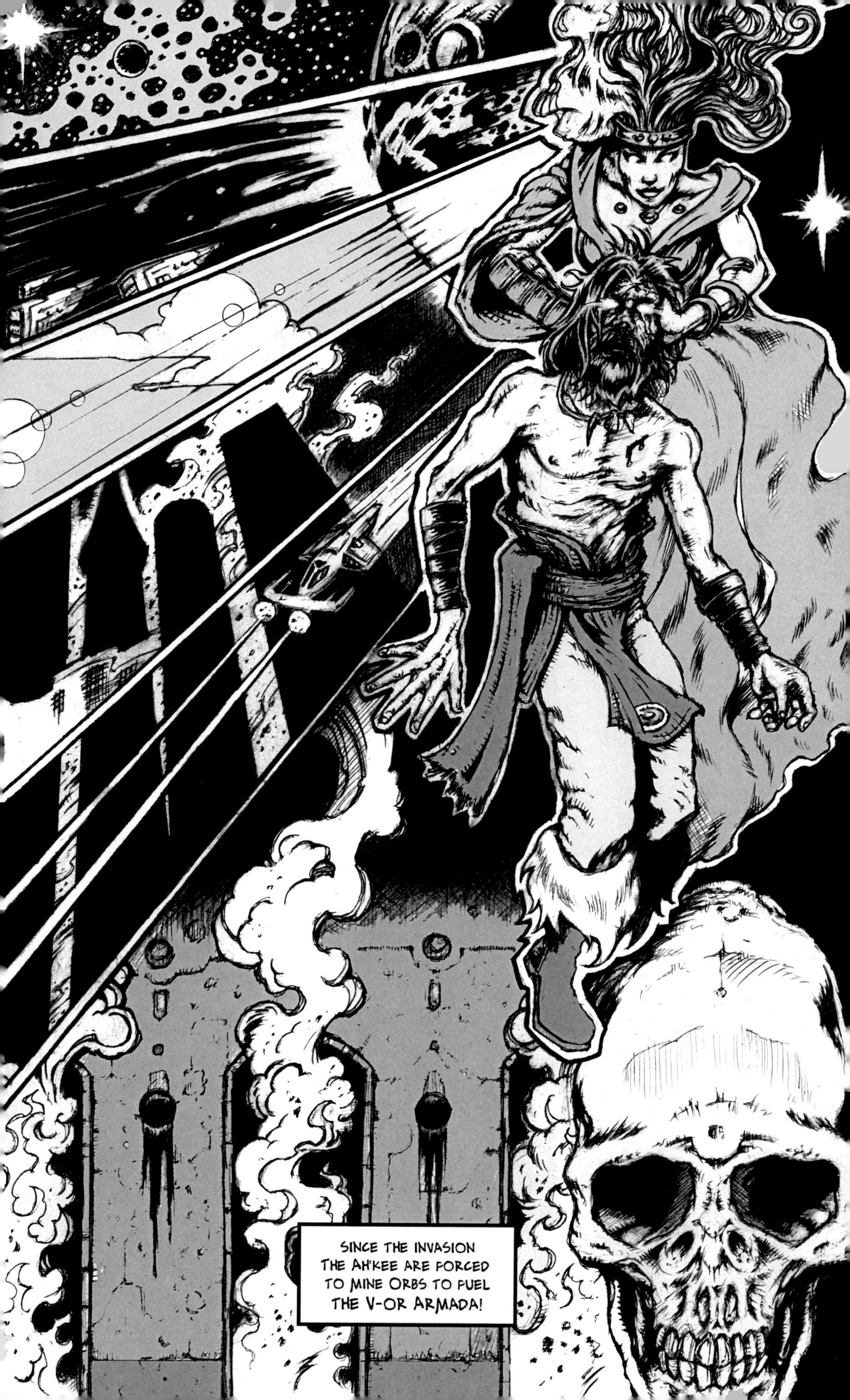
SINCE THE INVASION
THE AH'KEE ARE FORCED
TO MINE ORBS TO FUEL
THE V-OR ARMADA!

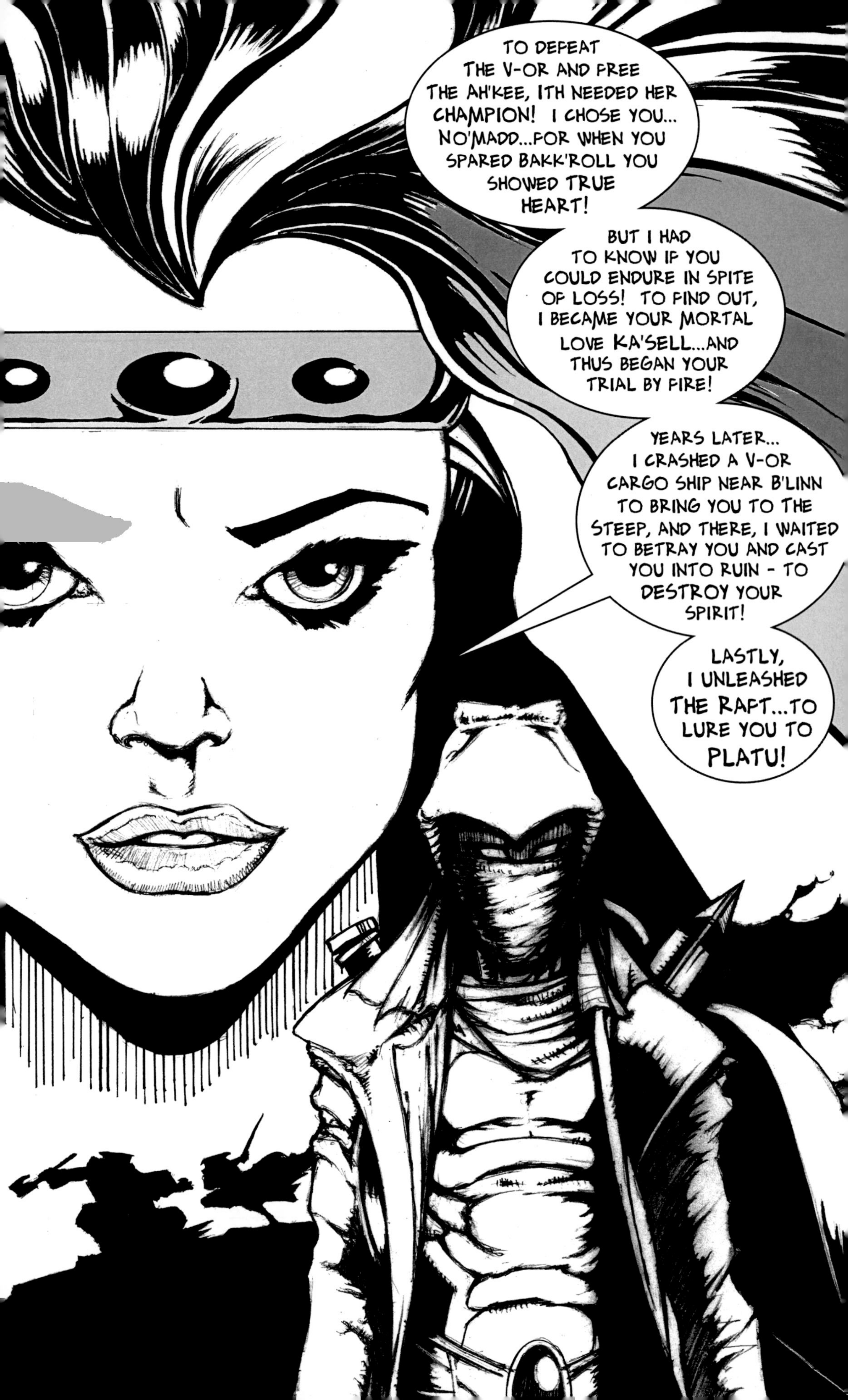
TO DEFEAT THE V-OR AND FREE THE AH'KEE, ITH NEEDED HER CHAMPION! I CHOSE YOU... NO'MADD...FOR WHEN YOU SPARED BAKK'ROLL YOU SHOWED TRUE HEART!
BUT I HAD TO KNOW IF YOU COULD ENDURE IN SPITE OF LOSS! TO FIND OUT, I BECAME YOUR MORTAL LOVE KA'SELL...AND THUS BEGAN YOUR TRIAL BY FIRE!
YEARS LATER... I CRASHED A V-OR CARGO SHIP NEAR B'LINN TO BRING YOU TO THE STEEP, AND THERE, I WAITED TO BETRAY YOU AND CAST YOU INTO RUIN - TO DESTROY YOUR SPIRIT!
LASTLY, I UNLEASHED THE RAFT...TO LURE YOU TO PLATU!

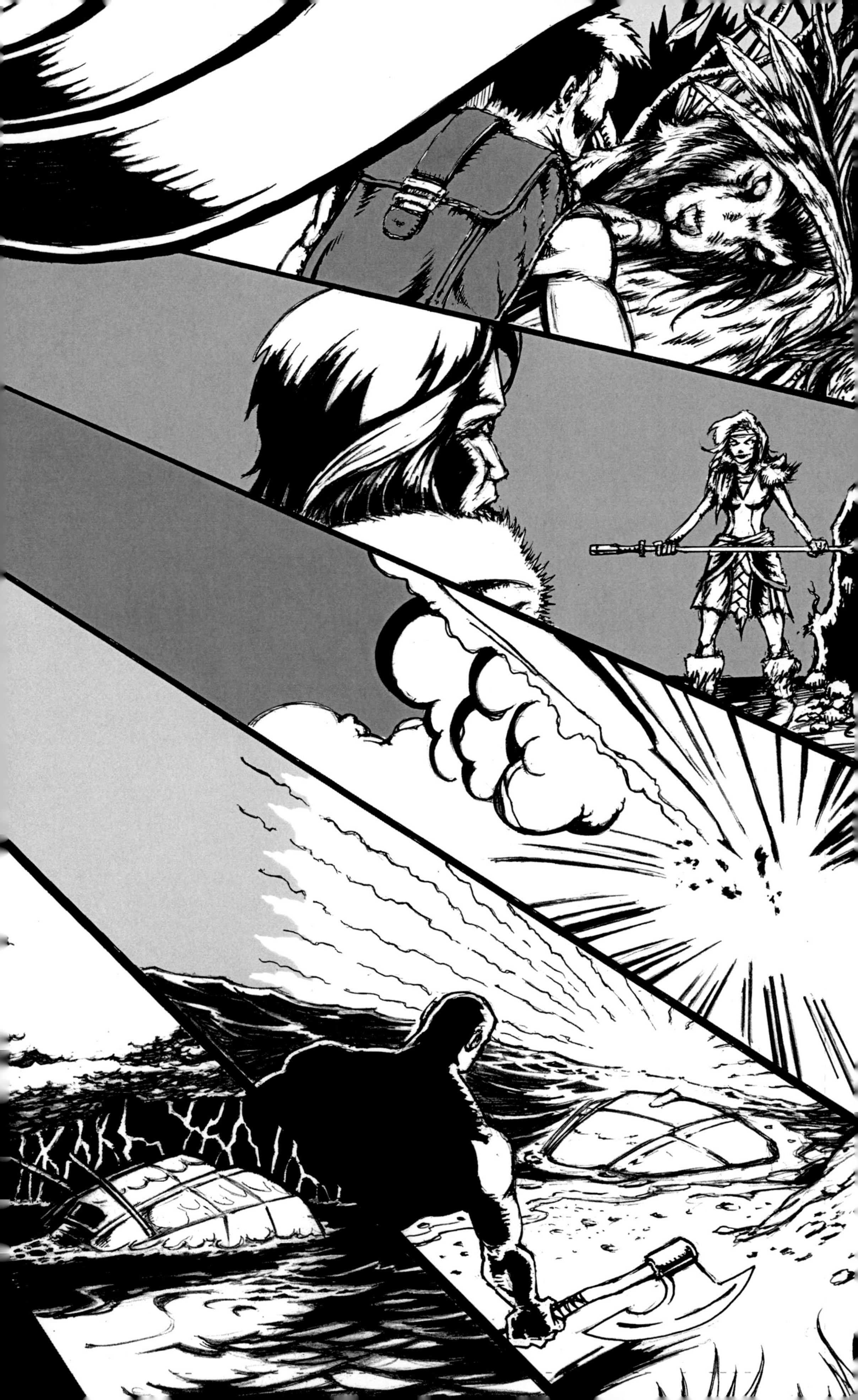

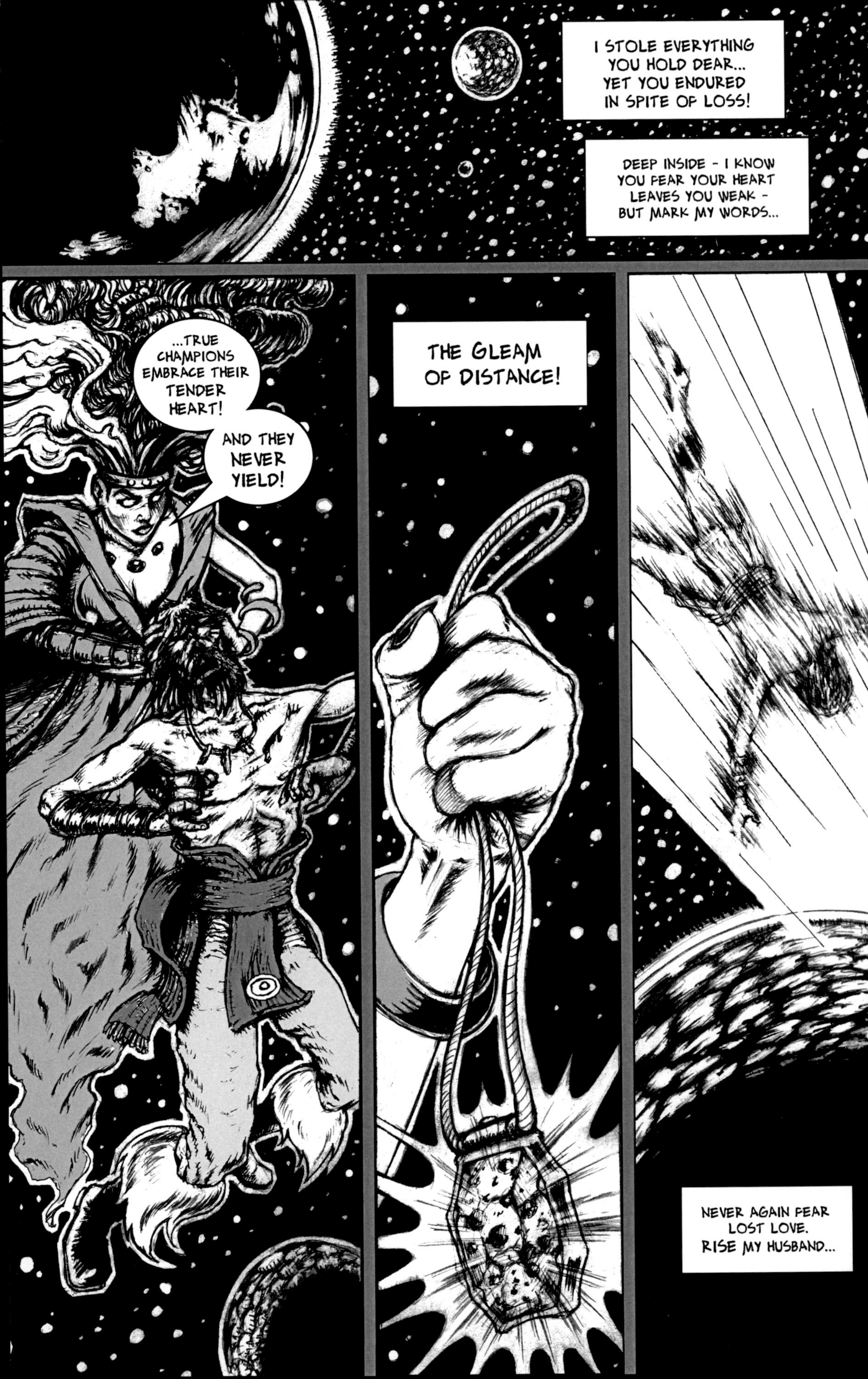

I STOLE EVERYTHING YOU HOLD DEAR... YET YOU ENDURED IN SPITE OF LOSS!
DEEP INSIDE - I KNOW YOU FEAR YOUR HEART LEAVES YOU WEAK - BUT MARK MY WORDS...
...TRUE CHAMPIONS EMBRACE THEIR TENDER HEART!
AND THEY NEVER YIELD!
THE GLEAM OF DISTANCE!
NEVER AGAIN FEAR LOST LOVE. RISE MY HUSBAND...

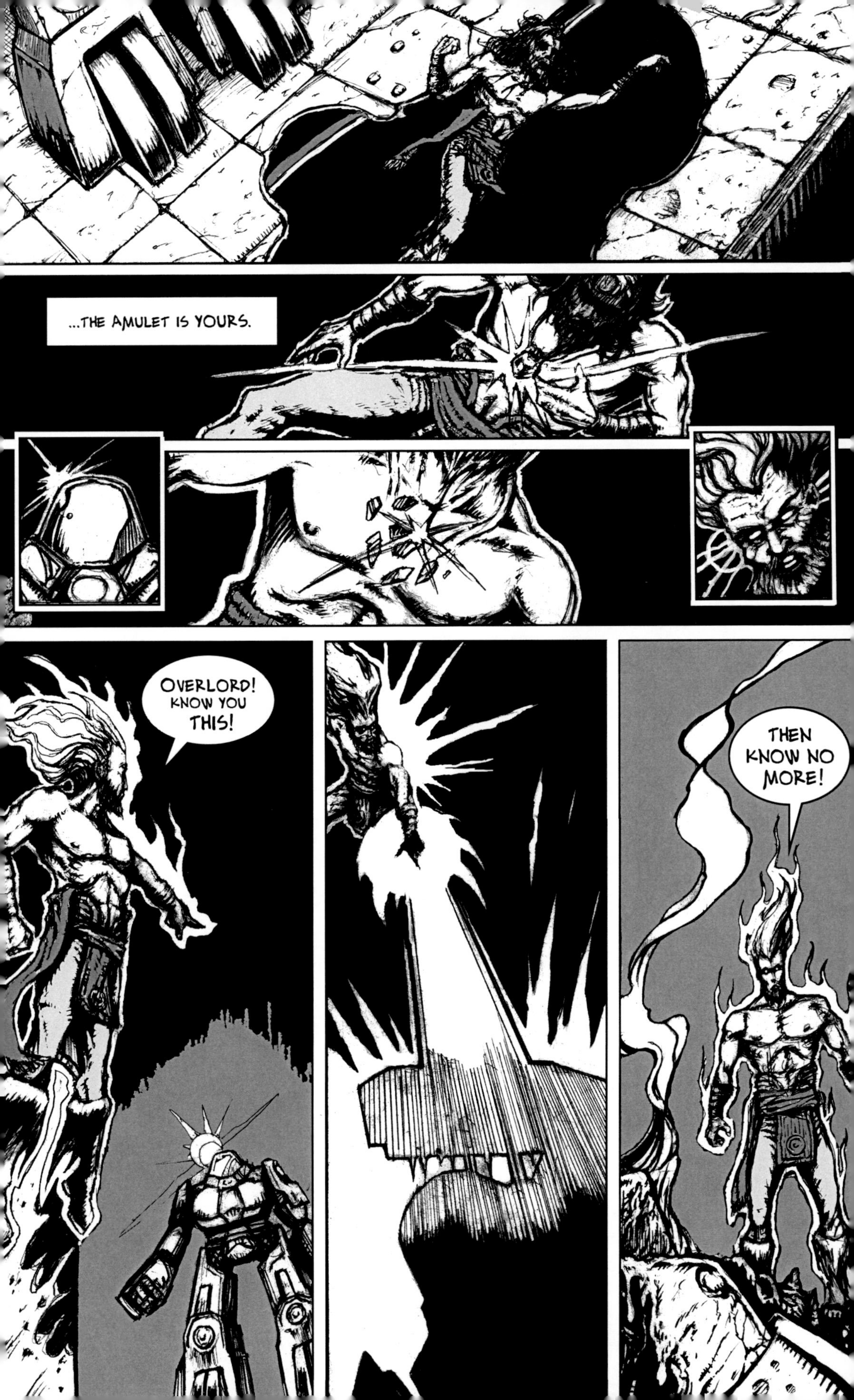
...THE AMULET IS YOURS.
OVERLORD! KNOW YOU THIS!
THEN KNOW NO MORE!

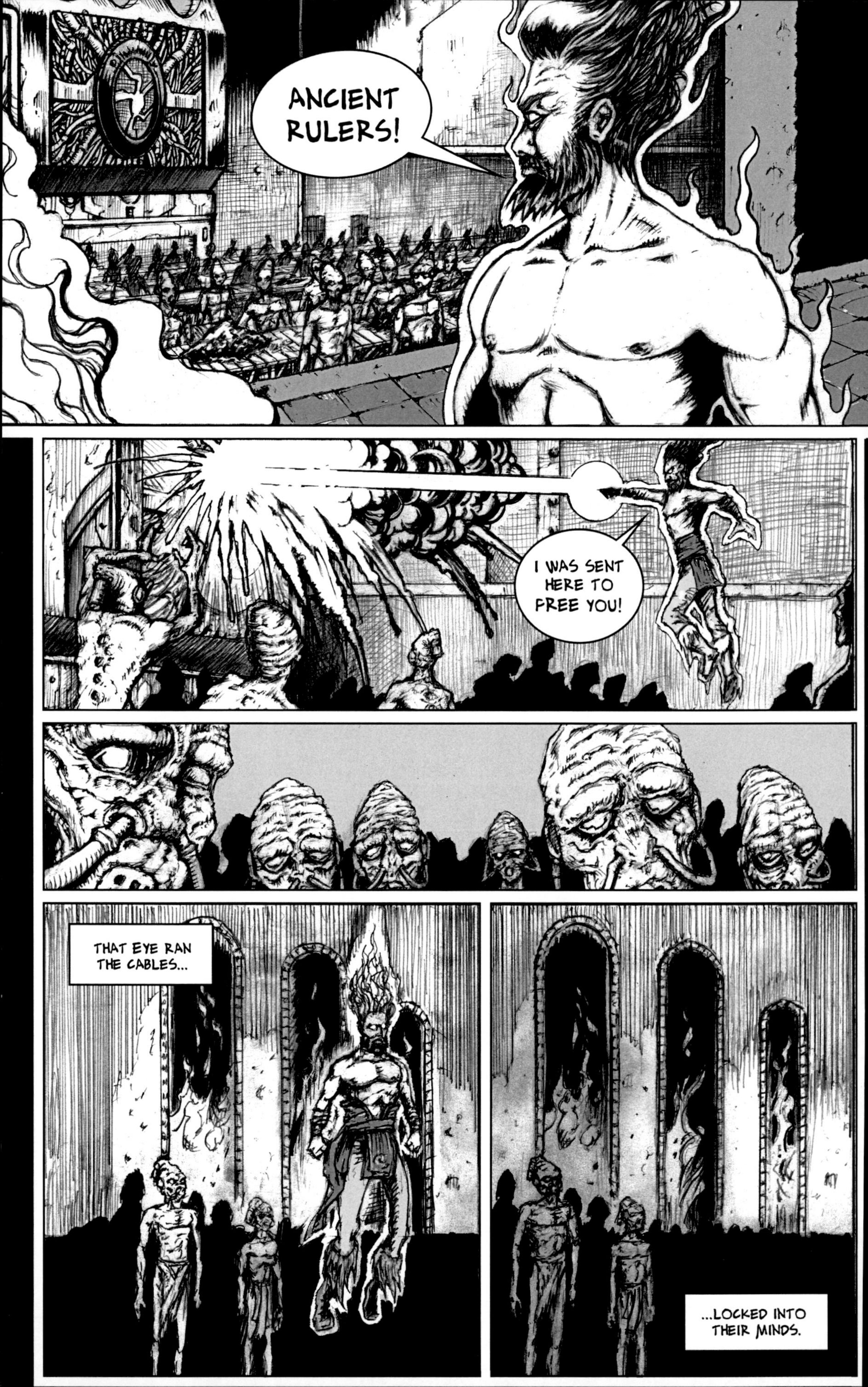
ANCIENT RULERS!
I WAS SENT HERE TO FREE YOU!
THAT EYE RAN THE CABLES...
...LOCKED INTO THEIR MINDS.

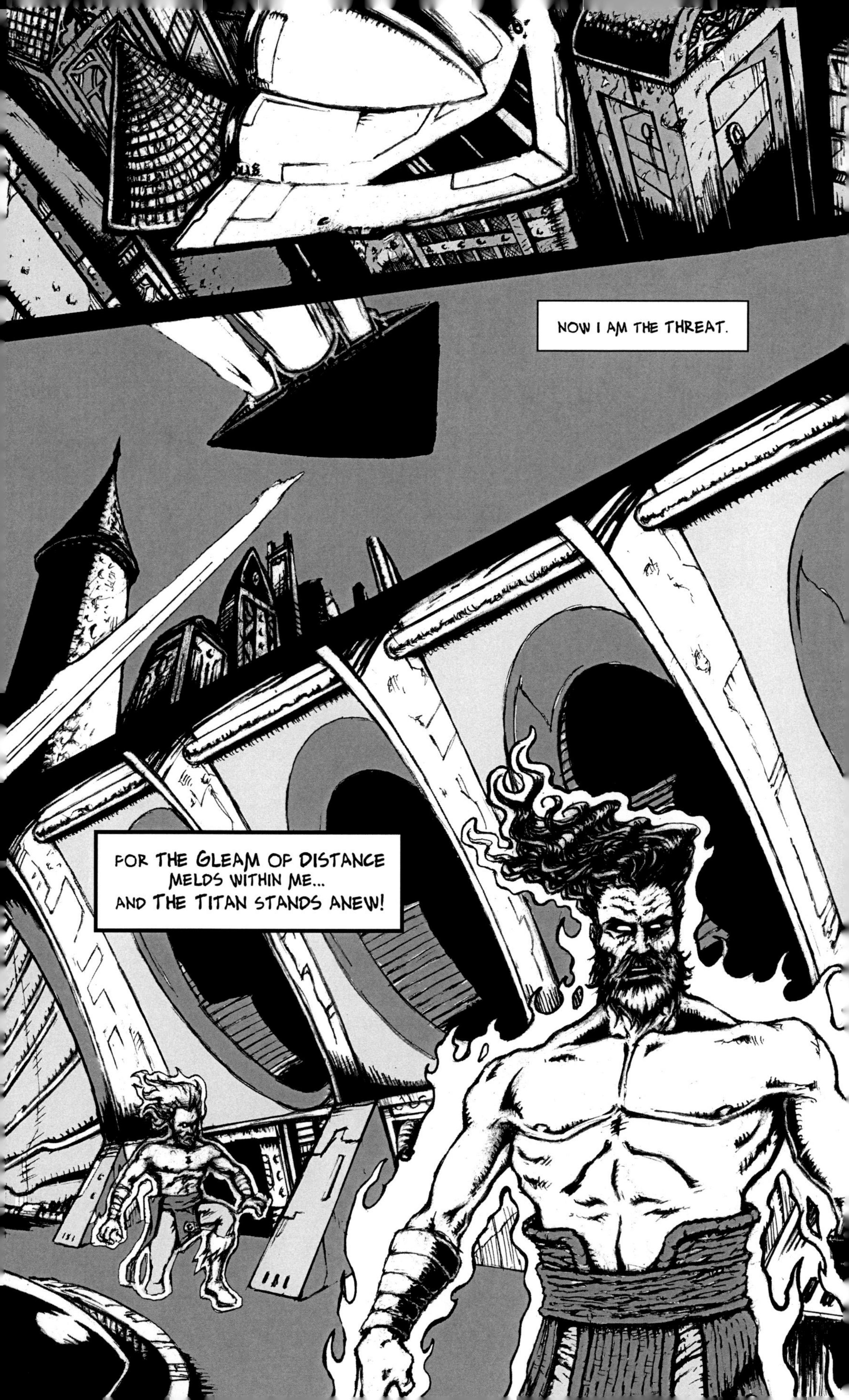
NOW I AM THE THREAT.
FOR THE GLEAM OF DISTANCE MELDS WITHIN ME... AND THE TITAN STANDS ANEW!

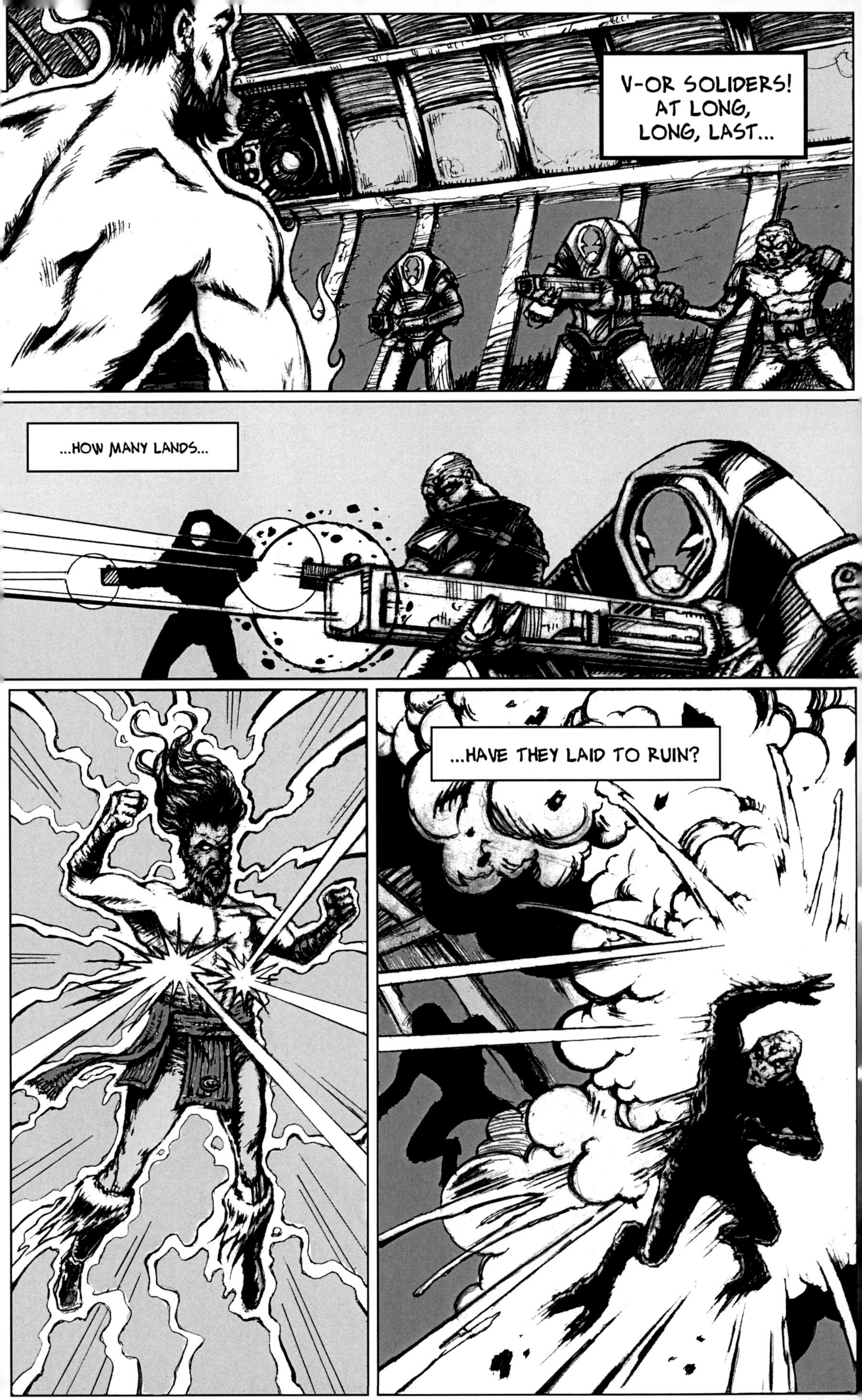
V-OR SOLIDERS! AT LONG, LONG, LAST...
...HOW MANY LANDS...
...HAVE THEY LAID TO RUIN?

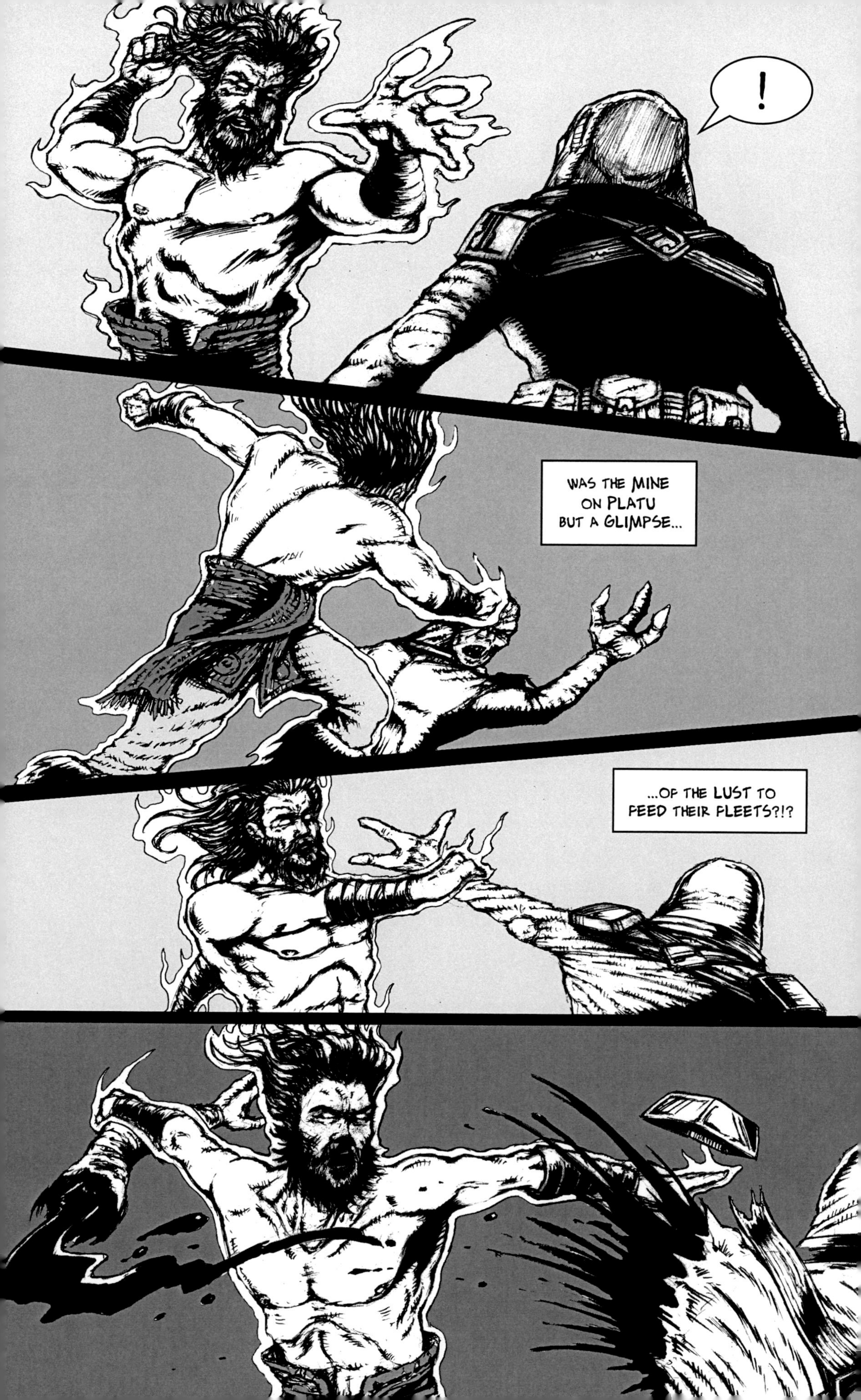
!
WAS THE MINE ON PLATU BUT A GLIMPSE...
...OF THE LUST TO FEED THEIR FLEETS?!?

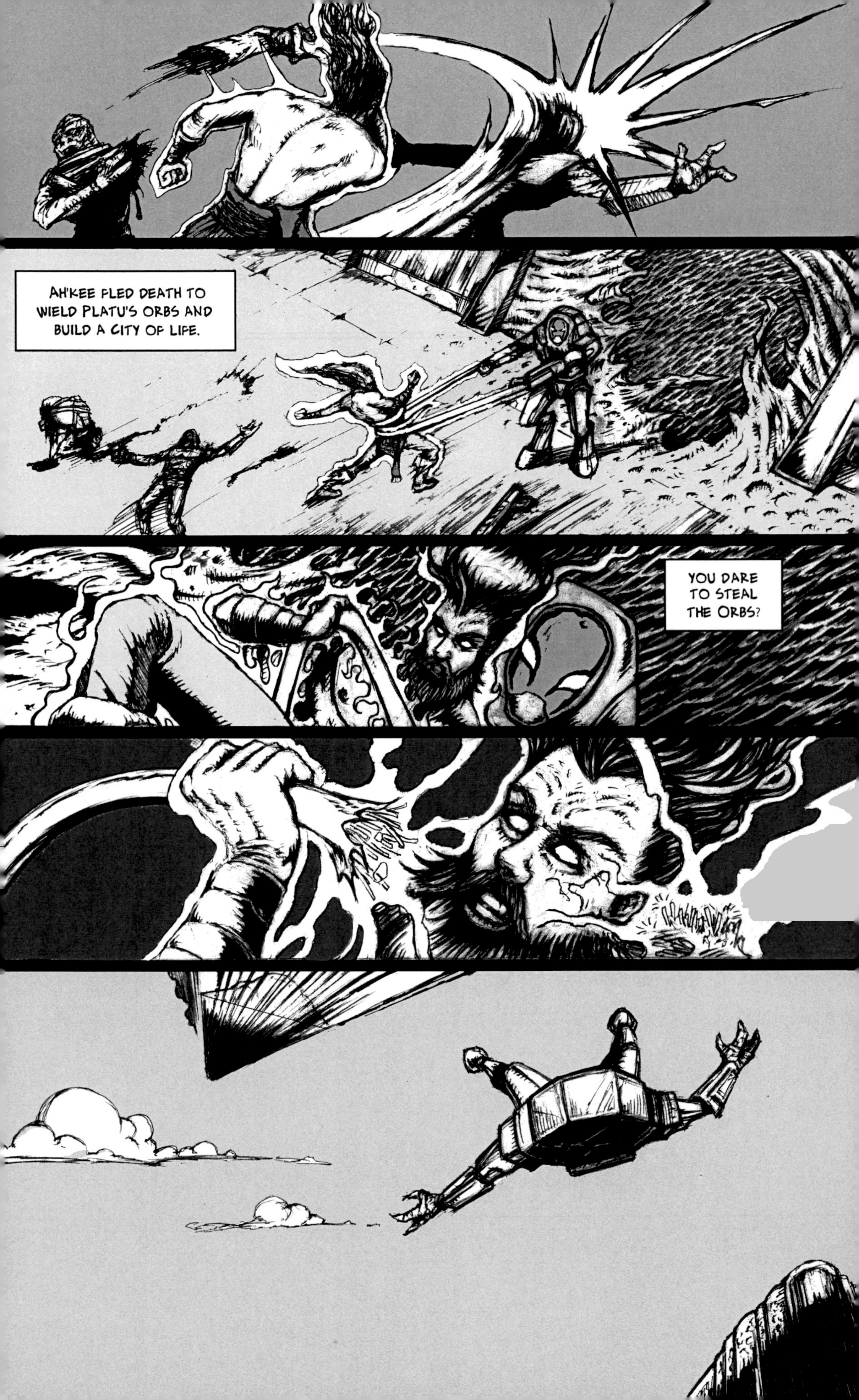
AH'KEE FLED DEATH TO WIELD PLATU'S ORBS AND BUILD A CITY OF LIFE.
YOU DARE TO STEAL THE ORBS?

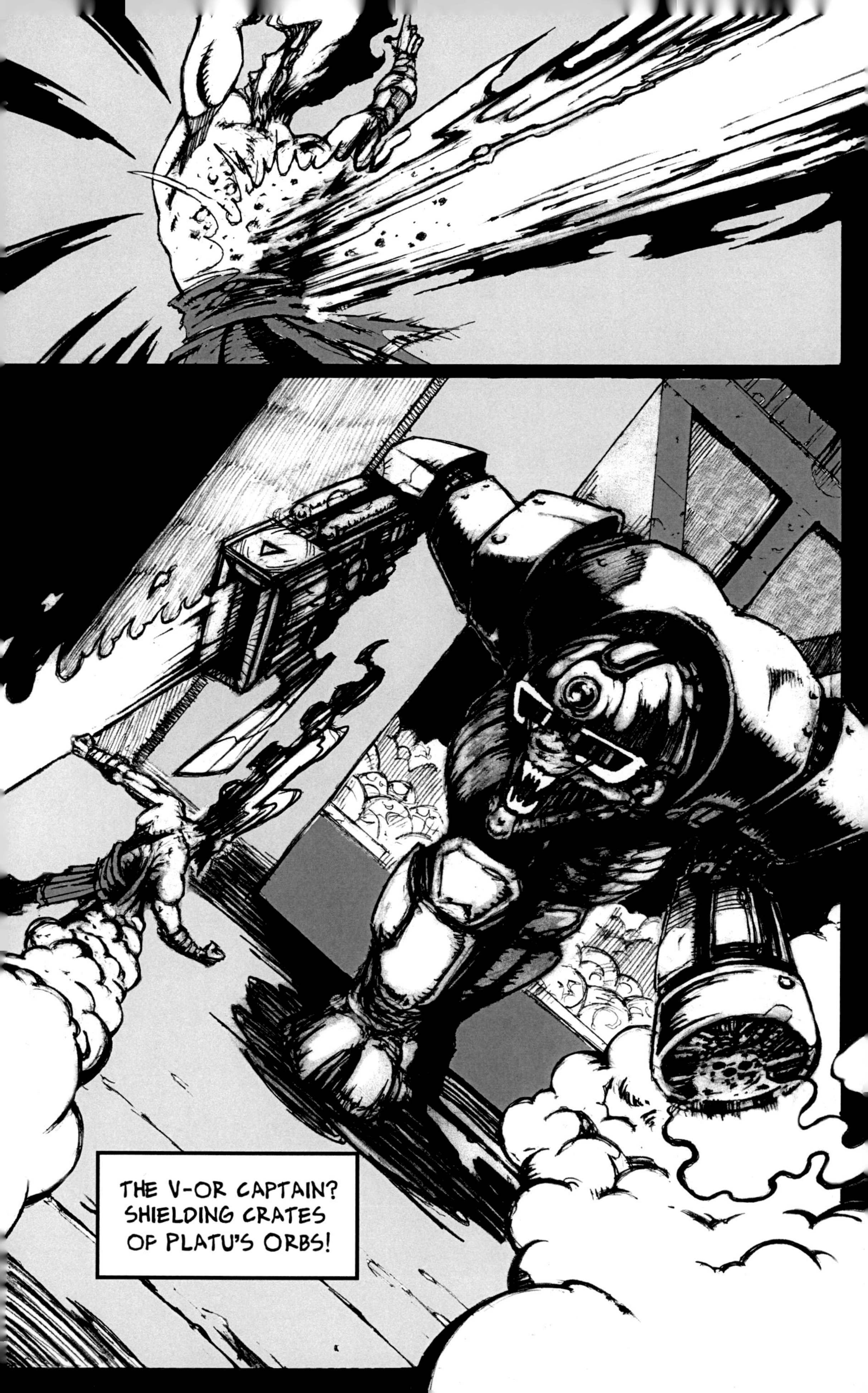
THE V-OR CAPTAIN? SHIELDING CRATES OF PLATU'S ORBS!

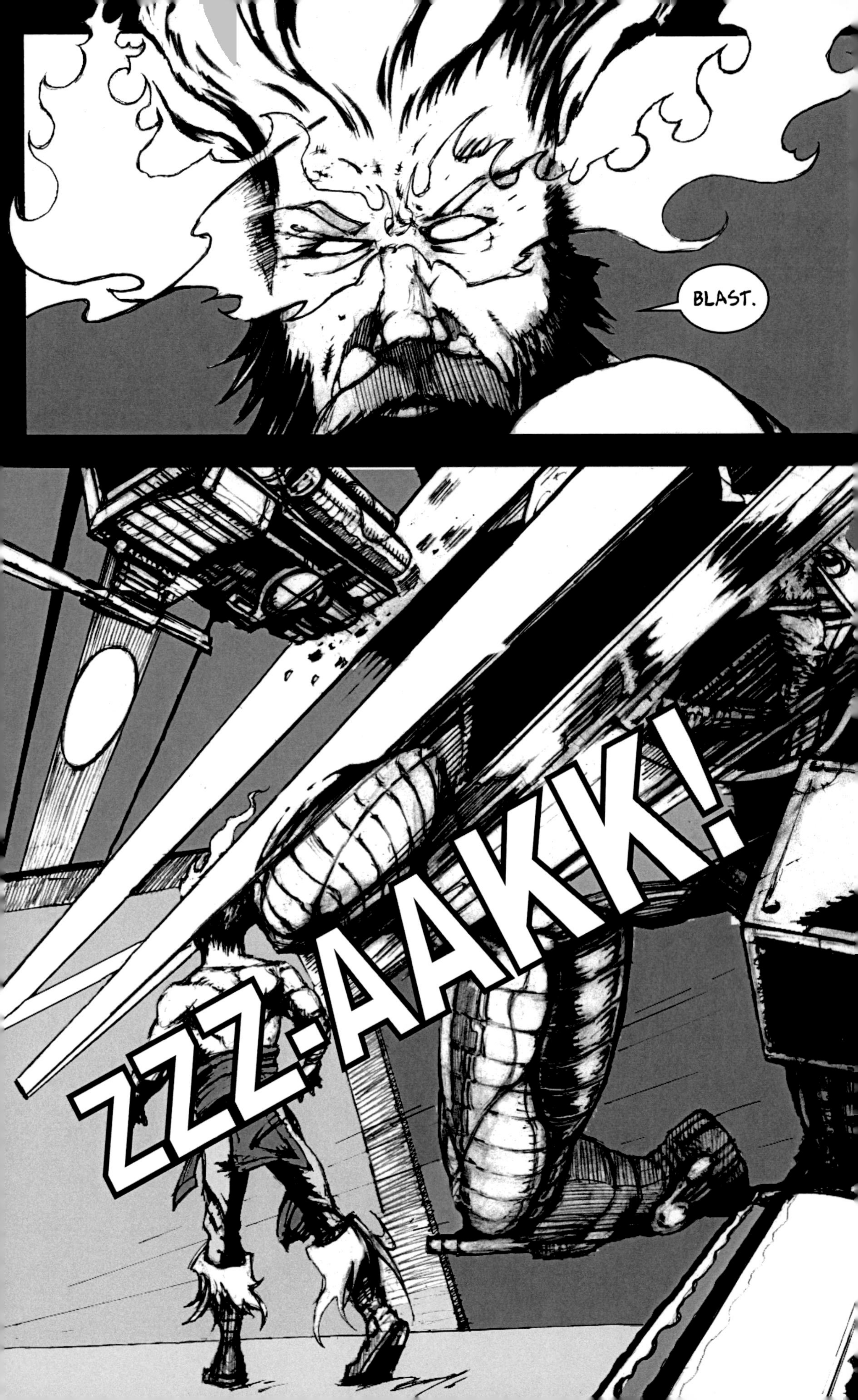
BLAST.
ZZZ-AAKK!

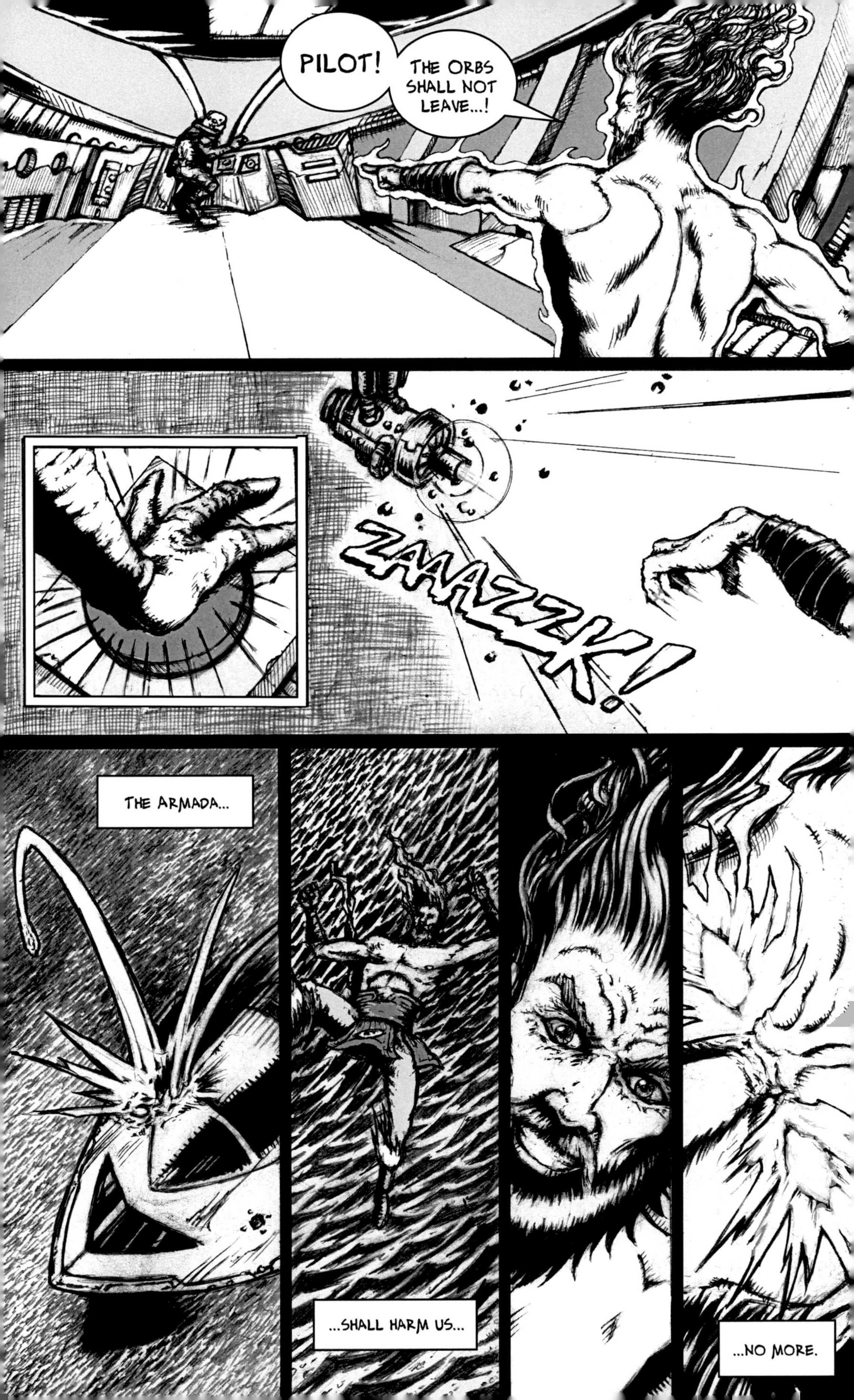
PILOT!
THE ORBS SHALL NOT LEAVE...!
ZAAAZZK!
THE ARMADA...
...SHALL HARM US...
...NO MORE.

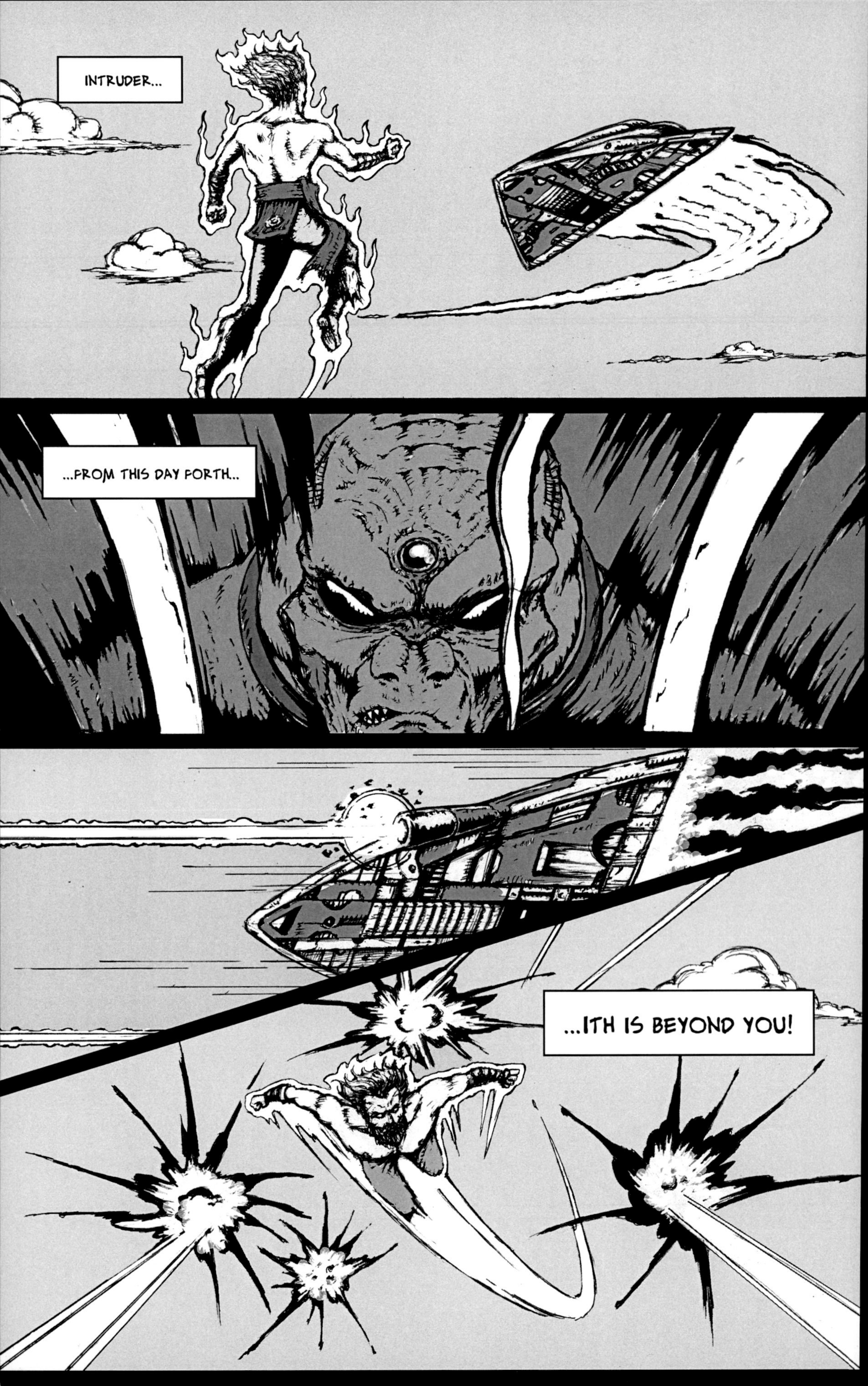
INTRUDER...
...FROM THIS DAY FORTH...
...ITH IS BEYOND YOU!

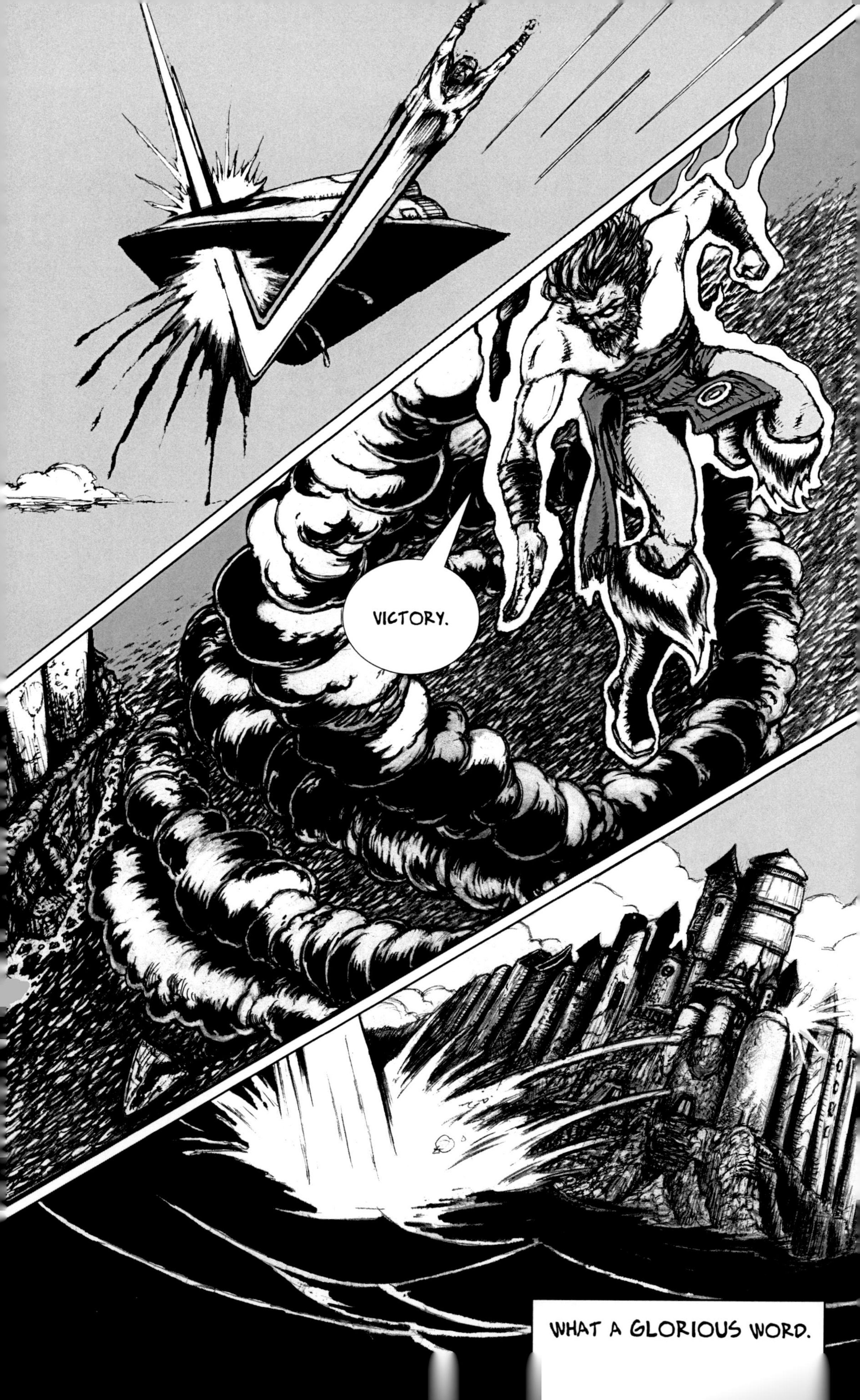
VICTORY.
WHAT A GLORIOUS WORD.

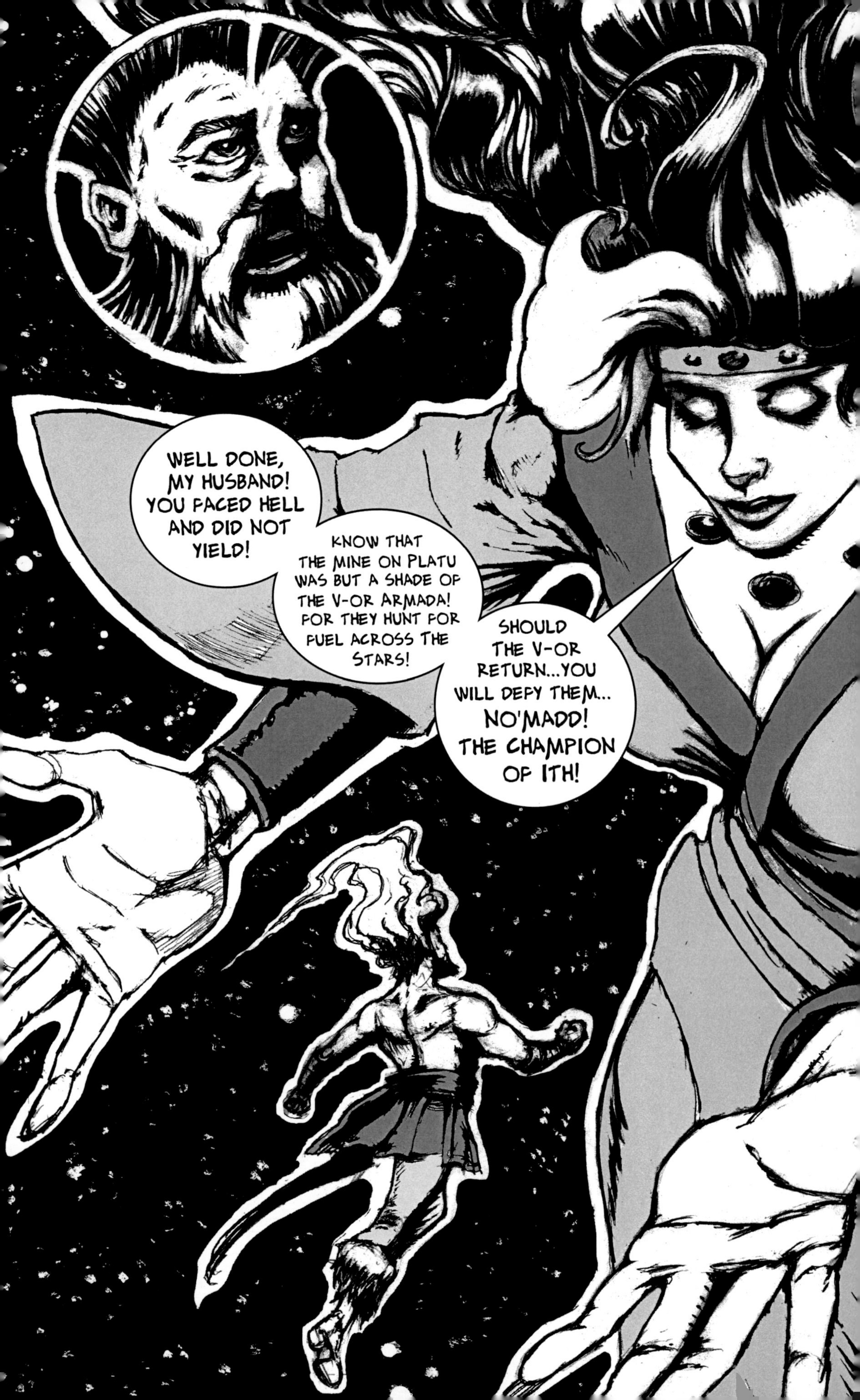
WELL DONE, MY HUSBAND! YOU FACED HELL AND DID NOT YIELD!
KNOW THAT THE MINE ON PLATU WAS BUT A SHADE OF THE V-OR ARMADA! FOR THEY HUNT FOR FUEL ACROSS THE STARS!
SHOULD THE V-OR RETURN...YOU WILL DEFY THEM... NO'MADD! THE CHAMPION OF ITH!

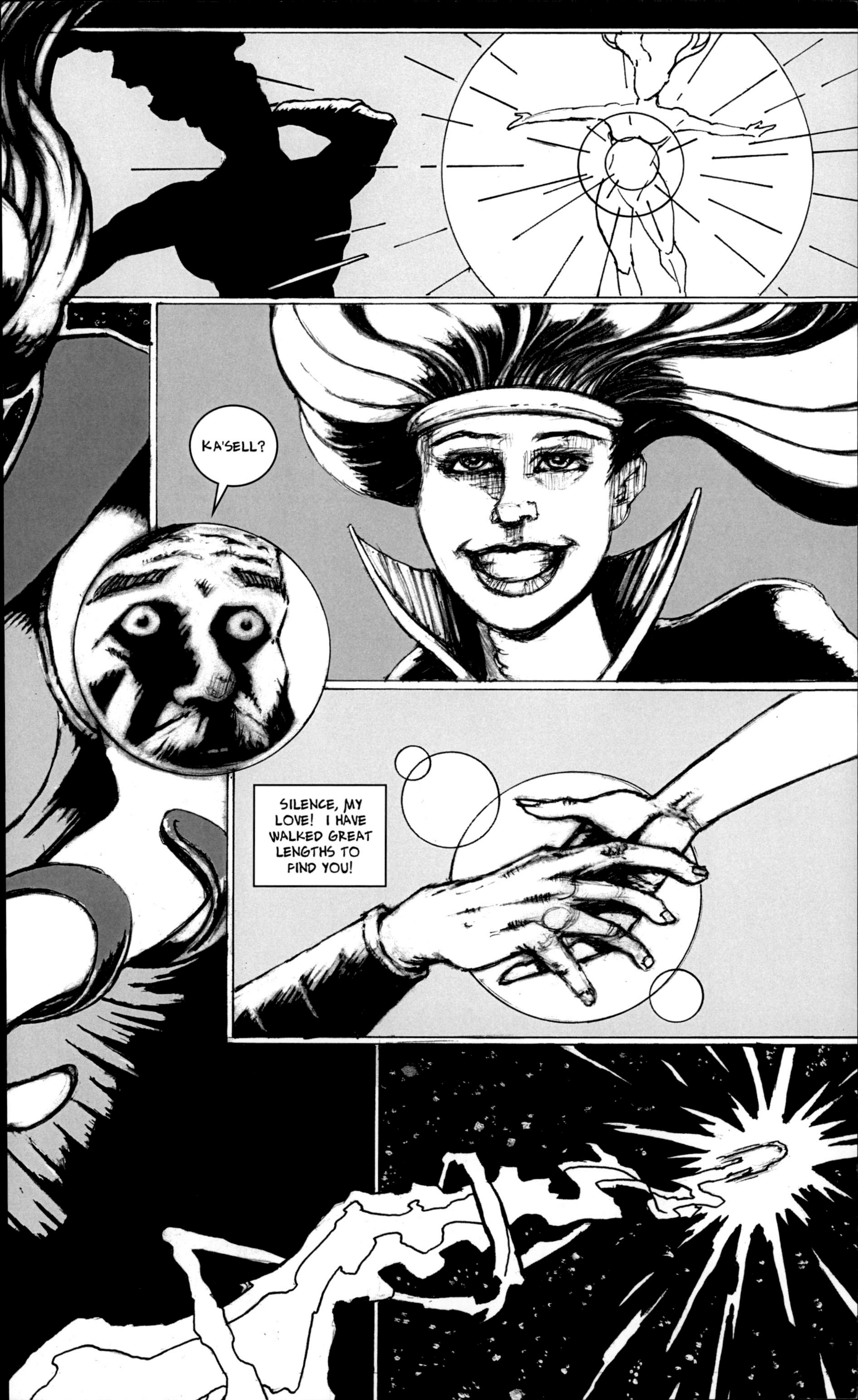
KA'SELL?
SILENCE, MY LOVE! I HAVE WALKED GREAT LENGTHS TO FIND YOU!

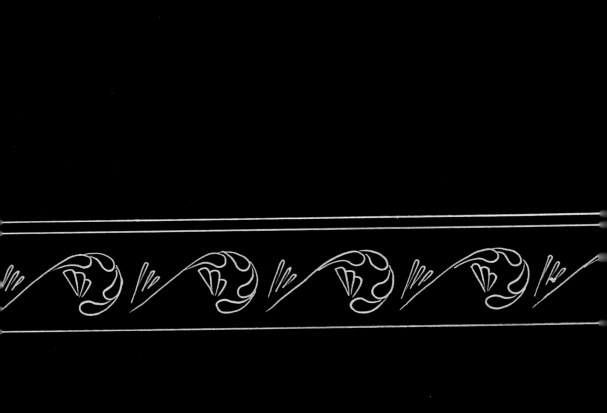

EPILOGUE

TION

"HUSBAND...

...WOULD YOU
KNOW MY SECRETS?"

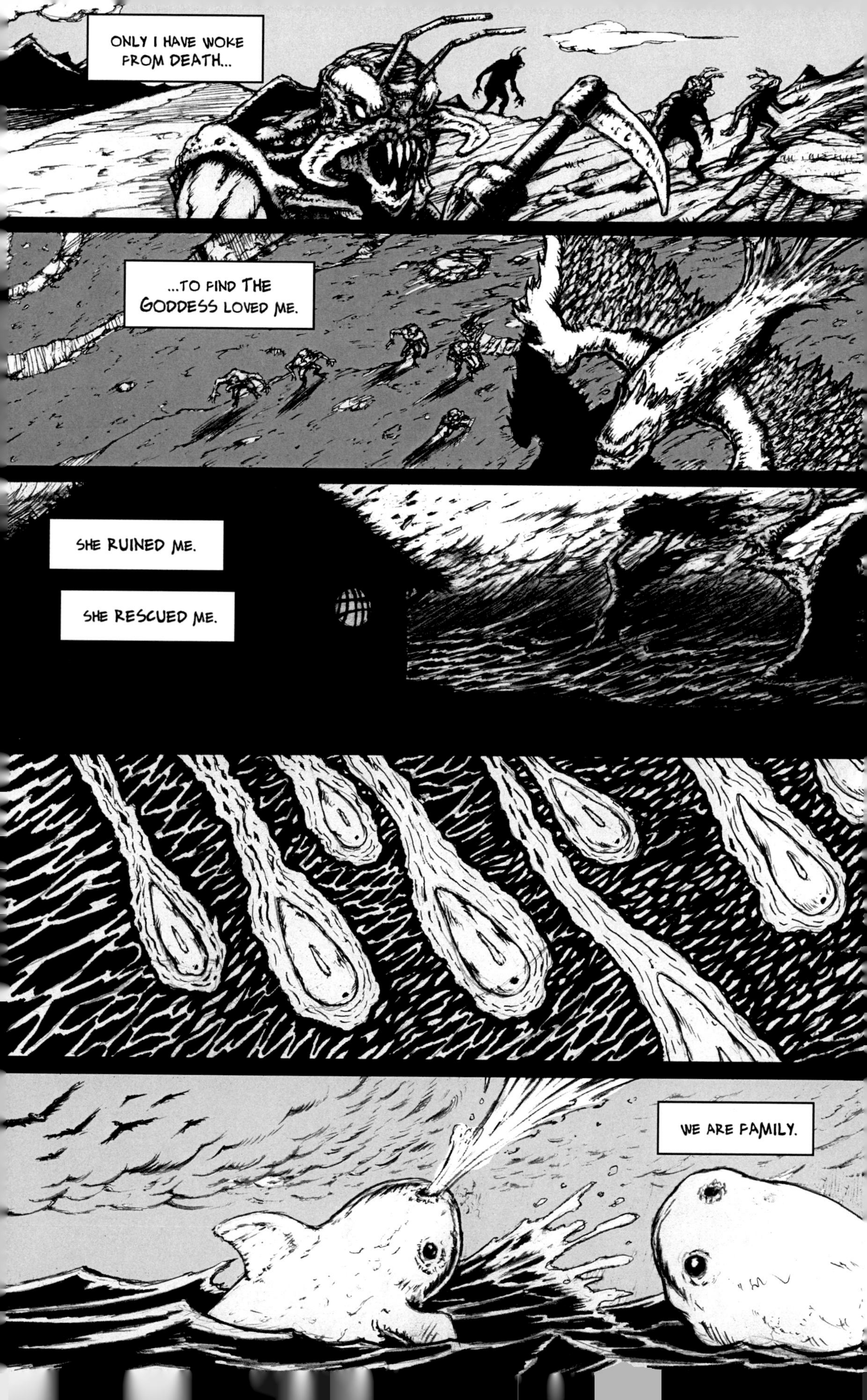
ONLY I HAVE WOKE FROM DEATH...
...TO FIND THE GODDESS LOVED ME.
SHE RUINED ME.
SHE RESCUED ME.
WE ARE FAMILY.

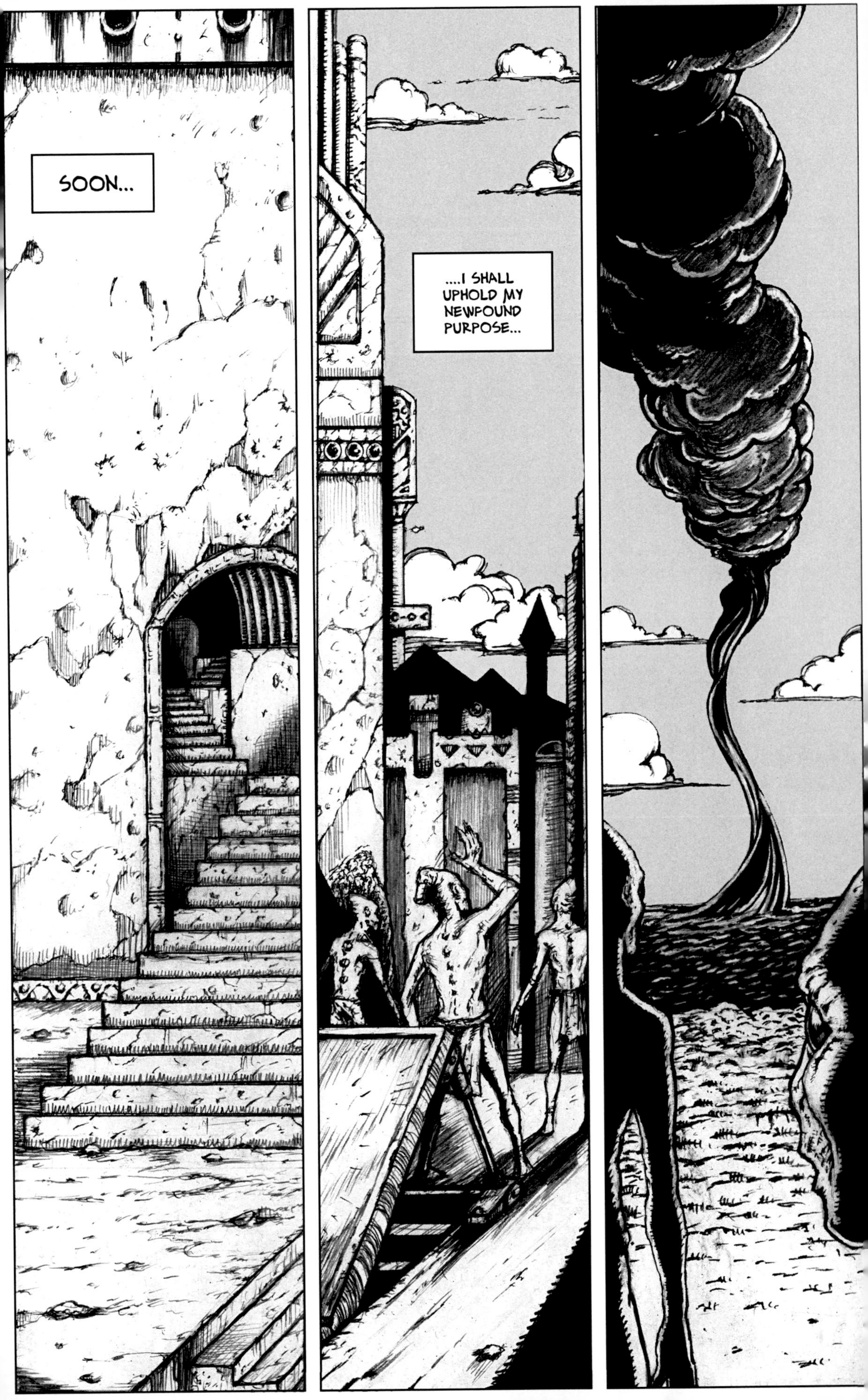
SOON...
....I SHALL UPHOLD MY NEWFOUND PURPOSE...

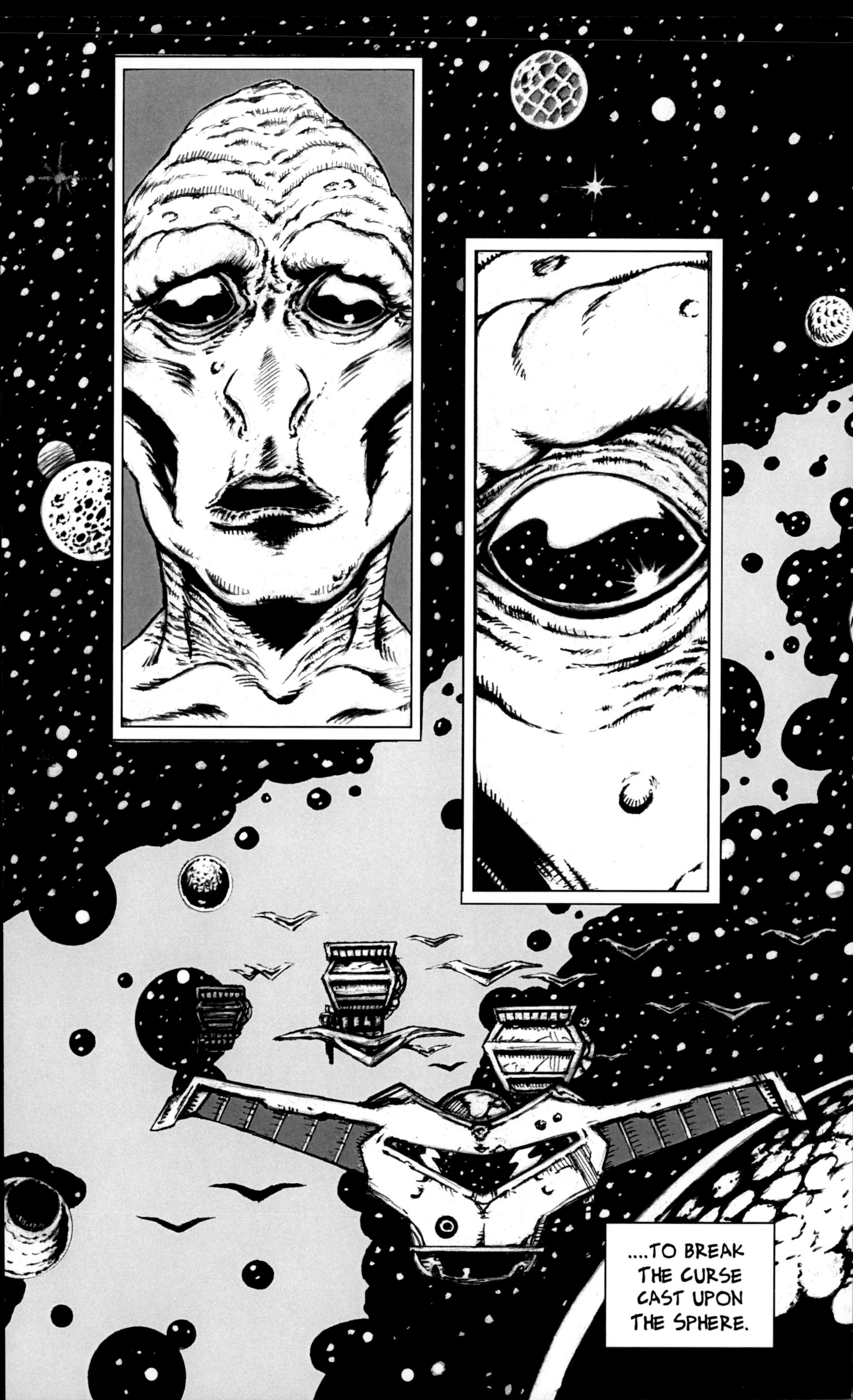
....TO BREAK THE CURSE CAST UPON THE SPHERE.

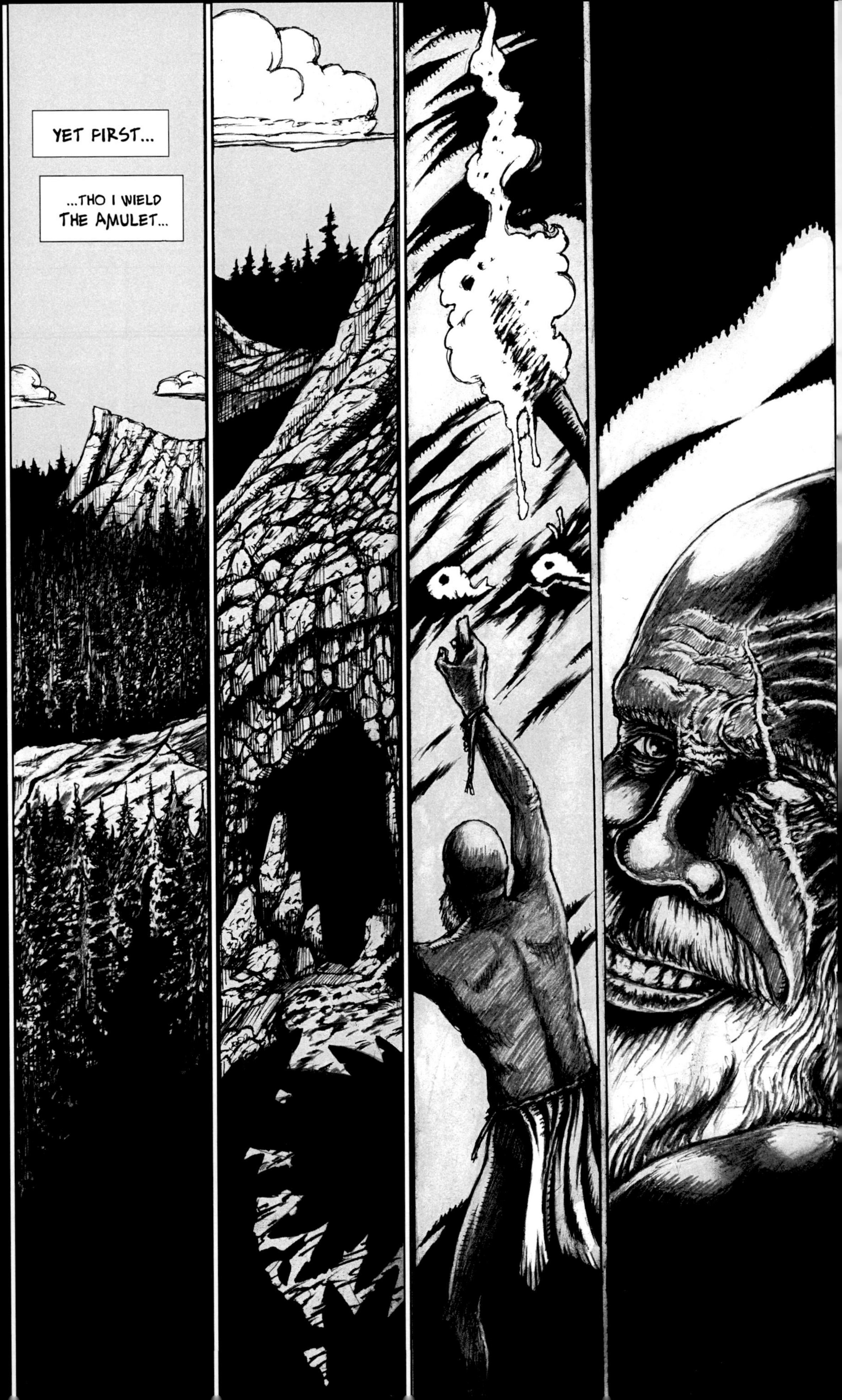
YET FIRST...
...THO I WIELD THE AMULET...

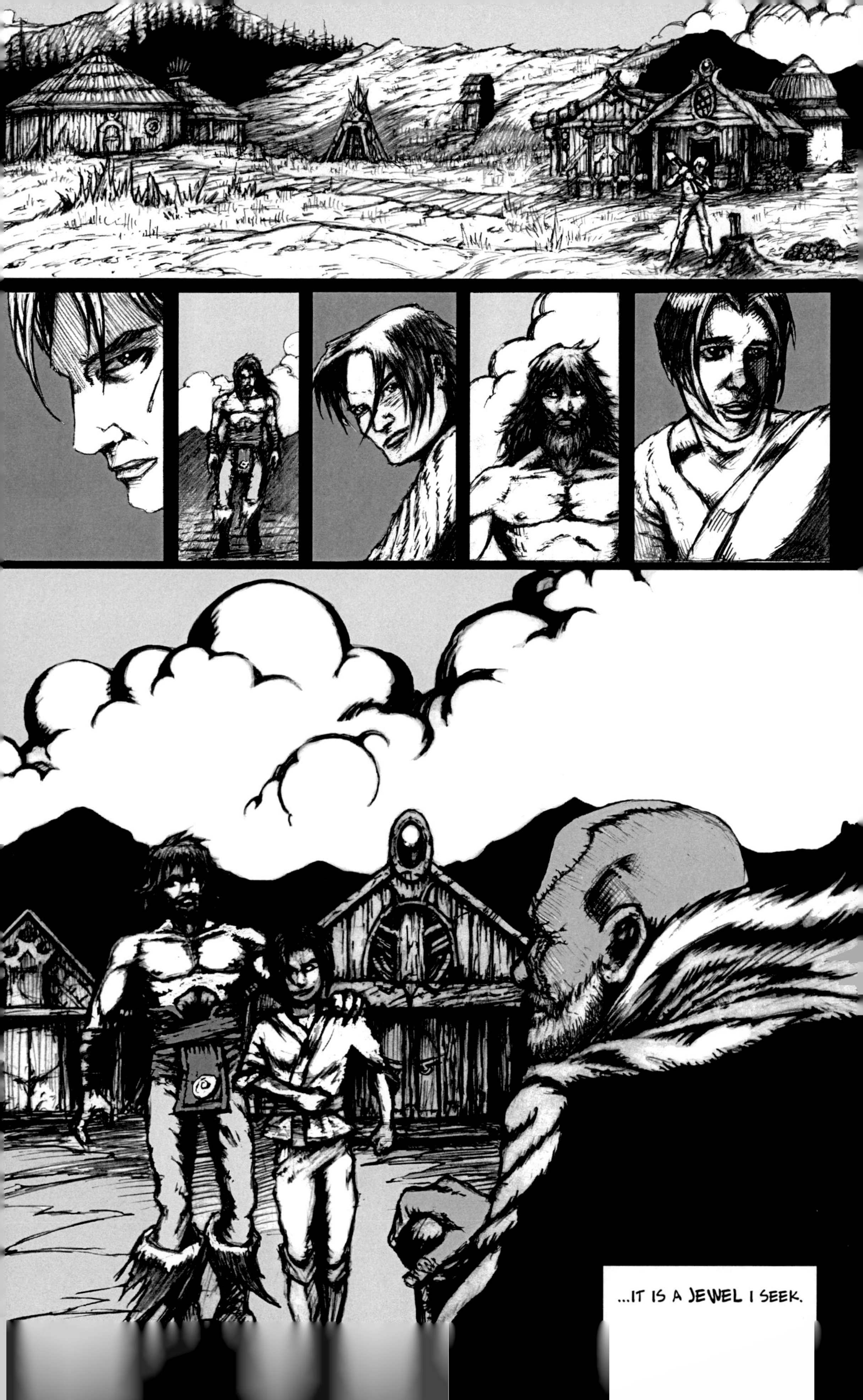
...IT IS A JEWEL I SEEK.

NOTE FROM THE AUTHOR

THANK YOU FOR READING THIS FAR!

I HOPE YOU WANT TO KNOW MORE ABOUT NO'MADD.

I AM WORKING ON HIS SECOND JOURNEY.

PLEASE FOLLOW MY PROGRESS AT:

NOMADD.NET

OR FIND ANY OF THE CREATIVE
MEMBERS ON FACEBOOK OR TWITTER, TO HELP
EXPAND UPON A NEW UNIVERSE.

FOR NOW, I AM JUST GLAD WE GOT NO'MADD HOME.

DREW

CREATOR BIOS

ANDREW KAFOURY

ANDREW IS FROM PORTLAND, OR.
HE GREW UP READING BATMAN, X-MEN, AND
TMNT. NO'MADD IS HIS FIRST
GRAPHIC NOVEL.

AKAFOURY@HOTMAIL.COM

TODD HERMAN

TODD HAS DRAWN FOR DARK HORSE,
TOP SHELF, DYNAMITE, AND NUMEROUS
OTHER PUBLISHERS. THIS IS
HIS FIRST FULL BOOK DESIGN.

JEFFERSONHOUSE@YAHOO.COM

SCOTT ROLLER

SCOTT LIVES IN PORTLAND, OR. HIS
PAST CREDITS INCLUDE RAPT IN FEAR
AND THE INDIE ANTHOLOGY INSECT BATH.

SCOTTY.ROLLER@GMAIL.COM

CHRIS FACCONE

CHRIS IS A PROFESSIONAL ILLUSTRATOR
WHO LIVES IN NEW JERSEY. HE IS
THE CREATOR OF SAVAGE CONQUEST.

CHRISFACCONEART.COM

No'Madd

THE CHAMPION OF ITH

KA'SELL
THE WALKING MOON

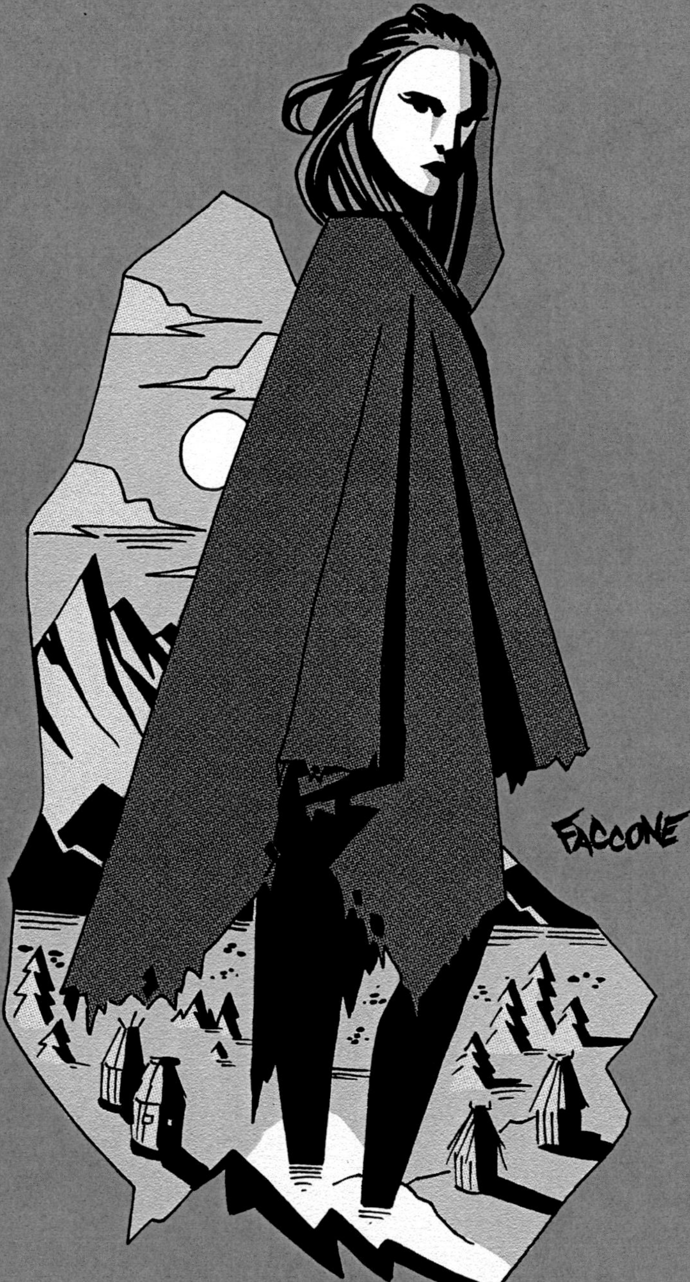
FACCONE

NOMADD.NET

TARON
THE HEIR OF DISTANCE

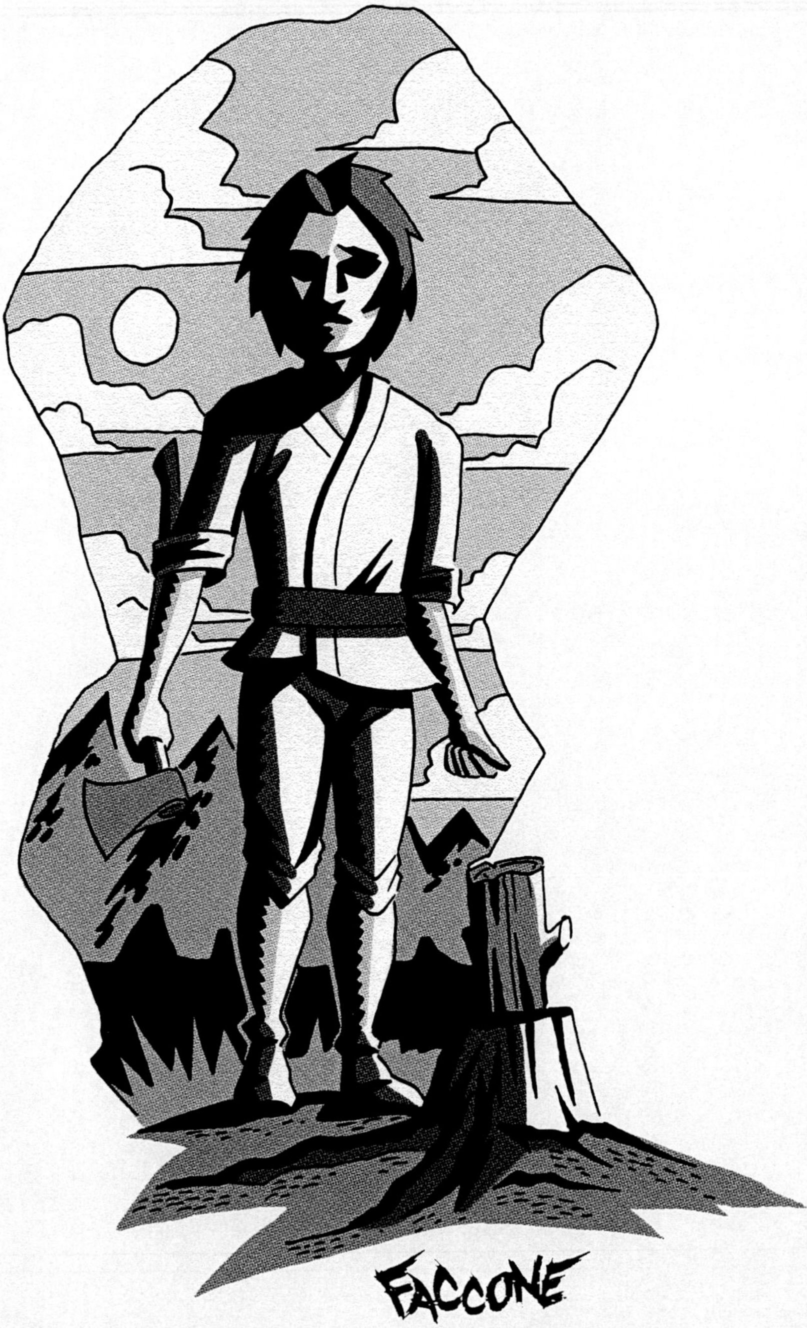
FACCONE

NOMADD.NET

WHISPERS
HERMIT OF THE STONES

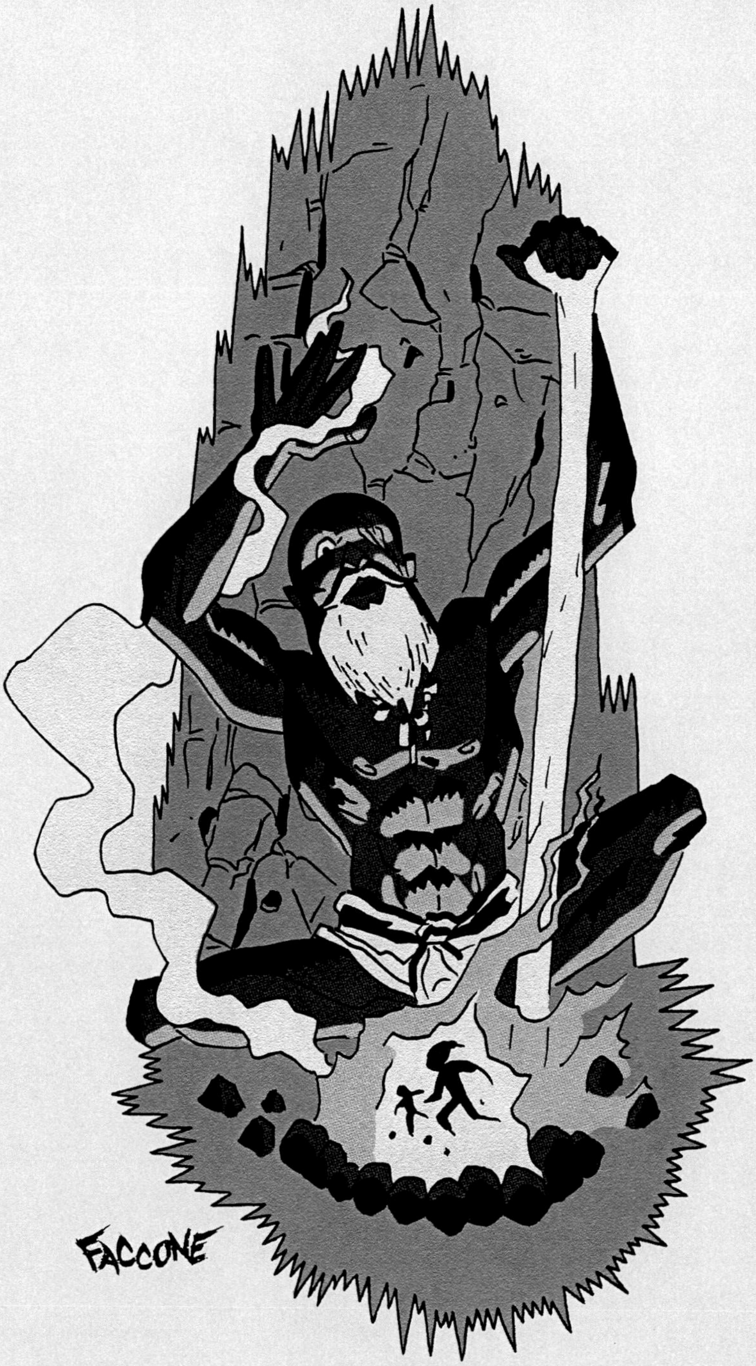
FACCONE

NOMADD.NET

SKREE
THE COLOSSAL

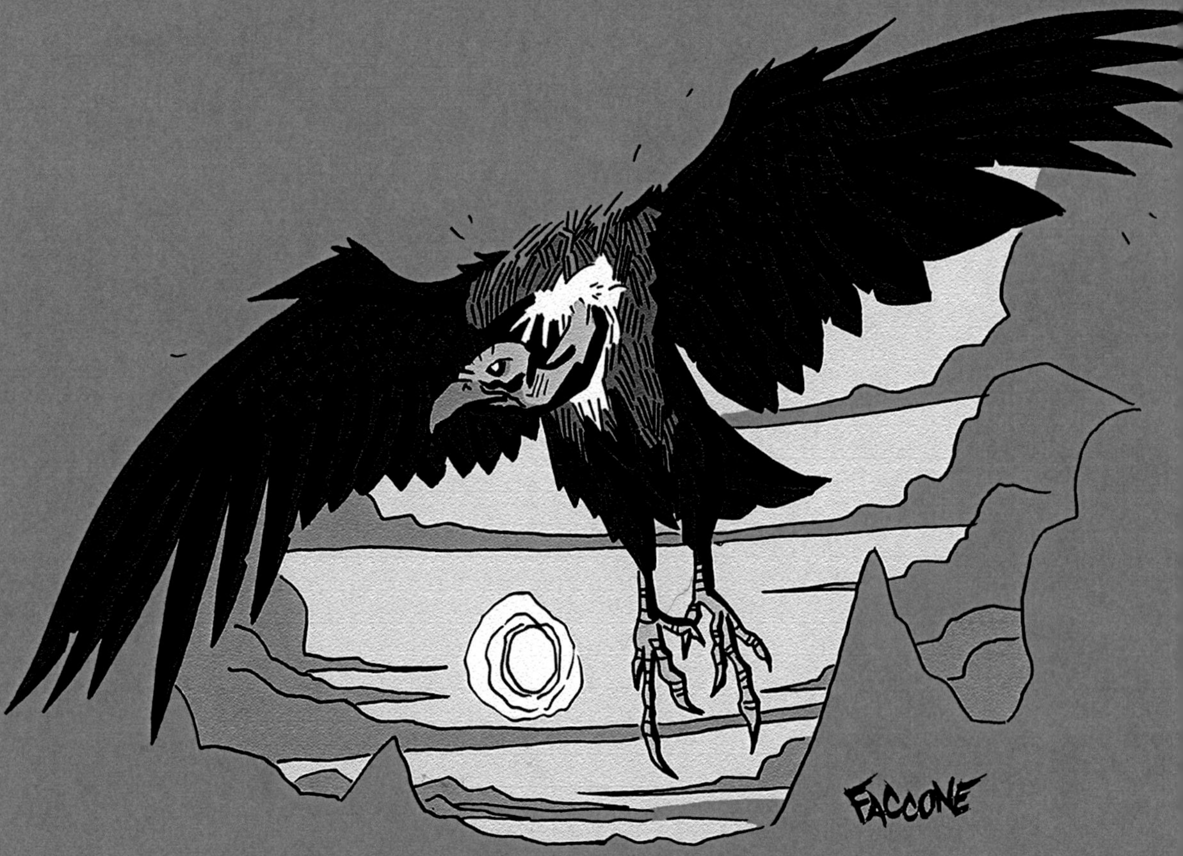
FACCONE

NOMADD.NET

GNATZ
SWARM OF THE PIT

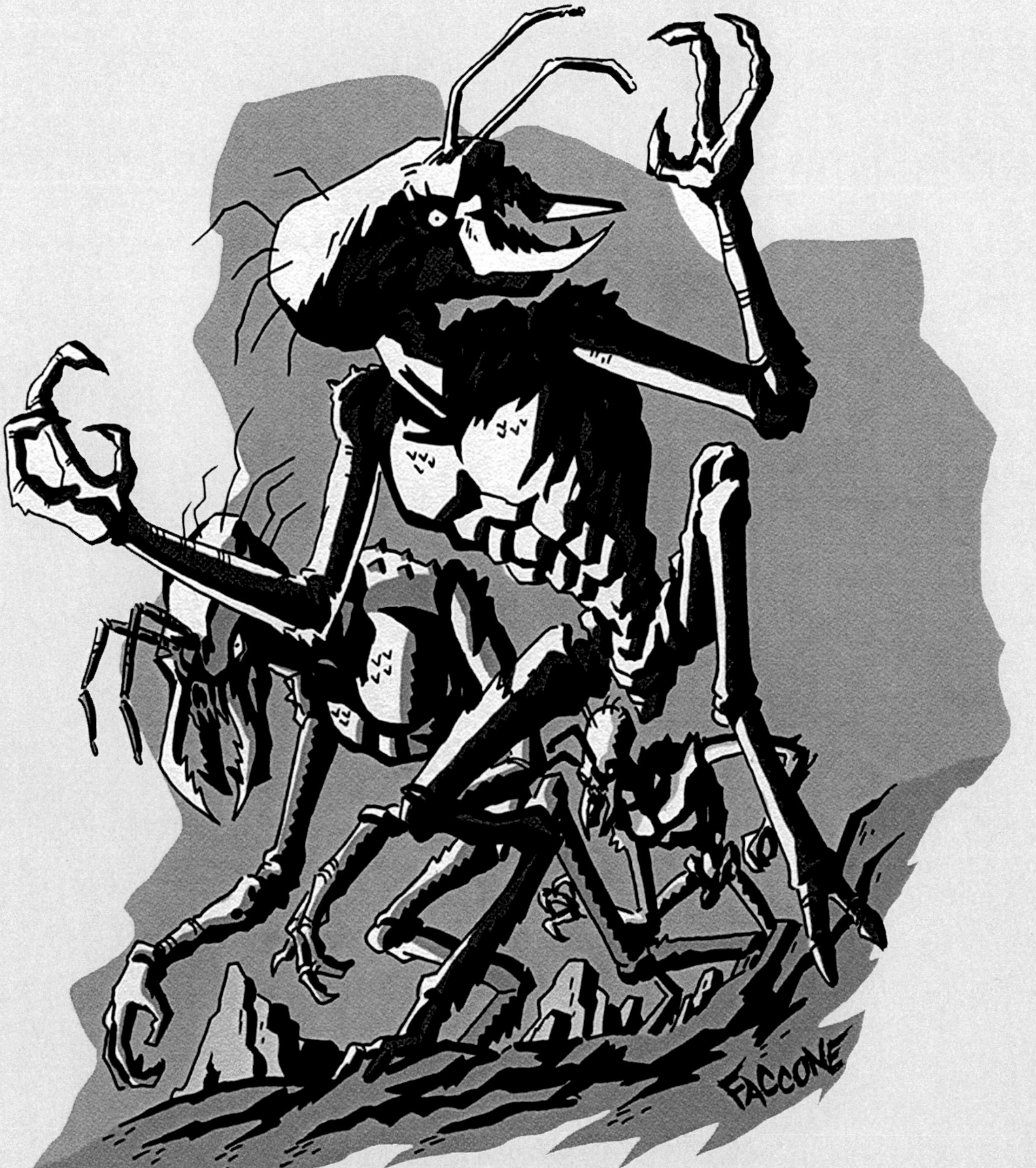
FACCONE

NOMADD.NET

WARLORD

GHOST OF THE STEEP

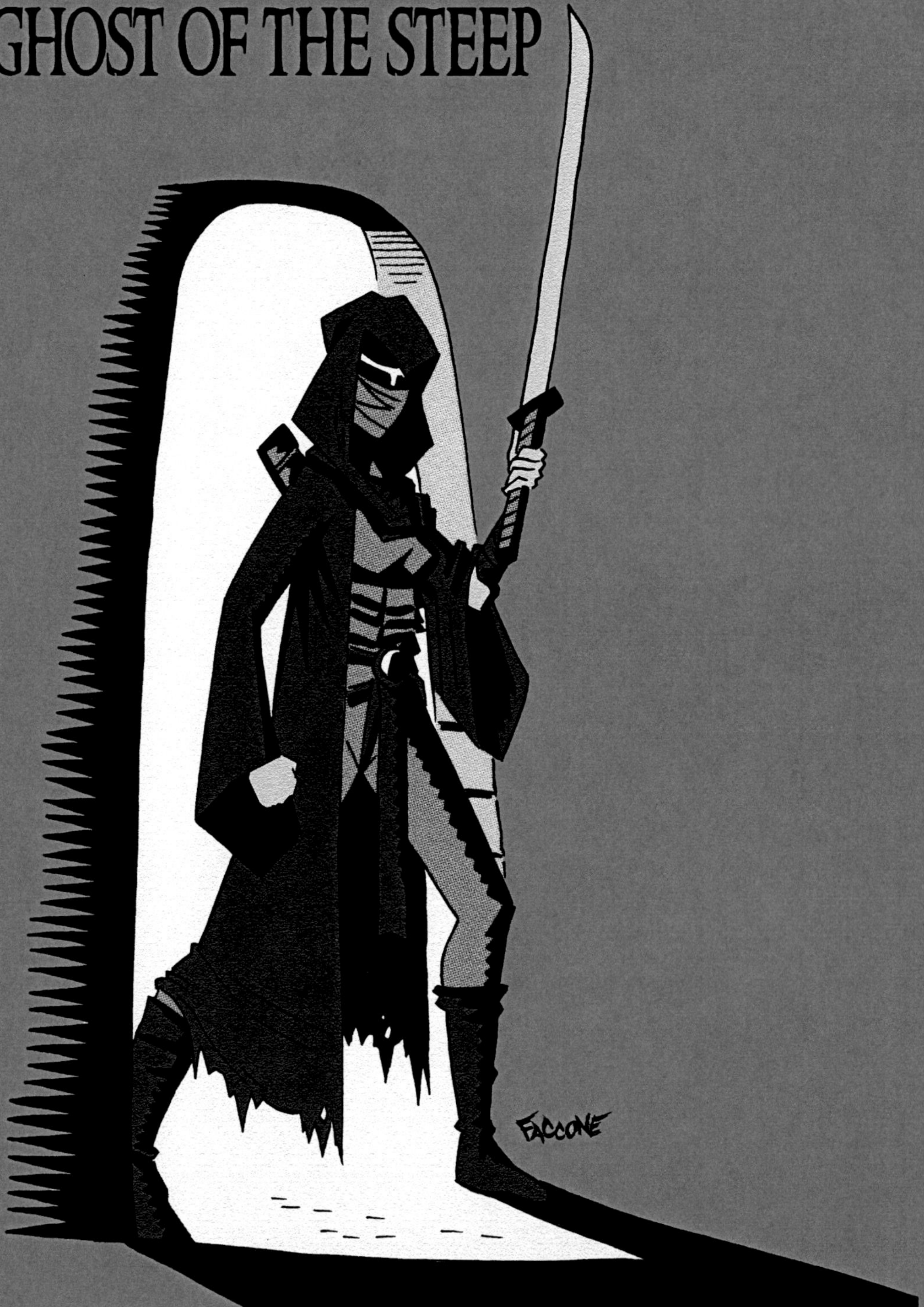

FACCONE

NOMADD.NET

BAKK'ROLL
THE SACRED FANG

VESP
BANE OF THE TIDES

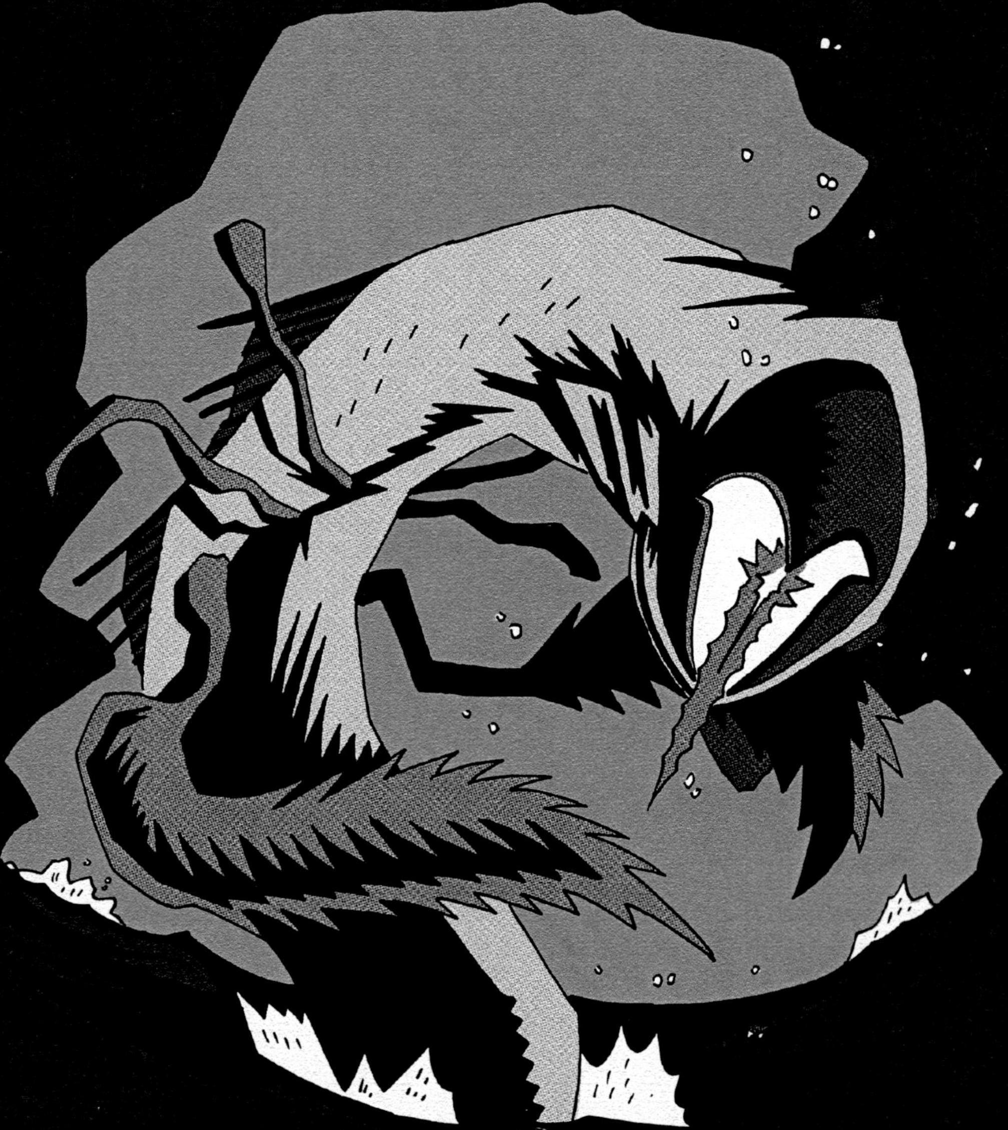

NOMADD.NET

BRUMM
THE HIDDEN SPIRIT

FACCONE

NOMADD.NET

SWOTH

THE GENTLE STEED

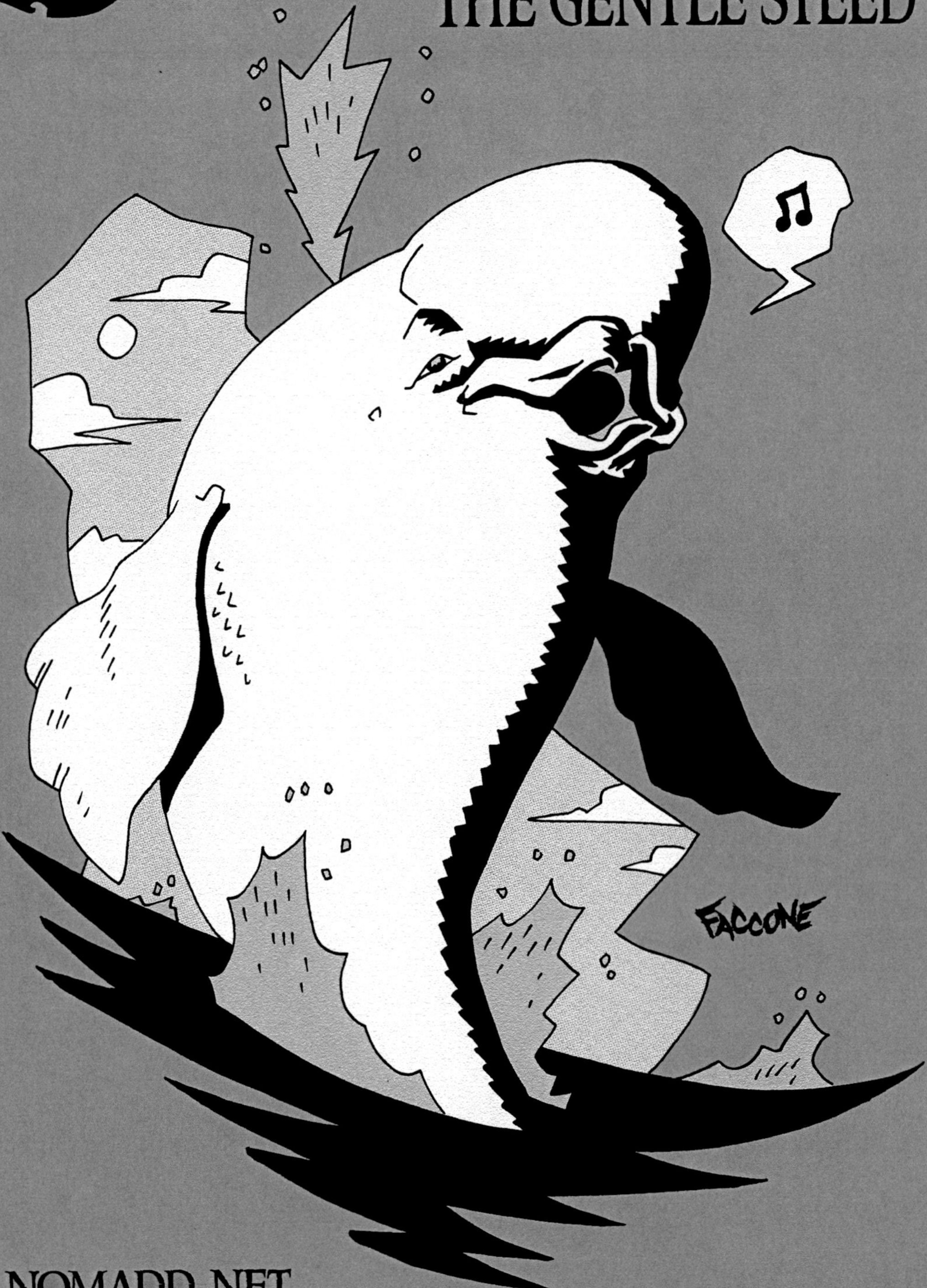
FACCONE

NOMADD.NET

AH'KEE
THE LOST RULERS

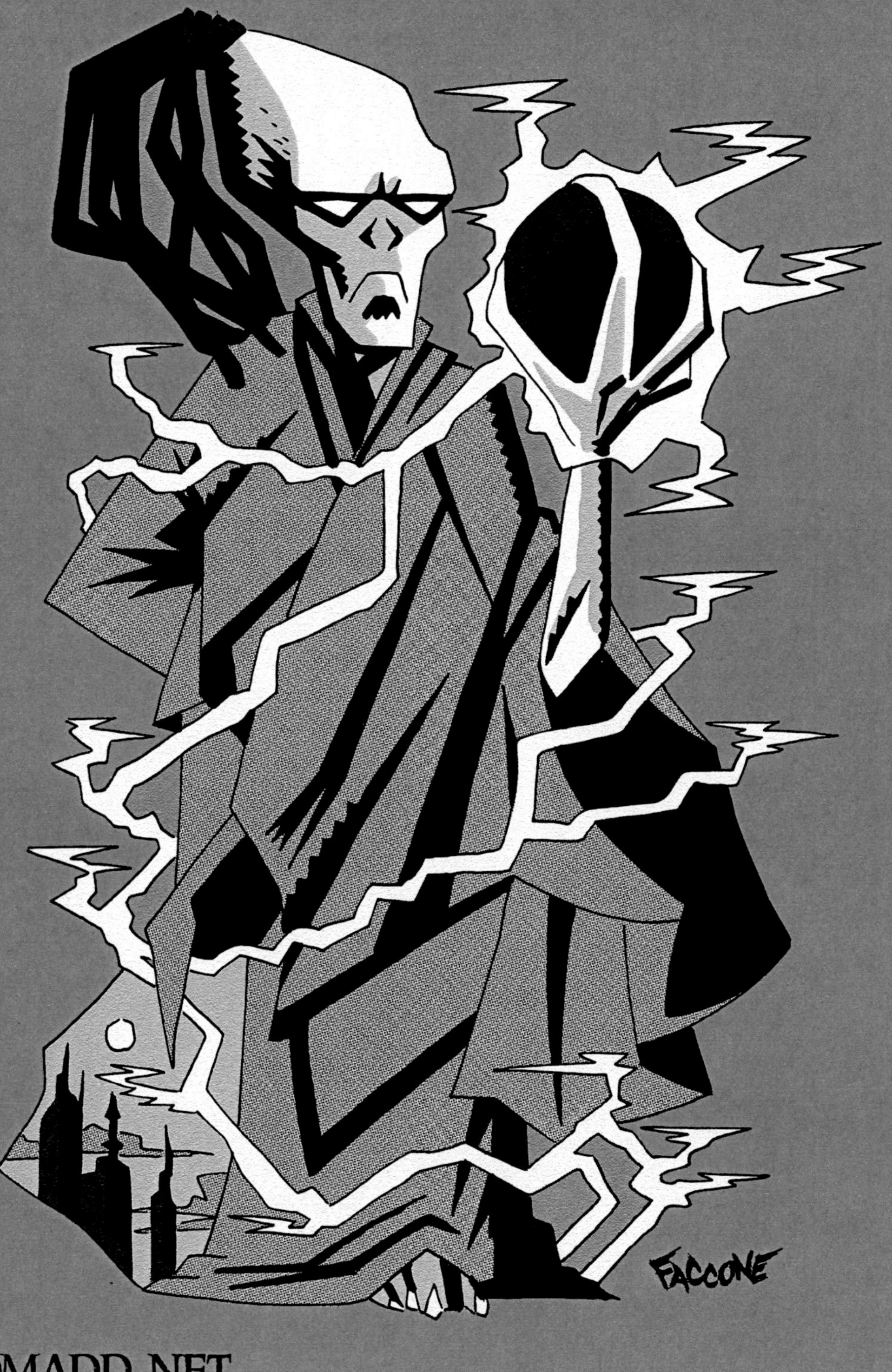
FACCONE

NOMADD.NET

OVERLORD

MASTER OF THE MINE

FACCONE

TION
THE DISTANT

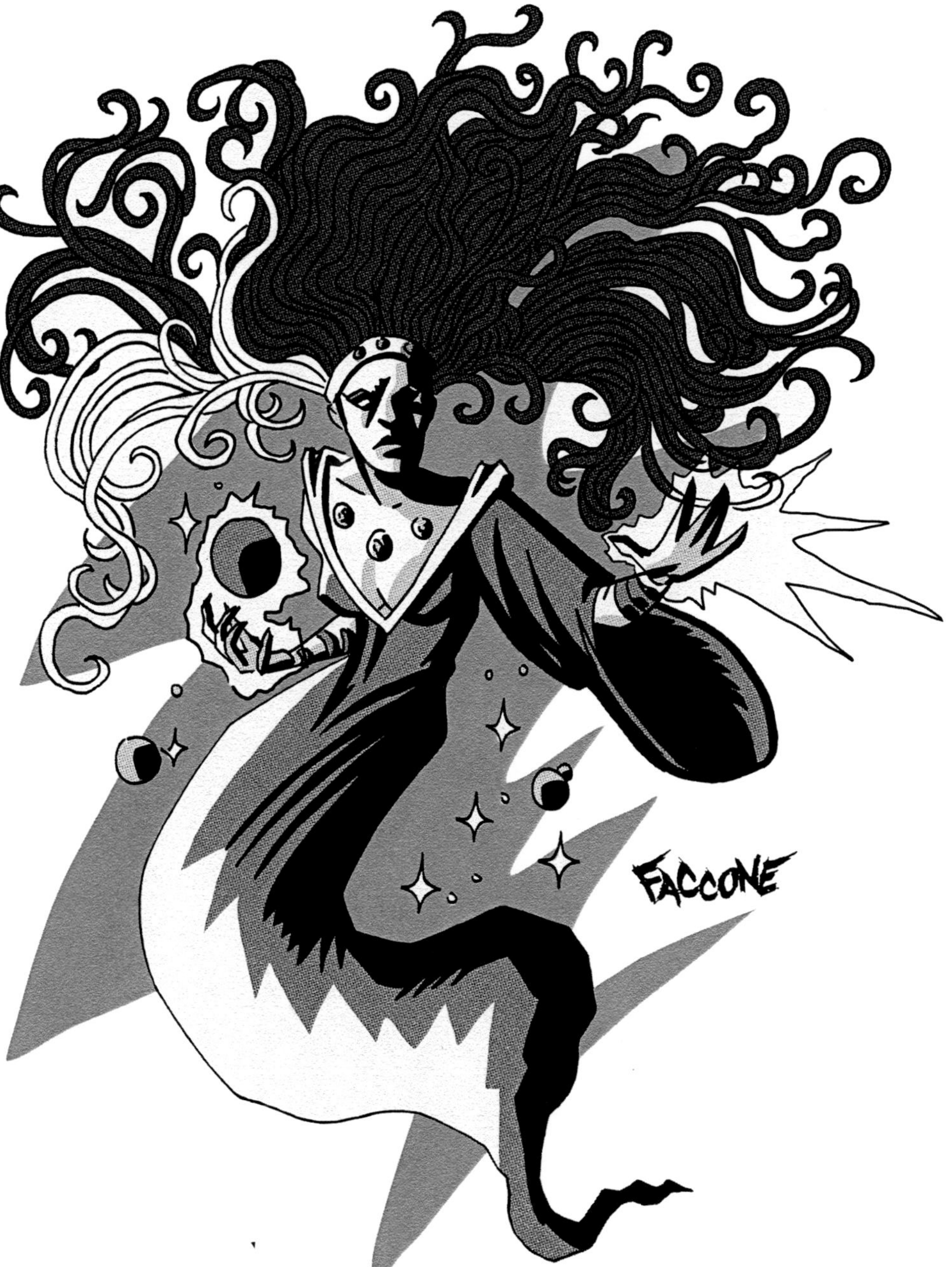
FACCONE

NOMADD.NET

V-OR
THE INTRUDERS

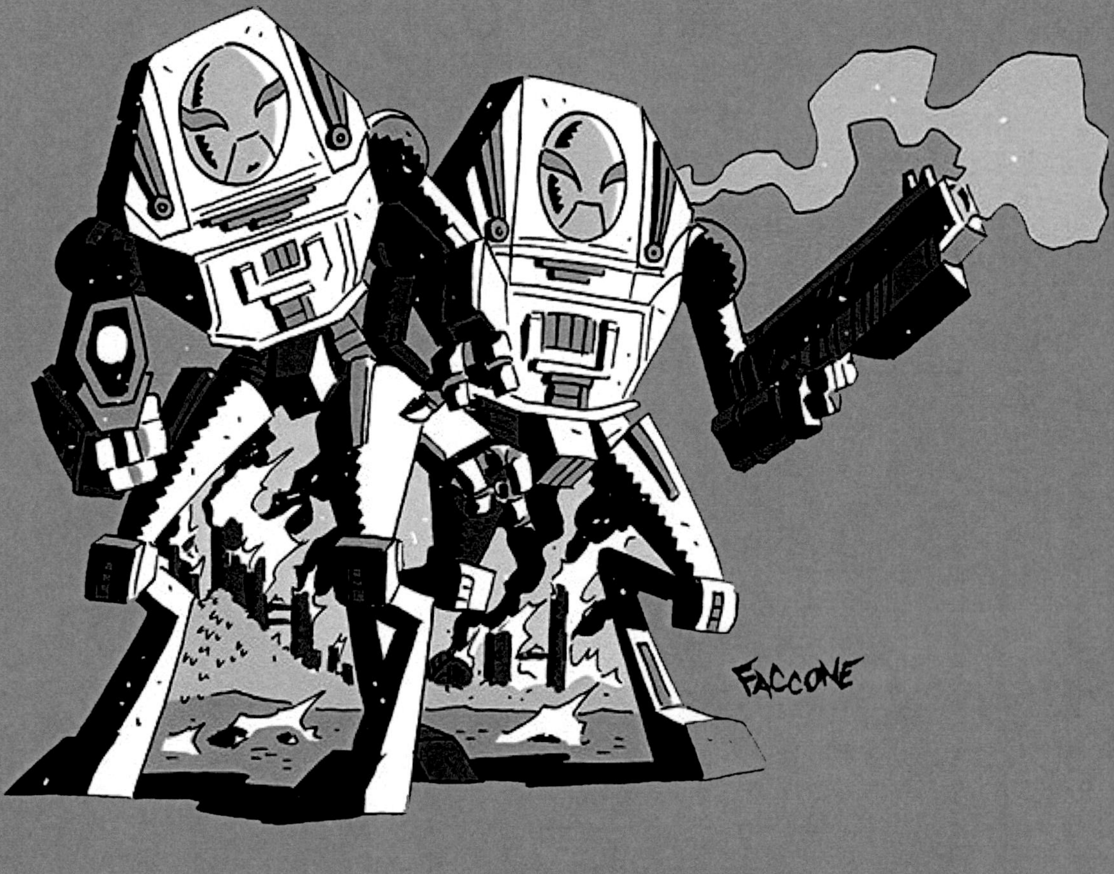
FACCONE

NOMADD.NET

CY-VOR
THE FORTRESS SHIELD

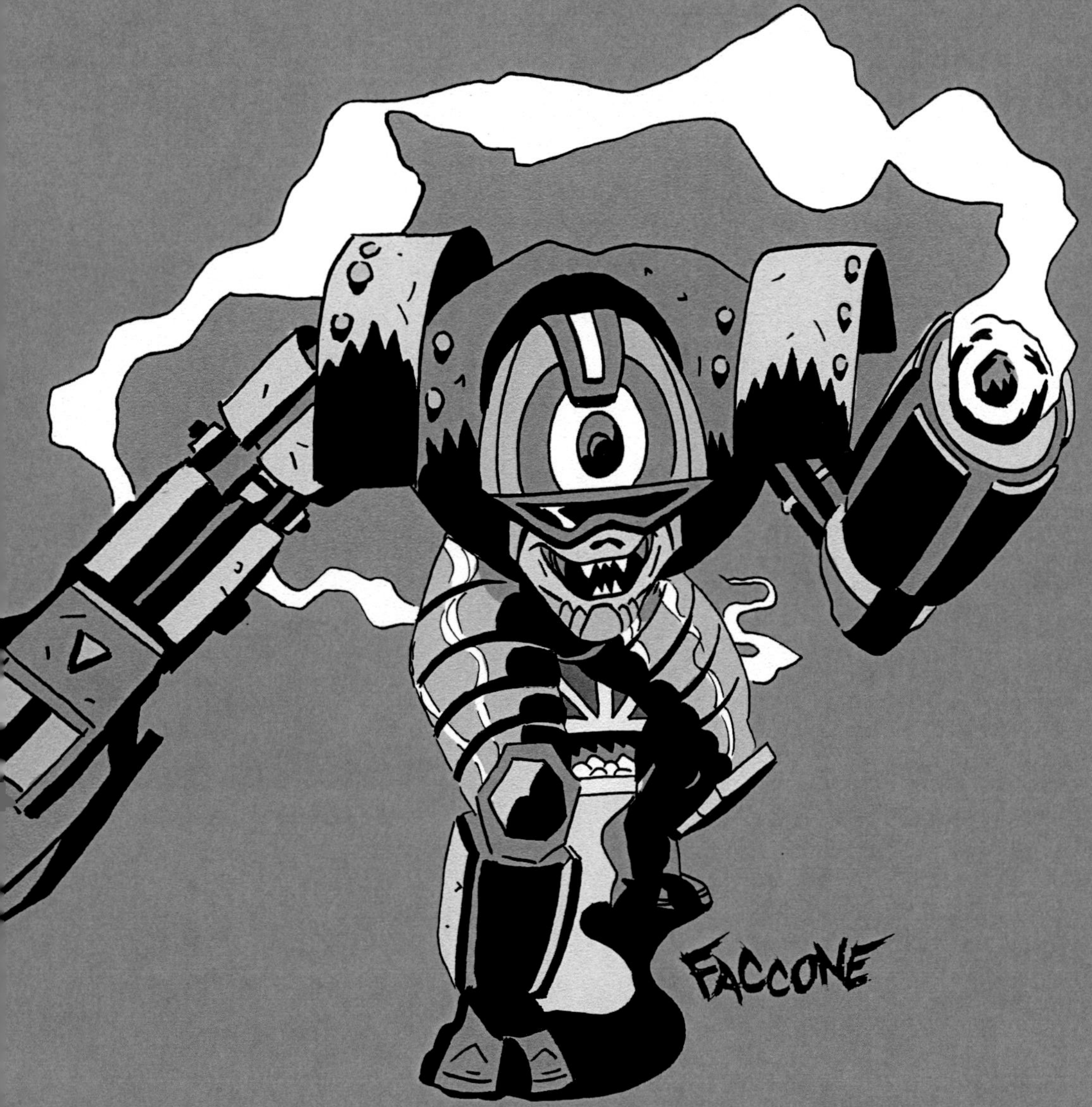
FACCONE

NOMADD.NET

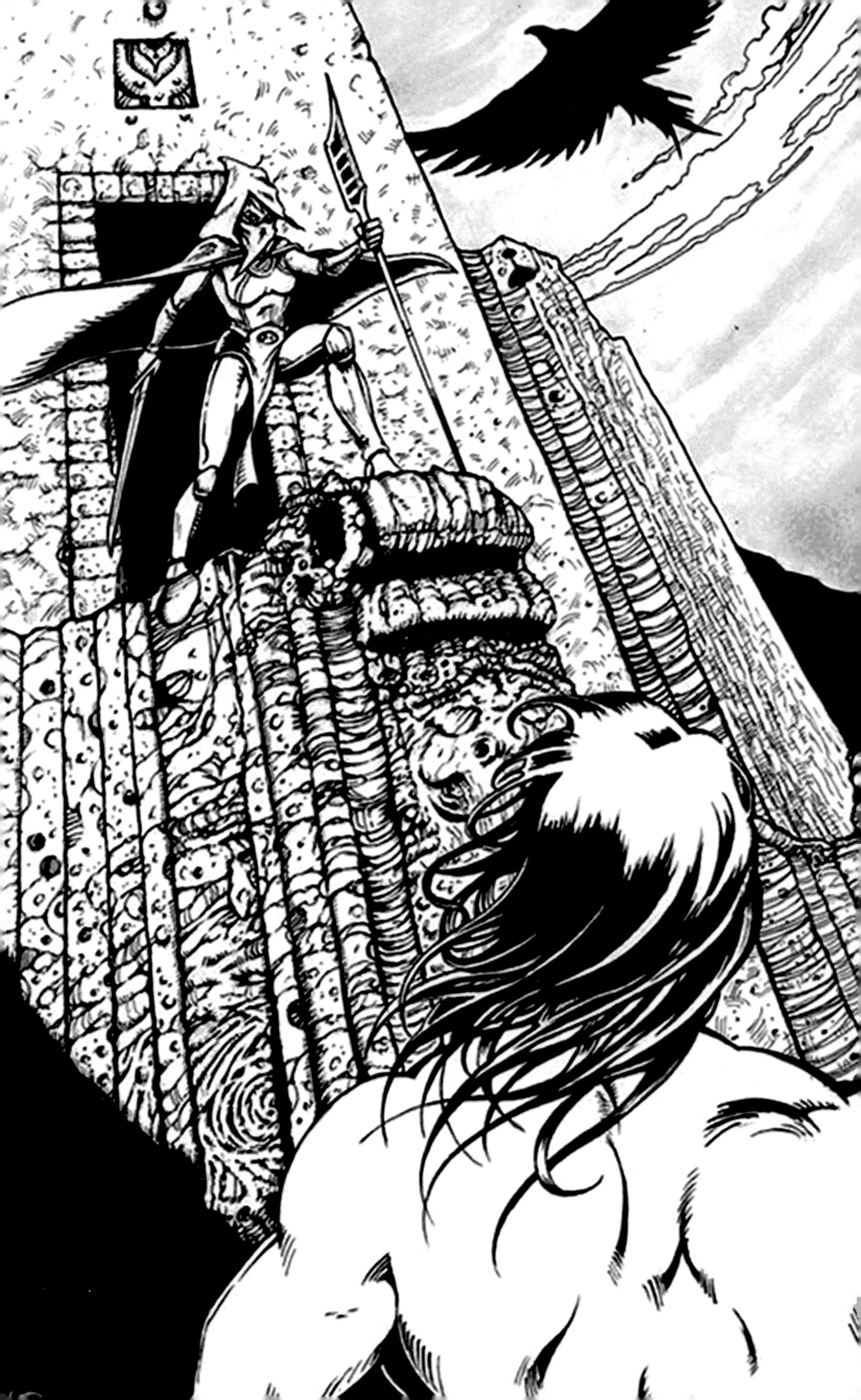

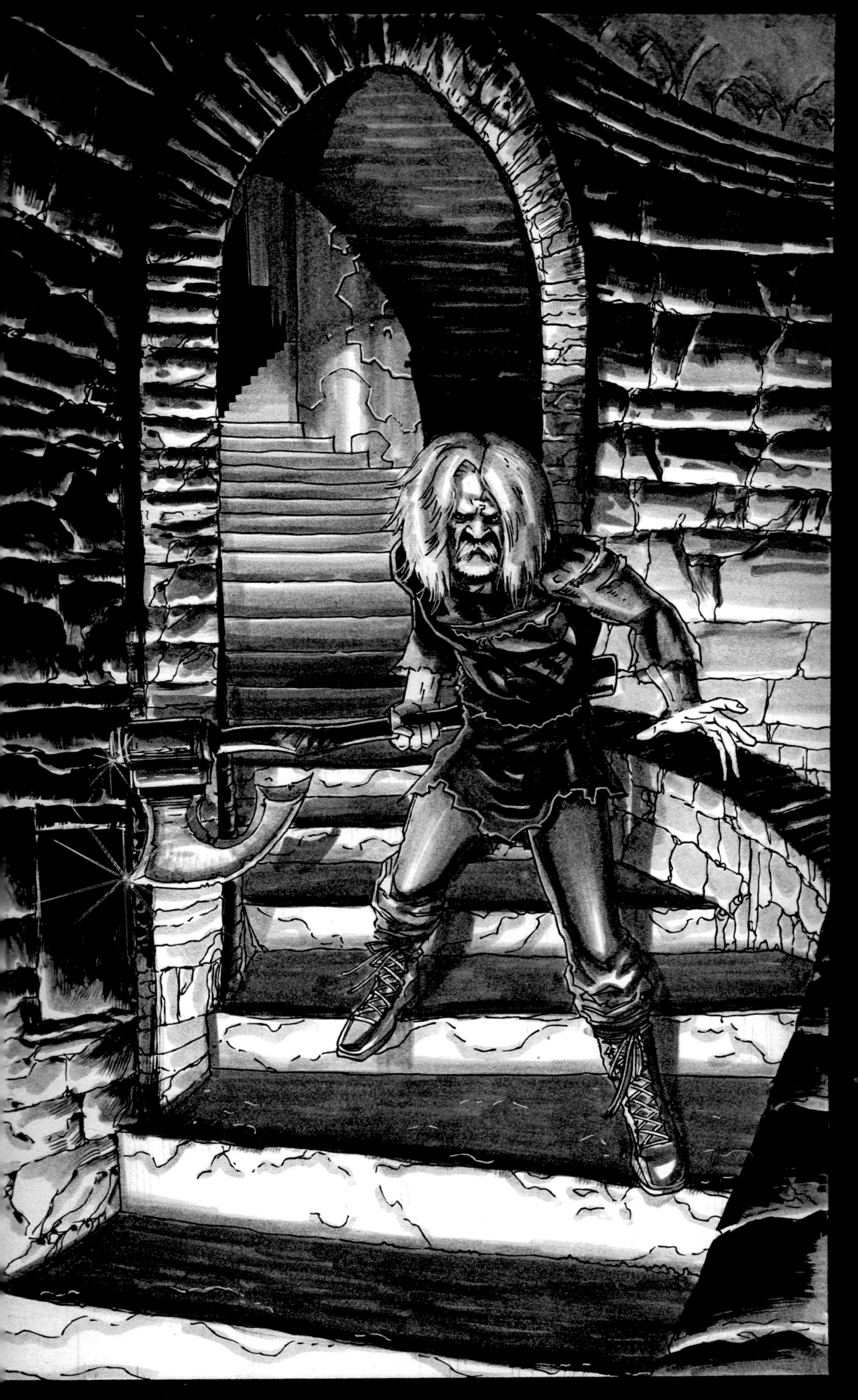

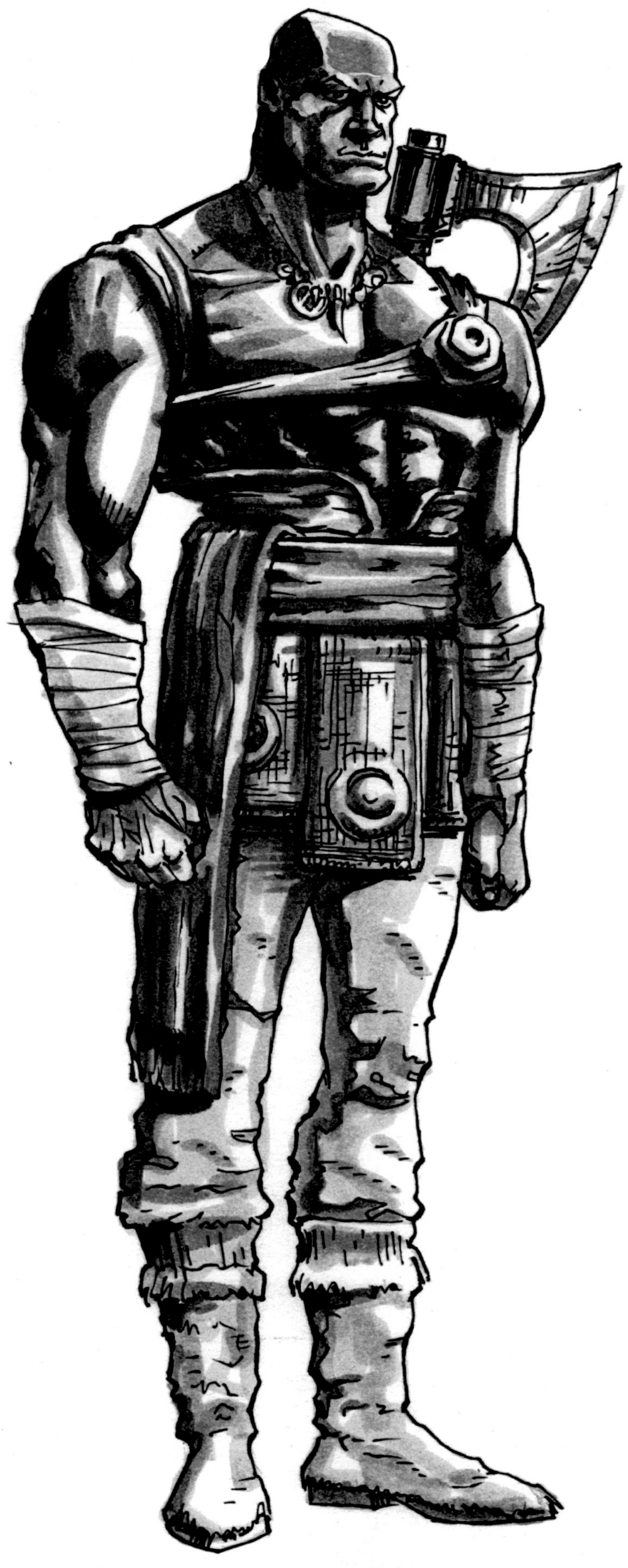